W9-BHJ-627

THE MARRIAGE OF
Bette and Boo

THE MARRIAGE OF
Bette and Boo

by
CHRISTOPHER DURANG

Grove Press
New York

Published by Grove Press, Inc.
920 Broadway
New York, N.Y. 10010

Library of Congress Cataloging-in-Publication Data

Durang, Christopher, 1949–
The marriage of Bette and Boo.

I. Title.
PS3554.U666M3   1987   812'.54   86-33468
ISBN 0-394-56071-X
ISBN 0-394-62347-9 (pbk.)

Manufactured in the United States of America

First Edition 1987

10 9 8 7 6 5 4 3 2 1

To my mother

The Marriage of Bette and Boo was first presented by the New York Shakespeare Festival (Joseph Papp, President) at the Public/Newman Theater in New York City on May 16, 1985. It was directed by Jerry Zaks; the scenery was by Loren Sherman; the costumes were by William Ivey Long; the lighting was by Paul Gallo; the original music was by Richard Peaslee; the hair was designed by Ron Frederick; the associate producer was Jason Steven Cohen; the production stage manager was James Harker; the stage manager was Pamela Singer. The cast was as follows:

Bette Brennan	*Joan Allen*
Margaret Brennan, her mother	*Patricia Falkenhain*
Paul Brennan, her father	*Bill McCutcheon*
Joan Brennan, her sister	*Mercedes Ruehl*
Emily Brennan, her sister	*Kathryn Grody*
Boo Hudlocke	*Graham Beckel*
Karl Hudlocke, his father	*Bill Moor*
Soot Hudlocke, his mother	*Olympia Dukakis*
Father Donnally/Doctor	*Richard B. Shull*
Matt	*Christopher Durang*

Understudies: Dalton Dearborn, Patrick Garner, Lizbeth MacKay, Rose Arrick, Ann Hilliary. During the final week, Mr. Dearborn and Ms. Hilliary played Karl and Soot.

The Marriage of Bette and Boo has a long history. A fifty minute version was presented at the Yale School of Drama and at the Williamstown Theatre's Second Company. The Public Theatre production was the premiere of the expanded version.

CHARACTERS

Bette Brennan
Margaret Brennan, *her mother*
Paul Brennan, *her father*
Joan Brennan, *her sister*
Emily Brennan, *her sister*
Boo Hudlocke
Karl Hudlocke, *his father*
Soot Hudlocke, *his mother*
Father Donnally
Doctor
Matt

SCENES

ACT ONE

Scene 1

All the characters, in various wedding apparel, stand together to sing: the **Brennan** *family, the* **Hudlocke** *family.* **Matthew** *stands apart from them.*

All *(sing)*:

> God bless Bette and Boo and Skippy,
> Emily and Boo,
> Margaret, Matt, and Betsy Booey,
> Mommy, Tommy too,
>
> Betty Betsy Booey Boozey,
> Soot, Karl, Matt, and Paul,
> Margaret Booey, Joanie Phooey,
> God bless us one and all.

(The characters now call out to one another.)

Bette: Booey? Booey? Skippy?

Boo: Pop?

Margaret: Emily, dear?

Bette: Booey?

Boo: Bette?

Karl: Is that Bore?

Soot: Karl? Are you there?

Joan: Nikkos!

Bette: Skippy! Skippy!

3

Emily: Are you all right, Mom?

Bette: Booey, I'm calling you!

Margaret: Paul? Where are you?

Joan: Nikkos!

Boo: Bette? Betsy?

Bette: Boo? Boo?

(Flash of light on the characters, as if their picture is being taken. Lights off the **Brennans** *and* **Hudlockes**. *Light on* **Matt**, *late twenties or so. He speaks to the audience.)*

Matt: If one looks hard enough, one can usually see the order that lies beneath the surface. Just as dreams must be put in order and perspective in order to understand them, so must the endless details of waking life be ordered and then carefully considered. Once these details have been considered, generalizations about them must be made. These generalizations should be written down legibly, and studied. *The Marriage of Bette and Boo.*

*(***Matt** *exits. Characters assume their places for photographs before the wedding.* **Boo** *stands to the side with his parents,* **Karl** *and* **Soot**. **Bette**, *in a wedding gown, poses for pictures with her family:* **Margaret**, *her mother;* **Emily**, *her sister, holding a cello;* **Joan**, *another sister, who is pregnant and is using nose spray, and* **Paul**, *her father.* **Bette**, **Margaret**, **Emily** *smile, looking out.* **Paul** *looks serious, fatherly.* **Joan** *looks sort of grouchy. Lights flash. They change positions.)*

Margaret: You look lovely, Bette.

Emily: You do. Lovely.

Margaret: A lovely bride. Smile for the camera, girls. *(Speaking out to either audience or to unseen photographer:)* Bette was always the most beautiful of my children. We used to say that Joanie was the most striking, but Bette was the one who looked beautiful all the time. And about Emily we used to say her health wasn't good.

Emily: That's kind of you to worry, Mom, but I'm feeling much better. My asthma is hardly bothering me at all today. *(Coughs lightly.)*

Margaret: Boo seems a lovely boy. Betsy, dear, why do they call him Boo?

Bette: It's a nickname.

Margaret: Don't you think Bette looks lovely, Joanie?

Joan *(without enthusiasm)*: She does. You look lovely, Bette.

Margaret: Where is Nikkos, dear?

Joan: He's not feeling well. He's in the bathroom.

Emily: Do you think we should ask Nikkos to play his saxophone with us, Joan dear?

Joan: A saxophone would sound ridiculous with your cello, Emily.

Emily: But Nikkos might feel left out.

Joan: He'll probably stay in the bathroom anyway.

Bette: Nikkos seems crazy. (**Joan** *glares at her.*) I wish you and Nikkos could've had a big wedding, Joanie.

Margaret: Well, your father didn't much like Nikkos. It just didn't seem appropriate. (**Emily** *coughs softly.*) Are you all right, Emily?

Emily: It's nothing, Mom.

Joan: You're not going to get sick, are you?

Emily: No. I'm sure I won't.

Margaret: Emily, dear, please put away your cello. It's too large.

Emily: I can't find the case.

(**Joan** *uses her nose spray.*)

Bette: I can't wait to have a baby, Joanie.

Joan: Oh yes?

Margaret *(out to front again)*: Betsy was always the mother of the family, we'd say. She and her brother Tom. Played with dolls all day long, they did. Now Joanie hated dolls. If you gave Joanie a doll, she put it in the oven.

Joan: I don't remember that, Mom.

Bette: I love dolls.

Emily: Best of luck, Bette. *(Kisses her; to* **Joan:***)* Do you think Nikkos will be offended if we don't ask him to play with us?

Joan: Emily, don't go on about it.

Emily: Nikkos is a wonderful musician.

Bette: So are you, Emily.

Margaret: I just hope he's a good husband. Booey seems very nice, Betsy.

Bette: I think I'll have a large family.

(Lights flash, taking a photo of of the **Brennans**. *Lights dim on them. Lights now pick up* **Boo**, **Karl**, *and* **Soot**, *who now pose for pictures.)*

Karl: It's almost time, Bore.

Boo: Almost, Pop.

Soot: Betsy's very pretty, Booey. Don't you think Betsy's pretty, Karl?

Karl: She's pretty. You're mighty old to be getting married, Bore. How old are you?

Boo: Thirty-two, Pop.

Soot: That's not old, Karl.

Karl: Nearly over the hill, Bore.

Soot: Don't call Booey "Bore" today, Karl. Someone might misunderstand.

Karl: Nobody will misunderstand.

(Photo flash. Enter **Father Donnally**. *The families take their place on either side of him.* **Bette** *and* **Boo** *come together, and stand before him.)*

Father Donnally: We are gathered here in the sight of God to join this man and this woman in the sacrament of holy matrimony. Do you, Bette. . . ?

Bette *(to* **Boo***)*: I do.

Father Donnally: And do you, Boo. . . ?

Boo *(to* **Bette***)*: I do.

Father Donnally *(sort of to himself)*: Take this woman to be your lawfully wedded . . . I do, I do. *(Back to formal sounding.)* I pronounce you man and wife.

(**Bette** *and* **Boo** *kiss.* **Karl** *throws a handful of rice at them, somewhat hostilely. This bothers no one.*)

Joan: Come on, Emily.

(**Emily** *and* **Joan** *step forward.* **Paul** *gets* **Emily** *a chair to sit in when she plays her cello. He carries a flute.*)

Emily: And now, in honor of our dear Bette's wedding, I will play the cello and my father will play the flute, and my wonderful sister Joanie will sing the Schubert Lied *Lachen und Weinen*, which translates as "Laughing and Crying." (**Joan** *gets in position to sing.* **Paul** *holds his flute to his mouth.* **Emily** *sits in her chair, puts the cello between her legs, and raises her bow. Long pause.*) I can't remember it.

Joan (*very annoyed*): It starts on A, Emily.

Emily (*tries again; stops*): I'm sorry. I'm sorry, Bette. I can't remember it.

(*Everyone looks a little disappointed and disgruntled with* **Emily**. *Photo flash. Lights change. Spot on* **Matt**.)

Scene 2

Matt *addresses the audience.*

Matt: When ordering reality, it is necessary to accumulate all the facts pertaining to the matter at hand. When all the facts are not immediately available, one must try to reconstruct them by considering oral history—hearsay, gossip, and apocryphal stories. And then with perseverance and intelligence, the analysis of these facts should bring about understanding. The honeymoon of Bette and Boo.

(**Matt** *exits. Enter* **Bette**, *still in her wedding dress. In the following speech, and much of the time,* **Bette** *talks cheerfully and quickly, making no visible connections between her statements.*)

Bette: Hurry up, Boo. I want to use the shower. (*Speaks to audience, who seem to her a great friend:*) First I was a tomboy. I used to climb trees and beat up my brother Tom. Then I used to try to break my sister Joanie's voice box because she liked to sing. She always scratched me though, so instead I tried to play Emily's cello. Except I don't have a lot of musical talent, but I'm very popular. And I know more about the cello than people who don't know anything. I don't like the cello, it's too much work and besides, keeping my legs open that way made me feel funny. I asked Emily if it made her feel funny and she didn't know what I meant; and then when I told her she cried for two whole hours and then went to confession twice, just in case the priest didn't understand her the first time. Dopey Emily. She means well. (*Calls offstage:*) Booey! I'm pregnant! (*To audience:*) Actually I couldn't be, because I'm a virgin. A married man tried to have an affair with me, but he was married and so it would have been pointless. I didn't know he was married until two months ago. Then I met Booey, sort of on the rebound. He seems fine, though. (*Calls out:*) Booey! (*To audience:*) I went to confession about the cello practicing, but I don't think the priest heard me. He didn't say anything. He didn't even give me a penance. I wonder if nobody was in there. But as long as your conscience is all right, then so is your soul. (*Calls, giddy, happy:*) Booey, come on! (end)

(**Bette** *runs off. Lights change. Spot on* **Matt**.)

Scene 3

Matt *addresses the audience.*

Matt: Margaret gives Emily advice.

*(**Matt** exits. Enter **Margaret**, **Emily**, holding her cello.)*

Emily: Mom, I'm so upset that I forgot the piece at the wedding. Bette looked angry. When I write an apology, should I send it to Bette, or to Bette *and* Boo?

Margaret: Emily, dear, don't go on about it.

*(Lights change. Spot on **Matt**.)*

Scene 4

Matt *addresses the audience.*

Matt: The honeymoon of Bette and Boo, continued.

*(**Matt** exits. Enter **Bette** and **Boo**, wrapped in a large sheet and looking happy. They stand smiling for a moment. They should still be in their wedding clothes—**Bette** minus her veil, **Boo** minus his tie and jacket.)*

Bette: That was better than a cello, Boo.

Boo: You're mighty good-looking, gorgeous.

Bette: Do you think I'm prettier than Polly Lydstone?

Boo: Who?

Bette: I guess you don't know her. I want to have lots of children, Boo. Eight. Twelve. Did you read *Cheaper by the Dozen?*

Boo: I have to call my father about a new insurance deal we're handling. *(Takes phone from beneath the sheets; talks quietly into it.)* Hello, Pop . . .

Bette *(to audience)*: Lots and lots of children. I loved the movie *Skippy* with Jackie Cooper. I cried and cried. I always loved little boys. Where is my pocketbook? Find it for me, Boo.

*(The pocketbook is in full sight, but **Bette** doesn't seem to notice it.)*

Boo: I'm talking to Pop, Bette. What is it, Pop?

Bette *(to audience)*: When I was a little girl, I used to love to mind Jimmy Winkler. "Do you want me to watch Jimmy?" I'd say to Mrs. Winkler. He was five years old and had short stubby legs. I used to dress him up as a lamp shade and walk him to town. I put tassels on his toes and taped doilies on his knees, and he'd scream and scream. My mother said, "Betsy, why are you crying about *Skippy*, it's only a movie, it's not real." But I didn't believe her. Bonnie Wilson was my best friend and she got tar all over her feet. Boo, where are you?

Boo: I'm here, angel. No, not you, Pop. No, I was talking to Bette. Here, why don't you speak to her? *(Hands **Bette** the phone.)* Here, Bette, it's Pop.

Bette: Hello there, Mr. Hudlocke. How are you? And Mrs. Hudlocke? I cried and cried at the movie *Skippy* because I thought it was real. Bonnie Wilson and I were the two stupidest in the class. Mrs. Sullivan used to say, "The two stupidest in math are Bonnie and Betsy. Bonnie, your grade is eight, and Betsy, your grade is five." Hello? Hello? *(To **Boo**:)* We must have been cut off, Boo. Where is my pocketbook?

Boo: Here it is, beautiful.

(**Boo** *gives her the pocketbook that has been in full sight all along.*)

Bette: I love you, Boo.

Scene 5

Emily sits at her cello.

Emily: I can't remember it. (*She gets up and addresses her chair.*) It starts on A, Emily. (*She sits down, tries to play.*) I'm sorry. I'm sorry, Bette. I can't remember it.

(*Enter* **Joan** *with scissors.*)

Joan: It may start on A, Emily. But it ends now.

(**Joan** *raises scissors up. Freeze and/or lights change.*)

Scene 6

Matt *addresses the audience.*

Matt: At the suggestion of *Redbook*, Bette refashions her wedding gown into a cocktail dress. Then she and Boo visit their in-laws. Bette is pregnant for the first time.

(**Matt** *exits.* **Bette**, **Boo**, **Karl**, **Soot**. **Bette** *is in a shortened, simplified version of her wedding dress.*)

Soot: How nice that you're going to have a baby.

Karl: Have another drink, Bore.

Bette *(to* **Soot***)*: I think Booey drinks too much. Does Mr. Hudlocke drink too much?

Soot: I never think about it.

Karl: Soot, get me and Bore another drink.

*(***Boo** *and* **Karl** *are looking over papers, presumably insurance.)*

Bette: Don't have another one, Boo.

Soot *(smiles, whispers)*: I think Karl drinks too much, but when he's sober he's really very nice.

Bette: I don't think Boo should drink if I'm going to have a baby.

Soot: If it's a boy, you can name him Boo, and if it's a girl you can call her Soot after me.

Bette: How did you get the name "Soot"?

Soot: Oh, you know. The old saying "She fell down the chimney and got covered with soot."

Bette: What saying?

Soot: Something about that. Karl might remember. Karl, how did I get the name "Soot"?

Karl: Get the drinks, Soot.

Soot: All right.

Karl *(to* **Bette***)*: Soot is the dumbest white woman alive.

Soot: Oh, Karl. *(Laughs, exits.)*

Bette: I don't want you to get drunk again, Boo. Joanie's husband Nikkos may lock himself in the bathroom, but he doesn't drink.

Boo: Bette, Pop and I are looking over these papers.

Bette: I'm your wife.

Boo: Bette, you're making a scene.

Karl: Your baby's going to be all mouth if you keep talking so much. You want to give birth to a mouth, Bette?

Bette: All right. I'm leaving.

Boo: Bette. Can't you take a joke?

Bette: It's not funny.

Karl: I can tell another one. There was this drunken airline stewardess who got caught in the propeller . . .

Bette: I'm leaving now, Boo. *(Exits.)*

Boo: Bette. I better go after her. *(Starts to exit.)*

Karl: Where are you going, Bore?

Boo: Bette's a little upset, Pop. I'll see you later.

*(**Boo** exits. Enter **Soot** with drinks.)*

Soot: Where's Booey, Karl?

Karl: He isn't here.

Soot: I know. Where did he go?

Karl: Out the door.

Soot: Did you say something to Bette, Karl?

Karl: Let's have the drinks, Soot.

Soot: You know, I really can't remember how everyone started calling me Soot. Can you, Karl?

Karl: Go into your dance, Soot.

Soot: Oh, Karl. *(Laughs.)*

Karl: Go get the veils and start in. The shades are down.

Soot: Karl, I don't know what you're talking about.

Karl: You're the dumbest white woman alive. I rest my case.

*(**Soot** laughs. Lights change.)*

Scene 7

Matt addresses the audience.

Matt: Bette goes to Margaret, her mother, for advice.

*(**Matt** exits. **Bette**, **Margaret**, **Emily** on the floor, writing a note. **Paul**, the father, is also present.)*

Bette: Mom, Boo drinks. And his father insulted me.

Margaret: Betsy, dear, marriage is no bed of roses.

Emily: Mom, is the phrase "my own stupidity" hyphenated?

Margaret: No, Emily. She's apologizing to Joanie again about forgetting the piece at the wedding. Joanie *was* very embarrassed.

Bette: How can I make Boo stop drinking?

Margaret: I'm sure it's not a serious problem, Betsy.

Bette: Poppa, what should I do?

Paul: W##hh, ah%#% enntgh oo sh#$w auns$$dr ehvg###ing%%#s ahm.

(NOTE TO READER AND/OR ACTOR: Paul is meant to be the victim of a stroke. His mind is still functioning well, but his

ability to speak is greatly impaired. Along these lines, I give him specific lines to say and be motivated by, but the audience and the other characters in the play should genuinely be unable to make out almost anything that he says—though they can certainly follow any emotional colorings he gives. I have found it useful for actors who read the part of Paul to say the lines written in the brackets, but to drop almost all of the consonants and to make the tongue go slack, so that poor Paul's speech is almost all vowels, mixed in with an occasional inexplicable group of consonants. Paul's first line up above—emphasizing that no one should be able to make out almost any of it—would be: "Well, I think you should consider giving things time.")

Bette: *What* should I do?

Paul *(angry that he can't be understood)*: On####%t ump oo%#% onoosns#$s. Eggh ing ahm#$. [Don't jump to conclusions. Give things time.]

Margaret: Paul, I've asked you not to speak. We can't understand you.

Emily: Mom, how do you spell "mea culpa"?

Margaret: Emily, Latin is pretentious in an informal letter. Joanie will think you're silly.

Emily: This one is to Father Donnally.

Margaret: M-E-A C-U-L-P-A.

Bette: Boo's father has given him a very bad example. *(Enter* **Joan**, *carrying a piece of paper.)* Oh, Joan, quick— do you think when I have my baby, it will make Boo stop . . .

Joan: Wait a minute. *(To* **Emily:***)* Emily, I got your note. Now listen to me closely. *(With vehemence:)* I *forgive* you, I *forgive* you, I *forgive* you.

Emily (*a bit startled*): Oh. Thank you.

Joan (*to* **Bette**): Now, what did you want?

Bette: Do you think when I have my baby, it will make Boo stop drinking and bring him and me closer together?

Joan: I have no idea.

Bette: Well, but hasn't your having little Mary Frances made things better between you and Nikkos? He isn't still disappearing for days, is he?

Joan: Are you trying to make me feel bad about my marriage?

Emily: I'm sorry, Joanie.

Joan: What?

Emily: If I made you feel bad about your marriage.

Joan: Oh, shut up. (*Exits.*)

Bette (*to* **Margaret**): She's so nasty. Did you punish her enough when she was little?

Margaret: She's just tired because little Mary Frances cries all the time. She really is a dreadful child.

Bette: I love babies. Poppa, don't you think my baby will bring Boo and me closer together?

Paul: Aszzs&* ot uh er#ry owowd#@ eeah oo ah uh ayee, ehtte. [That's not a very good reason to have a baby, Bette.]

(**Bette** *looks at* **Paul** *blankly. Lights change.*)

Scene 8

Matt *addresses the audience.*

Matt: Twenty years later, Boo has dinner with his son.

(Boo *and* **Matt** *sit at a table.)*

Boo: Well, how are things up at Dartmouth, Skip? People in the office ask me how my Ivy League son is doing.

Matt: It's all right.

Boo: Are there any pretty girls up there?

Matt: Uh huh.

Boo: So what are you learning up there?

Matt: Tess of the d'Urbervilles is a masochist.

Boo: What?

Matt: It's a novel we're reading. *(Mumbles.) Tess of the d'Urbervilles.*

Boo *(laughs):* A man needs a woman, son. I miss your mother. I'd go back with her in a minute if she wanted. She's not in love with her family anymore, and I think she knows that drinking wasn't that much of a problem. I think your old man's going to get teary for a second. I'm just an old softie. **(Boo** *blinks his eyes, wipes them.* **Matt** *exits, embarrassed.* **Boo** *doesn't notice but addresses the chair as if* **Matt** *were still there.)* I miss your mother, Skip. Nobody should be alone. Do you have any problems, son, you want to talk over? Your old man could help you out.

(Boo *waits for an answer. Lights change.)*

Scene 9

Matt *addresses the audience.*

Matt: The first child of Bette and Boo.

(**Matt** *exits. Enter* **Boo, Karl, Soot, Margaret, Emily** *with her cello,* **Joan, Paul.** *They all stand in a line and wait expectantly. Enter the* **doctor***, who is played by the same actor who plays Father Donnally.)*

Doctor: She's doing well. Just a few more minutes. *(Exits.)*

Emily: Oh God, make her pain small. Give me the pain rather than her. *(Winces in pain.)*

Margaret: Emily, behave, this is a hospital.

Boo: Pop, I hope it's a son.

Karl: This calls for a drink. Soot, get Bore and me a drink.

Soot: Where would I go?

Karl: A drink, Soot.

Soot: Karl, you're teasing me again.

Karl: All right, I won't talk to you.

Soot: Oh, please. Please talk to me. Booey, talk to your father.

Boo: Come on, Pop. We'll have a drink afterwards.

Soot: Karl, I'll get you a drink. *(To* **Margaret***:)* Where would I go? *(To* **Karl***:)* Karl?

Karl: This doctor know what he's doing, Bore?

Soot: Karl? Wouldn't you like a drink?

Emily: It's almost here. *(Having an experience of some sort.)* Oh no, no, no no no no.

Margaret: Emily!

Karl: This Betsy's sister, Bore?

Boo: Pop, I hope it's a boy.

Karl: You were a boy, Bore. *(Enter the **doctor**, holding the baby in a blue blanket.)* This is it, Bore.

Emily: In the name of the Father, and of the Son, and of the Holy Ghost.

Doctor: It's dead. The baby's dead. *(He drops it on the floor.)*

Emily *(near collapse)*: Oh no!

Joan: I win the bet.

Margaret: I'm here, Betsy, it's all right. *(**Paul** picks up the baby.)* Paul, put the baby down. That's disrespectful.

Paul: Buh uh ayee ah#$# ehh#! [But the baby's not dead.]

Margaret: Don't shout. I can understand you.

Paul *(to **doctor**)*: Uh ayee ah#$# ehh#! Yrr uh ahherr, ann## oo ee, uh ayee ah#$# ehh#! [The baby's not dead. You're a doctor, can't you see, the baby's not dead.]

Doctor *(takes the baby)*: Oh, you're right. It's not dead. Mr. Hudlocke, you have a son.

Karl: Congratulations, Bore.

Emily: Thank you, God. *(Enter **Bette**, radiant. She takes the baby.)*

Bette *(to audience)*: We'll call the baby Skippy.

Emily: It has to be a saint's name, Bette.

Bette: Mind your business, Emily.

Margaret: Betsy, dear, Emily's right. Catholics have to be named after saints. Otherwise they can't be baptized.

Boo: Boo.

Margaret: There is no Saint Boo.

Emily: We should call it Margaret in honor of Mom.

Bette: It's a boy.

Emily: We should call him Paul in honor of Dad.

Margaret: Too common.

Soot: I always liked Clarence.

Joan: I vote for Boo.

Margaret *(telling her to behave)*: Joanie.

Karl: Why not name it after a household appliance?

Soot: Karl. *(Laughs.)*

Karl: Egg beater. Waffle iron. Bath mat.

Bette *(to audience)*: Matt. I remember a little boy named Matt who looked just like a wind-up toy. We'll call him Matt.

Boo: It's a boy, Pop.

Emily: Is Matt a saint's name, Bette?

Bette: Matthew, Emily. Maybe if you'd finally join the convent, you'd learn the apostles' names.

Emily: Do you think I should join a convent?

Bette *(to audience)*: But his nickname's going to be Skippy. My very favorite movie.

(Lights change.)

Scene 10

Matt *addresses the audience.*

Matt: *My Very Favorite Movie,* an essay by Matthew Hudlocke. My very favorite movie . . . are . . . *Nights of Cabiria, 8½, Citizen Kane, L'Avventura, The Seventh Seal, Persona, The Parent Trap, The Song of Bernadette, Potemkin, The Fire Within, The Bells of St. Mary's, The Singing Nun, The Dancing Nun, The Nun on the Fire Escape Outside My Window, The Nun That Caused the Chicago Fire, The Nun Also Rises, The Nun Who Came to Dinner, The Caucasian Chalk Nun, Long Day's Journey into Nun, None But the Lonely Heart,* and *The Nun Who Shot Liberty Valance.*

Page two. In the novels of Thomas Hardy, we find a deep and unrelieved pessimism. Hardy's novels, set in his home town of Wessex, contrast nature outside of man with the human nature inside of man, coming together inexorably to cause human catastrophe. The sadness in Hardy—his lack of belief that a benevolent God watches over human destiny, his sense of the waste and frustration of the average human life, his forceful irony in the face of moral and metaphysical questions—is part of the late Victorian mood. We can see something like it in A. E. Housman, or in Emily's life. Shortly after Skippy's birth, Emily enters a convent, but then leaves the convent due to nerves. Bette becomes pregnant for the second time. Boo continues to drink. If psychiatrists had existed in nineteenth century Wessex, Hardy might suggest Bette and Boo seek counseling. Instead he has no advice to give them, and in 1886 he writes *The Mayor of Casterbridge*. This novel is one of Hardy's greatest successes, and Skippy studies it in college. When he is little, he studies *The Wind in the Willows* with Emily. And when he is very little, he studies drawing with Emily.

(**Emily**, **Matt**. **Emily** *has brightly colored construction paper and crayons.*)

Emily: Hello, Skippy, dear. I thought we could do some nice arts and crafts today. Do you want to draw a cat or a dog?

Matt: A dog.

Emily: All right, then I'll do a cat. *(They begin to draw.)* Here's the head, and here's the whiskers. Oh dear, it looks more like a clock. Oh, Skippy, yours is very good. I can tell it's a dog. Those are the ears, and that's the tail, right?

Matt: Yes.

Emily: That's very good. And you draw much better than Mary Frances. I tried to interest her in drawing Babar the elephant the other day, but she doesn't like arts and crafts, and she scribbled all over the paper, and then she had a crying fit. *(Sits back.)* Oh dear. I shouldn't say she doesn't draw well, it sounds like a criticism of Joanie.

Matt: I won't tell.

Emily: Yes, but it would be on my conscience. I better write Joanie a note apologizing. And really, Mary Frances draws *very* well, I didn't mean it when I said she didn't. She probably had a headache. I think I'll use this nice pink piece of construction paper to apologize to Joanie, and I'll apologize about forgetting the piece at your mother's wedding too. I've never been sure Joanie's forgiven me, even though she says she has. I don't know what else I can do except apologize. I don't have any money.

Matt: Your cat looks very good. It doesn't look like a clock.

Emily: You're such a comfort, Skippy. I'll be right back. Why don't you pretend your dog is real, and you can teach it tricks while I'm gone.

(Emily *exits.* **Matt** *makes "roll over" gesture to drawing, waits for response. Lights change.* **Matt** *exits.)*

Scene 11

Bette *enters, carrying a chair. She sits on the chair.*

Bette *(to audience and/or herself)*: I'm going to pretend that I'm sitting in this chair. Then I'm going to pretend that I'm going to have another baby. And then I'm going to have another, and another and another. I'm going to pretend to have a big family. There'll be Skippy. And then all the A. A. Milne characters. Boo should join AA. There'll be Eeyore and Pooh Bear and Christopher Robin and Tigger . . . My family is going to be like an enormous orphanage. I'll be their mother. Kanga and six hundred Baby Roos. Baby Roo is Kanga's baby, but she's a mother to them all. Roo and Tigger and Pooh and Christopher Robin and Eeyore and Owl, owl, ow, ow, ow, ow, ow, ow, ow, ow! I'm giving birth, Mom. Roo and Tigger and Boo and Pooh and Soot and Eeyore and Karl and Betsy and Owl . . .

(Enter quickly: **Boo**, **Karl**, **Soot**, **Margaret**, **Paul**, **Emily**, **Joan**. *They stand in their same hospital positions. Enter the* **doctor** *with the baby in a blue blanket.)*

Doctor: The baby's dead. *(Drops it on the floor.)*

Margaret: Nonsense. That's what he said about the last one, didn't he, Paul?

Doctor: This time it's true. It *is* dead.

Bette: Why?

Doctor: The reason the baby is dead is this: Mr. Hudlocke has Rh positive blood.

Karl: Good for you, Bore!

Doctor: Mrs. Hudlocke has Rh negative blood.

Bette: Like Kanga.

Doctor: And so the mother's Rh negative blood fights the baby's Rh positive blood and so: the mother kills the baby.

Emily *(rather horrified)***:** Who did this??? The mother did this???

Karl: You married a winner, Bore.

Boo: The baby came. And it was dead. *(Picks up baby.)*

Soot: Poor Booey.

Bette: But I'll have other babies.

Doctor: The danger for your health if you do and the likelihood of stillbirth are overwhelming considerations.

Boo: The baby came. And it was dead.

Bette: Mama, tell him to go away.

Margaret: There, there. Say something to her, Paul.

(**Paul** *says nothing. Lights change.*)

Scene 12

Matt *addresses the audience.*

Matt: Bette and Margaret visit Emily, who is in a rest home due to nerves.

(**Matt** *exits.* **Emily** *with her cello.* **Bette**, **Margaret**. **Bette** *seems very depressed, and keeps looking at the floor or looking off.*)

Emily: Oh, Mom, Bette. It's so good to see you. How are you feeling, Bette, after your tragedy?

Margaret: Emily, don't talk about it. Change the subject.

Emily (*trying desperately to oblige*): Um . . . um . . . uh . . .

Margaret (*looking around slightly*): This is a very nice room for an institution. Bette, look up. Do you like the doctors, Emily?

Emily: Yes, they're very good to me.

Margaret: They should be. They're very expensive. I was going to ask your brother Tom for some money for your stay here, but he's really not . . . Oh, I didn't mean to mention Tom. Forget I said anything.

Emily: Oh, what is it? Is he all right?

Margaret: I shouldn't have mentioned it. Forget it, Emily.

Emily: But what's the matter with him? Is he ill? Oh, Mom . . .

Margaret: Now, Emily, don't go on about it. That's a fault of yours. If you had stayed in the convent, maybe you could have corrected that fault. Oh, I'm sorry. I didn't mean to bring up the convent.

Emily: That's all right, Mom. *(Silence.)*

Margaret: Besides, whatever happens, happens. Don't look that way, Emily. Change the subject.

Emily: Um . . . uh . . .

Margaret: There are many pleasant things in the world, think of them.

Emily *(trying hard to think of something; then)*: How is Skippy, Bette?

Bette: Who?

Emily: Skippy.

Bette *(to **Margaret**)*: Who?

Margaret: She means Baby Roo, dear.

Bette: Oh, Roo. Yes. *(Stares off in distance blankly.)*

Emily: Is he well?

Margaret *(telling **Emily** to stop)*: He's fine, dear, Looks just like his mother.

Emily: He's a lovely child. I look forward to seeing him when I finally leave here and get to go . . . *(Gets teary.)*

Margaret: Emily, the doctors told me they're sure you're not here for life. Isn't that right, Bette. *(Whispers to **Emily**:)* The doctors say Bette shouldn't have any more babies.

Emily: Oh dear. And Bette's a wonderful mother. Bette, dear, don't feel bad, you have the one wonderful child, and maybe someday God will make a miracle so you can have more children.

Bette (*the first sentence she's heard*): I can have more children?

Emily: Well, maybe God will make a *miracle* so you can.

Bette: I can have a miracle?

Emily: Well, you pray and ask for one.

Margaret: Emily, miracles are very fine . . .

Emily: Oh, I didn't think, I shouldn't have . . .

Margaret: But now you've raised Betsy's hopes . . .

Emily: Oh, Bette, listen to Mom . . . I'm so sorry . . .

Bette: I CAN HAVE MORE CHILDREN!

Margaret: That's right, Betsy. Emily, I know you didn't mean to bring this up . . .

Emily: I'm so stupid . . .

Margaret: But first you start on your brother Tom who has a spastic colon and is drinking too much . . .

Emily: Oh no!

Bette (*very excited, overlapping with* **Margaret**): I CAN HAVE MORE CHILDREN, I CAN HAVE MORE CHILDREN, I CAN HAVE MORE CHILDREN . . . (*etc.*)

Margaret (*overlapping with* **Bette**): . . . and has been fired and there's some crazy talk about him and some boy in high school, which I'm sure isn't true, and even if it is . . .

Emily: Tom's all right, isn't he, it isn't true . . .

Bette: . . . I CAN HAVE MORE CHILDREN! . . . *(etc.)*

Margaret: I didn't mean to tell you, Emily, but you talk and talk . . .

Bette: . . . I CAN HAVE MORE CHILDREN, I CAN HAVE MORE CHILDREN . . .

Emily: Oh, Mom, I'm so sorry, I . . .

Margaret: . . . and *talk* about a thing until you think your head is going to explode . . .

Emily *(overlapping still)*: I'm so sorry, I . . . WAIT! *(Silence.* **Emily** *sits at her cello with great concentration, picks up the bow.)* I think I remember it. *(Listens, tries to remember the piece from the wedding, keeps trying out different opening notes.* **Margaret** *looks between the two girls.)*

Margaret: I wish you two could see yourselves. *(Laughs merrily.)* You're both acting very funny. *(Laughs again.)* Come on, Betsy.

*(***Margaret** *and* **Bette** *exit, cheerful.* **Emily** *keeps trying to remember. Lights change.)*

Scene 13

Matt *addresses the audience.*

Matt: Bette seeks definition of the word "miracle" from Father Donnally.

*(***Matt** *exits.* **Bette**, **Father Donnally**. *She kneels to him in the confessional, blesses herself.)*

Father Donnally: Hello, Bette, how are you?

Bette: I'm feeling much better after my tragedy.

Father Donnally: It's a cross to bear.

Bette: Have you ever read *Winnie the Pooh*, Father? Most people think it's for children, but I never read it until I was an adult. The humor is very sophisticated.

Father Donnally: I'll have to read it sometime.

Bette: Do you believe in miracles, Father?

Father Donnally: Miracles rarely happen, Bette.

Bette: I do too! Thank you, Father. You've helped me make a decision.

(Lights change.)

Scene 14

Matt *addresses the audience.*

Matt: Soot gives Bette some advice.

(Matt *exits.* **Bette,** *pregnant,* **Boo, Soot, Karl.***)*

Bette: And then Father Donnally said that I should just keep trying and that even if this baby died, there would be at least one more baby that would live, and then I would be a mother as God meant me to be. Do you agree, Soot?

Soot: I've never met this Father Donnally. Karl, Pauline has a retarded daughter, doesn't she? LaLa is retarded, isn't she? I mean, she isn't just slow, is she?

Bette: I don't care if the child's retarded. Then that's God's will. I love retarded children. I like children more than I like people. Boo, you're drinking too much, it's not fair to me. If this baby dies, it's going to be your fault.

Boo: I don't think Father Donnally should have encouraged you about this. That's what I think.

Bette: He's a priest. *(To* **Soot:***)* Did you ever see Jackie Cooper as a child? I thought he was much cuter than Shirley Temple, what do you think, Soot?

Karl: Bore, my wife Soot hasn't said one sensible thing in thirty years of marriage . . .

Soot: Oh, Karl . . . *(Laughs, flattered.)*

Karl: But your little wife had just said more senseless things in one ten-minute period than Soot here has said in thirty years of bondage.

Soot: Oh, Karl. I never was one for talking.

Bette *(to* **Karl***):* Look here, you. I'm not afraid of you. I'm not going to let Boo push me to a breakdown the way you've pushed Soot. I'm stronger than that.

Soot: Oh my. *(Laughs.)* Sit down, dear.

Karl: Tell the baby-maker to turn it down, Bore.

Boo: Bette, sit down.

Bette: I want a marriage and a family and a home, and I'm going to have them, and if you won't help me, Boo, I'll have them without you. *(Exits.)*

Karl: Well, Bore, I don't know about you and your wife. Whatever one can say against your mother, and it's most everything *(Soot laughs)*, at least she didn't go around dropping dead children at every step of the way like some goddamned giddy farm animal.

Soot: Karl, you shouldn't tease everyone so.

Karl: I don't like the way you're behaving today, Soot. *(Exits.)*

Soot (*looks back to where* **Bette** *was*): Bette, dear, let me give you some advice. Oh, that's right. She left. (*A moment of disorientation; looks at* **Boo**.) Boo, Karl's a lovely man most of the time, and I've had a very happy life with him, but I hope you'll be a little kinder than he was. Just a little. Anything is an improvement. I wish I had dead children. I wish I had two hundred dead children. I'd stuff them down Karl's throat. (*Laughs.*) Of course, I'm only kidding. (*Laughs some more.*)

(*Lights change.*)

Scene 15

Matt *addresses the audience.*

Matt: Now the Mayor of Casterbridge, when drunk, sells his wife and child to someone he meets in a bar. Now Boo is considerably better behaved than this. Now the fact of the matter is that Boo isn't really an alcoholic at all, but drinks simply because Bette is such a terrible, unending nag. Or perhaps Boo *is* an alcoholic, and Bette is a terrible, unending nag in *reaction* to his drinking so much, and also because he just isn't "there" for her, any more than Clym Yeobright is really there for Eustacia Vye in *The Return of the Native*, although admittedly Eustacia Vye is very neurotic, but then so is Bette also.

Or perhaps it's the fault of the past history of stillbirths and the pressures that that history puts on their physical relationship. Perhaps blame can be assigned totally to the Catholic Church. Certainly Emily's guilt about leaving the convent and about everything else in the world can be blamed largely on the Catholic Church. (*Pleased.*) James Joyce can be blamed on the Catholic Church; but not really Thomas Hardy. And then in 1896 Hardy writes *Jude the Obscure*. And when Skippy is nine, Bette goes to the hospital for the third time. The third child of Bette and Boo.

(**Matt** *exits. Lights change.*)

Scene 16

Everyone assembles, except for **Bette**. **Boo**, **Karl**, **Soot**, **Margaret**, **Paul**, **Joan**, **Emily**. *They wait. Enter the* **doctor**. *He drops the baby on the floor, exits. Pause. Lights change.*

Scene 17

Bette *on the telephone, late at night.*

Bette: Hello, Bonnie? This is Betsy. Betsy. *(To remind her:)* "Bonnie, your grade is eight, and Betsy, your grade is five." Yes, it's me. How are you? Oh, I'm sorry, I woke you? Well, what time is it? Oh, I'm sorry. But isn't Florida in a different time zone than we are? Oh. I thought it was. Oh well.

Bonnie, are you married? How many children do you have? Two. That's nice. Are you going to have any more? Oh, I think you should. Yes, I'm married. To Boo. I wrote you. Oh, I never wrote you? How many years since we've spoken? Since we were fifteen. Well, I'm not a very good correspondent. Oh dear, you're yawning, I guess it's too late to have called. Bonnie, do you remember the beach and little Jimmy Winkler? I used to dress him up as a lamp shade, it was so cute. Oh. Well, do you remember when Miss Willis had me stand in the corner, and you stand in the wastebasket, and then your grandmother came to class that day? I thought you'd remember that. Oh, you want to go back to sleep?

Oh, I'm sorry. Bonnie, before you hang up, I've lost two babies. No, I don't mean misplaced, stupid, they died. I go through the whole nine-month period of carrying them, and then when it's over, they just take them away. I don't even see the bodies. Hello? Oh, I thought you weren't there. I'm sorry, I didn't realize it was so late. I thought Florida as Central Time or something. Yes, I got twelve in geography or something, you remember? "Betsy, your grade is twelve and Bonnie, your grade is . . ." What did you get in geography? Well, it's not important anyway. What? No, Boo's not home. Well, sometimes he just goes to a bar and then he doesn't come home until the bar closes, and some of them don't close at all and so he gets confused what time it is. Does your husband drink? Oh, that's good. What's his name? Scooter? Like bicycle? I like the name Scooter. I love cute things. Do you remember Jackie Cooper in *Skippy* and his best friend Sukey? I cried and cried. Hello, are you still there? I'm sorry, I guess I better let you go back to sleep. Goodbye, Bonnie, it was good to hear your voice. *(Hangs up.)*

(Lights change.)

Scene 18

Matt *addresses the audience.*

Matt: Several months later, Bette and Boo have the two families over to celebrate Thanksgiving.

(Bette, **Matt**. **Bette** *is on the warpath.)*

Bette (*calling off, nasty*): Come *up* from the cellar, Boo. I'm not going to say it again. They're going to be here. (*To* **Matt:**) He's hidden a bottle behind the furnace.

Matt: Please stop shouting.

Bette: Do you smell something on his breath?

Matt: I don't know. I didn't get that close.

Bette: Can't you go up and kiss him?

Matt: I can't go up and kiss him for no reason.

Bette: You're so unaffectionate. There's nothing wrong with a ten-year-old boy kissing his father.

Matt: I don't want to kiss him.

Bette: Well, I think I smelled something. (*Enter* **Boo**.)

Boo: What are you talking about?

Bette: You're always picking on me. I wasn't talking about anything. Set the table, SKippy. (**Matt** *exits.*)

Boo: When are they all coming?

Bette: When do you think they're coming? Let me smell your breath.

Boo: Leave my breath alone.

Bette: You've been drinking. You've got a funny look in your eye.

(*Enter* **Matt**, *holding some silverware.*)

Matt: Something's burning in the oven.

Bette: Why can't you stop drinking? You don't care enough about me and Skippy to stop drinking, do you?

Matt: It's going to burn.

Bette: You don't give me anything to be grateful for. You're just like your father. You're a terrible example to Skippy. He's going to grow up neurotic because of you.

Matt: I'll turn the oven off. *(Exits.)*

Boo: Why don't you go live with your mother, you're both so perfect.

Bette: Don't criticize my mother.

*(Enter **Joan** and **Emily**. **Joan** has a serving dish with candied sweet potatoes. **Emily** has a large gravy boat dish.)*

Emily: Happy Thanksgiving, Bette.

Bette: Hush, Emily. You're weak, Boo. It's probably just as well the other babies have died.

Emily: I brought the gravy.

Bette: We don't care about the gravy, Emily. I want you to see a priest, Boo.

Boo: Stop talking. I want you to stop talking.

*(Enter **Margaret** and **Paul**. **Paul** is holding a large cake.)*

Margaret: Hello, Betsy dear.

Bette: He's been drinking.

Margaret: Let's not talk about it. Hello, Boo, Happy Thanksgiving.

Boo: Hello.

*(Enter **Soot** and **Karl**. **Soot** is carrying a candelabra.)*

Soot: Hello, Margaret.

Margaret: How nice to see you. Paul, you remember Mrs. Hudlocke?

Paul: Icse oo ee oo, issizzse uhoch##. Iht oo ab uhull ineing uh arreeng ace####? [Nice to see you, Mrs. Hudlocke. Did you have trouble finding a parking place?]

Soot: I guess so. *(To everybody:)* I brought a candelabra.

Bette *(to* **Soot***):* You're his mother, I want you to smell his breath.

Boo: SHUT UP ABOUT MY BREATH!

(**Boo** *accidentally knocks into* **Emily**, *who drops the gravy on the floor.*)

Bette: You've spilled the gravy all over the rug!

Emily: I'm sorry.

Bette: Boo did it!

Boo: I'll clean it up, I'll clean it up. *(Exits.)*

Bette: I think he's hidden a bottle in the cellar.

Emily: Joanie didn't drop the sweet potatoes.

Soot: Are we early? *(Laughs)*

Karl: Pipe down, Soot.

(**Boo** *enters with a vacuum cleaner. All watch him as he starts to vacuum up the gravy.*)

Bette: What are you doing? Boo!

Boo: I can do it!

Bette: You don't vacuum gravy!

Boo: I can do it!

Bette: Stop it! You're ruining the vacuum!

Soot: Oh dear. Let's go. *(Laughs.)* Good-bye, Booey.

*(**Karl** and **Soot** exit.)*

Joan: I knew we shouldn't have had it here.

Margaret: Come on, Betsy. Why don't you and Skippy stay with us tonight?

Bette: YOU DON'T VACUUM GRAVY!

Margaret: Let it alone, Betsy.

Bette: You don't vacuum gravy. You don't vacuum gravy. You don't vacuum gravy!

Boo *(hysterical)*: WHAT DO YOU DO WITH IT THEN? TELL ME! WHAT DO YOU DO WITH IT?

Bette *(quieter, but very upset)*: You get warm water, and a sponge, and you sponge it up.

*(**Bette** and **Boo** stare at one another, spent.)*

Emily: Should we put the sweet potatoes in the oven?

*(**Matt** exits.)*

Joan: Come on, Emily. Let's go home.

Margaret: Betsy, if you and Skippy want to stay at our house tonight, just come over. Good-bye, Boo.

Emily *(calls)*: Good-bye, Skippy.

*(**Margaret**, **Joan**, **Emily**, and **Paul** exit. Enter **Matt** with a pan of water and two sponges. He hands them to **Bette**. **Bette** and **Boo** methodically sponge up the gravy. Music to the "Bette and Boo" theme in the background.)*

Boo (*quietly*): Okay, we'll soak it up with the sponge. That's what we're doing. We're soaking it up. (*They more or less finish with it.*) I'm going to take a nap.

(**Boo** *lies down where he is, and falls asleep.*)

Bette: Boo? Boo? Booey? Boo?

(*Enter* **Soot.**)

Soot: Did I lose an earring in here? Oh dear. He's just asleep, isn't he?

Bette: Boo? Boo.

Soot: He must have gotten tired. (*Holds up earring, to* **Matt:**) If you should see it, it looks like this one. (*Laughs.*) Booey? (*Laughs.*) I think he's asleep. Good-bye, Booey. (*Exits.*)

Bette: Boo? Booey?

Matt: Please don't try to wake him up. You'll just argue.

Bette: All right. I won't try to wake him. (*Pause.*) Boo. Booey. (*She pushes his shoulder slightly.*) Boo. (*To* **Matt:**) I just want to get through to him about the gravy. (*To* **Boo:**) Boo. You don't vacuum gravy. Are you awake, Boo? Boo? I wonder if he's going to sleep through the night. I can wait. Boo. Booey.

(**Bette** *looks at* **Matt**, *then back at* **Boo**. **Matt** *looks at both of them, then out to audience, exhausted and trapped, but with little actual expression on his face. Lights dim. End Act I.*)

ACT TWO

Scene 19

Bette, **Boo**, **Father Donnally** *down center*. **Matt** *to the side. All the others stand together as they did in the beginning to sing the "Bette and Boo" theme. Music introduction to the theme is heard.*
All *(except* **Bette**, **Boo**, **Father Donnally**, **Matt** *sing):*

Ninety-nine bottles of beer on the wall,
Ninety-nine bottles of beer,
Take one down, pass it around,
Ninety-eight bottles of beer on the wall.

Ninety-eight bottles of beer on the wall,
Ninety-eight bottles of beer . . . *(etc.)*

(They keep singing this softly under the following scene.)

Boo *(holding up a piece of paper)*: I pledge, in front of Father Donnally, to give up drinking in order to save my marriage and to make my wife and son happy.

Father Donnally: Now sign it, Boo.

*(***Boo*** signs it.)*

Bette *(happy)*: Thank you, Boo. *(Kisses him; to* **Father Donnally:***)* Should you bless him or something?

Father Donnally: Oh, I don't know. Sure. *(Blesses them.)* In the name of the Father, Son, and Holy Ghost. Amen.

Bette: Thank you, Father.

Father Donnally: All problems can be worked out, can't they?

Bette: Yes, they can.

Father Donnally: Through faith.

Bette: And willpower. Boo, let's have another baby.

Those Singing (*finishing*):

> Take one down, pass it around,
> God bless us one and all!

(*Lights change.*)

Scene 20

Bette *and* **Boo** *dance. Perhaps no music in the background.*

Bette: This is fun to go dancing, Boo. We haven't gone since before our honeymoon.

Boo: You're mighty pretty tonight, gorgeous.

Bette: I wonder if Bonnie Wilson grew up to be pretty. We were the two stupidest in the class. I don't think Joanie's marriage is working out. Nikkos is a louse.

Boo: I think the waiter thought I was odd just ordering ginger ale.

Bette: The waiter didn't think anything about it. You think everyone's looking at you. They're not. Emily said she's going to pray every day that this baby lives. I wonder what's the matter with Emily.

Boo: Your family's crazy.

Bette: Don't criticize my family, Boo. I'll get angry. Do you think I'm prettier than Polly Lydstone?

Boo: Who?

Bette: You're going to have to make more money when this baby comes. I think Father Donnally is very nice, don't you? Your father is terrible to your mother. My father was always sweet to my mother.

Boo: I think the waiter thinks I'm odd.

Bette: What is it with you and the waiter? Stop talking about the watier. Let's just have a nice time. *(They dance in silence.)* Are you having a nice time?

Boo: You're lookin' mighty pretty tonight, Bette.

Bette: Me too, Boo.

They dance, cheered up. Lights change.)

Scene 21

Matt *addresses the audience.*

Matt: *Holidays,* an essay by Matthew Hudlocke. Holidays were invented in 1203 by Sir Ethelbert Holiday, a sadistic Englishman. It was Sir Ethelbert's hope that by setting aside specific days on which to celebrate things—the birth of Christ, the death of Christ, Beowulf's defeat over Grendel—that the population at large would fall into a collective *deep* depression. Holidays would regulate joy so that anyone who didn't feel joyful on those days would feel bad. Single people would be sad they were single. Married people would be sad they were married. Everyone would feel disappointment that their lives had fallen so far short of their expectations.

A small percentage of people, sensing the sadism in Sir Ethelbert's plan, did indeed pretend to be joyful at these appointed times; everyone else felt intimidated by this small group's excessive delight, and so never owned up to being miserable. And so, as time went on, the habit of celebrating holidays became more and more ingrained into society.

Eventually humorists like Robert Benchley wrote mildly amusing essays poking fun at the impossibility of enjoying holidays, but no one actually spoke up and attempted to abolish them.

And so, at this time, the Thanksgiving with the gravy having been such fun, Bette and Boo decided to celebrate the holiday of Christmas by visiting the Hudlockes.

(*Maybe a bit of Christmas music.* **Emily** *sits near* **Karl** *and* **Soot**. **Boo** *is off to one side, drinking something.* **Bette** *is off to another side, looking grim; she is also looking pregnant.* **Matt** *sits on floor near* **Emily** *or* **Soot**.)

Emily: I think Christmas is becoming too commercial. We should never forget whose birthday we are celebrating.

Soot: That's right. Whose birthday are we celebrating?

Emily: Our Lord Savior.

Soot: Oh yes, of course. I thought she meant some relative.

Emily: Jesus.

Soot: It's so nice of you to visit us today, Emily. I don't think I've seen you since you were away at that . . . well . . . away. (*Laughs.*)

Emily: Skippy asked me to come along, but I'm enjoying it.

Karl: Soot, get Bore and me another drink.

Bette: IF BOO HAS ANOTHER DRINK, I AM GOING TO SCREAM AND SCREAM UNTIL THE WINDOWS BREAK! I WARN YOU! *(Pause.)*

Karl *(looks at Bette)*: You're having another baby, woman?

Boo: I told you, Pop. Besty has a lot of courage.

Karl: You're trying to kill Betsy, bore?

Bette: I'm going to lie down in the other room. *(To Boo:)* Skippy will tell me if you have another drink. *(Exits.)*

Karl: You sound like quite a scout, Skip. Is Skip a scout, Bore?

Boo: What, Pop?

Karl: Is Skip a scout, Bore?

Soot: I was a Brownie.

(Re-enter Bette.)

Bette: Boo upsets Skippy's stomach. *(Sits down.)* I'm not leaving the room. *(Pause.)*

Soot *(to Emily)*: My friend Lottie always comes out to visit at Christmas time . . .

Karl: Her friend Lottie looks like an onion.

Soot: Karl always says she looks like an onion. *(Doing her best:)* But this year Lottie won't be out till after New Year's.

Karl: She may look like an onion, but she smells like a garbage disposal.

Soot: Oh, Karl. Because this year Lottie slipped on her driveway and broke her hip because of all the ice.

Karl: And she tastes like a septic tank.

Soot: So when Lottie gets here she's going to have a cast on her . . . Karl, where would they put the cast if you broke your hip?

Karl: Lottie doesn't have hips. She has pieces of raw whale skin wrapped around a septic tank in the middle.

Soot: Karl doesn't like Lottie.

Karl: That's right.

Soot: Karl thinks Lottie smells, but I think he's just kidding.

Bette: HOW CAN YOU SMELL HER WITH ALCO-HOL ON YOUR BREATH?

Boo: Oh God.

Karl: What did you say, woman?

Bette: You're too drunk to smell anything.

Boo: Will you lay off all this drinking talk?

Karl (*holds up his drink*): I think it's time your next still-born was baptized, don't you, Soot?

Soot: Karl . . .

(**Karl** *pours his drink on* **Bette's** *lap.* **Bette** *has hysterics. Lights change.*)

Scene 22

Matt *addresses the audience.*

Matt: Twenty years later, Boo has dinner with his son.

(**Boo**, **Matt**.)

Boo: Well, how are things up at Dartmouth, Skip? People in the office ask me how my Ivy League son is doing.

Matt: It's all right.

Boo: Are there any pretty girls up there?

Matt: Uh huh.

Boo: So what are you learning up there?

Matt: Tess of the d'Urbervilles is a . . . I'm not up at Dartmouth anymore. I'm at Columbia in graduate school.

Boo: I know that. I meant Columbia. How is it?

Matt: Fine.

Boo: Why are you still going to school?

Matt: I don't know. What do you want me to do?

Boo: I don't know. Your mother and I got divorced, you know.

Matt: Yes, I know. We have discussed this, you know.

Boo: I don't understand why she wanted a divorce. I mean, we'd been separated for several years, why not just leave it at that?

Matt: She wants to feel independent, I guess.

Boo: I thought we might get back together. You know, I always found your mother very charming when she wasn't shouting. A man needs a woman, son. I think your old man's going to get teary for a second. Do you have any problems you want to talk over? (*Blinks his eyes.*) I'm just an old softie.

(**Matt** *steps out of the scene.* **Boo** *stays in place.*)

Matt *(to audience)*: At about the same time, Bette also has dinner with her son.

(Bette, Matt.)

Bette: Hello, Skippy, dear. I made steak for you, and mashed potatoes and peas and cake. How many days can you stay?

Matt: I have to get back tomorrow.

Bette: Can't you stay longer?

Matt: I really have to get back.

Bette: You never stay long. I don't have much company, you know. And Polly Lydstone's son goes to her house for dinner twice a week, and her daughter Mary gave up her apartment and lives at home. And Judith Rankle's son moved home after college and commutes forty minutes to work.

Matt: And some boy from Pingry School came home after class and shot both his parents. So what?

Bette: There's no need to get nasty.

Matt: I just don't want to hear about Polly Lydstone and Judith Rankle.

Bette: You're the only one of my children that lived. You should see me more often.

(Matt *looks aghast.)*

Matt: That's not a fair thing to say.

Bette: You're right. It's not fair of me to bring up the children that died; that's beside the point. I realize Boo and I must take responsibility for our own actions. Of course, the Church wasn't very helpful at the time, but nonetheless we had brains of our own, so there's no point in assigning blame. I must take responsibility for wanting children so badly that I foolishly kept trying over and over, hoping for miracles. Did you see the article in the paper, by the way, about how they've discovered a serum for people with the Rh problem that would have allowed me to have more babies if it had existed back then?

Matt: Yes, I did. I wondered if you had read about that.

Bette: Yes, I did. It made me feel terribly sad for a little while; but then I thought, "What's past is past. One has no choice but to accept facts." And I realized that you must live your own life, and I must live mine. My life may not have worked out as I wished, but still I feel a deep and inner serenity, and so you mustn't feel bad about me because I am totally happy and self-sufficient in my pretty sunlit apartment. And now I'm going to close my eyes, and I want you to go out into the world and live your life. Good-bye. God bless you. (*Closes her eyes.*)

Matt (*to audience*): I'm afraid I've made that conversation up totally.

(*They start the scene over.*)

Bette: Hello, Skippy, dear. I made steak for you, and mashed potatoes and peas and cake. You know, you're the only one of my children that lived. How long can you stay?

Matt: Gee, I don't know. Uh, a couple of days. Three years. Only ten minutes, my car's double-parked. I could stay eight years if I can go away during the summer. Gee, I don't know.

(Lights change.)

Scene 23

Matt *addresses the audience.*

Matt: Back in chronology, shortly after the unpleasant Christmas with the Hudlockes, Bette brings Boo back to Father Donnally.

*(***Matt** *exits.* **Bette**, **Boo**, **Father Donnally**. **Bette** *in a foul temper.)*

Boo *(reading)*: I pledge in front of Father Donnally to give up drinking in order to save my marriage and to make my wife and son happy, and this time I mean it.

Bette: Read the other part.

Boo *(reading)*: And I promise to tell my father to go to hell.

Father Donnally: Oh, I didn't see that part.

Bette: Now sign it. *(***Boo** *signs it. Crossly, to* **Father Donnally:**) Now bless us.

Father Donnally: Oh, all right. In the name of the Father, Son, and Holy Ghost. Amen.

Bette: Now let's go home. *(***Bette** *and* **Boo** *cross to another part of the stage;* **Father Donnally** *exits.)* Now if you give up drinking for good this time, maybe God will let this next baby live, Boo.

Boo: Uh huh.

Bette: And I'm going to go to Mass daily. And Emily is praying.

Boo: Uh huh.

Bette: You're not very talkative, Boo.

Boo: I don't have anything to say.

Bette: Well, you should have something to say. Marriage is a fifty-fifty proposition.

Boo: Where do you pick up these sayings? On the back of matchpacks?

Bette: Why are you being nasty? Have you had a drink already?

Boo: No, I haven't had a drink already. I just find it very humiliating to be constantly dragged in front of that priest all the time so he can hear your complaints about me.

Bette: You have an idiotic sense of pride. Do you think he cares what you do? And if you don't want people to know you drink, then you shouldn't drink.

Boo: You are obsessed with drinking. Were you frightened at an early age by a drunk? What is the matter with you?

Bette: What is the matter with *you?*

Boo: What is the matter with *you?*

Bette: What is the matter with you?

Boo: What is the matter with you?

(This argument strikes them both funny, and they laugh. Lights change.)

Scene 24

Matt *addresses the audience.*

Matt: Shortly after the second pledge, Bette and Skippy visit the Brennans to celebrate Joanie's birthday. Boo stays home, drunk or sulking, it's not clear.

(**Margaret**, **Paul**, **Bette**, **Emily**, **Joan**, *and* **Matt**. **Joan** *looks pregnant;* **Bette** *also looks pregnant.* **Margaret** *comes downstage and addresses the audience.*)

Margaret: All my children live home, it's so nice. Emily's here, back from the rest home. And Joanie's here because her marriage hasn't worked out and somebody has to watch all those children for her while she's working, poor thing. And Tom's here sometimes, when he gets fired or when his spastic colon is acting up really badly. Then he always goes off again, but I bet he ends up here for good eventually! (*Chuckles, pleased.*) The only one who hasn't moved back home is Betsy, because she's so stubborn, but maybe she'll end up here too someday. I just love having the children home, otherwise there'd be no one to talk to—unless I wanted to learn sign language with Paul. (*Laughs.*) Sometimes I'm afraid if I had to choose between having my children succeed in the world and live away from home, or having them fail and live home, that I'd choose the latter. But luckily, I haven't had to choose! (*Smiles, returns to the scene.*) Come on, everybody, let's celebrate Joanie's birthday, and don't anybody mention that she's pregnant with yet another baby.

Bette: Every time I look at you, you're using nose spray.

Joan: You just got here.

Bette: But the last time I was here. You're going to give yourself a sinus infection.

Joan: I already have a sinus infection.

Margaret: The girls always fight. It's so cute. Now, girls.

Bette: Well, you use too much nose spray. You might hurt the baby inside you.

Joan: Let's drop the subject of babies, shall we?

Bette: I can't imagine why you're pregnant again.

Emily: Happy birthday, Joan! (*Everyone looks at her.*) I made the cake. I better go get it. (*Exits.*)

Margaret: Where's Booey, Bette?

Bette: He's home, drunk or sulking, Skippy and I can't decide which. Where's Nikkos, Joan?

Joan: Under a truck, I hope.

Bette: Well, you married him. Everyone told you not to.

Margaret: Let's change the subject. How are you doing in school, Skippy?

Matt (*glum*): Fine.

Margaret: Isn't that nice?

Bette: Skippy always gets A's. Is little Mary Frances still getting F's? Maybe if you were home more, she'd do better.

Joan: I can't afford to be home more. I don't have a life of leisure like you do.

(*Enter **Emily** with the cake.*)

Emily: Happy birthday, Joan.

Bette: Hush, Emily. If I had several children, I'd *make* time to spend with them.

Joan: You have a home and a husband, and I don't have either.

Bette: Well, it's your own fault.

Emily: Please don't argue, Bette.

Bette: Why do you say "Bette"? Why not "Joanie"? She's the one arguing.

Emily: Don't anybody argue.

Margaret: Don't excite yourself, Emily.

Joan: You see what your talking has done? You're going to give Emily another breakdown.

Emily: That's sweet of you to worry, Joanie, but I'm all right.

Bette *(to Joan):* You're just a neurotic mess. You're going to ruin your children.

Joan: Well, it's lucky you only have one to ruin, or else the mental ward wouldn't have just Emily in it.

(**Emily** *has an asthma attack.*)

Margaret: This cake looks very nice, Emily. Why don't we all have some. I bet Skippy would like a piece.

(**Margaret** *cuts the cake and passes it around.*)

Emily: We forgot to have Joanie blow out the candles.

Joan: There aren't any candles on the cake.

Emily: Oh, I forgot them. I'm sorry, Joanie.

Joan: Why should I have candles? I don't have anything else.

Margaret: Poor Joanie.

Bette: The dough's wet. Don't eat it, Skippy, it'll make you sick.

Emily: It isn't cooked right?

Bette: It's wet, it's wet. You didn't cook it enough.

Joan: I don't like cake anyway.

Margaret: Poor Joanie.

Bette: Everything's always "poor Joanie." But her baby's going to live.

Emily: Oh, Bette.

Joan: Well, maybe we'll both have a miracle. Maybe yours'll live and mine'll die.

Emily: Oh, Joanie.

Bette: Stop saying that, Emily.

Margaret: Girls, girls. This isn't conversation for the living room. Or for young ears.

Paul (*choking on cake*): #%#%#%GHGHR#%#%#** - ***** **#@#@#********.

Margaret: Paul, stop it. Stop it.

Paul *falls over dead. Lights change.)*

Scene 25

Matt puts a sheet over **Paul** *and addresses the audience.*

Matt: The funeral of Paul Brennan.

(Paul *in a chair with a sheet over him. Present are* **Matt,** **Bette, Boo, Margaret, Emily, Joan.***)*

Margaret: Paul was a fine husband. Good-bye, Paul. *(Teary.)*

Bette: Boo, thank you for being sober today. *(Kisses him.)* Look how happy it makes Skippy.

Boo: Skippy's drunk.

Bette: That's not funny.

(Enter **Father Donnally.***)*

Father Donnally: Dearly bereaved, Paul Brennan was a fine man, and now he's dead. I didn't know Paul very well, but I imagine he was a very nice man and everyone spoke well of him. Though he wasn't able to speak well of them. *(Laughs; everyone looks faintly appalled.)*

It's going to be hard not to miss him, but God put his children on this earth to adapt to circumstances, to do His will.

I was reminded of this fact the other morning, when I saw my colored garbage man collecting the refuse as I was on my way to say Mass. "Good morning, Father," he said. "Nice day." "And what's your name?" I said. "Percival Pretty, Father," he said. I smiled a little more and then I said, "And how are you—Percival?" And he said, "I'm doing the will of God, Father. God saw fit to take my little Buttermilk to Him, and now I'm emptying the garbage." "And who is little Buttermilk?" I said, and he said, "Why, Buttermilk was my daughter who broke her neck playing on the swings." And then he smiled. Colored folk have funny ideas for names. I knew one colored woman who named her daughter "January 22nd." It wasn't easy to forget *her* birthday!) *(Everyone looks appalled again.)*

But I think Percival Pretty's smile is a lesson for us all, and so now when I think of Paul Brennan, I'm going to smile. *(Smiles.)* And then nothing can touch you. *(Shakes hands with* **Margaret***.)* Be strong, dear.

Emily: Thank you, Father, for your talk.

Joan *(to* **Paul***'s dead body):* I've turned against Greeks after Nikkos. You were right, Dad, you were right!

Margaret: Thank you, Joanie. That was a nice gesture.

Father Donnally: Hello, Bette. Hello, Boo. You're putting on weight, Bette.

Bette: It's nothing. *(Sadly.)* I mean, it will be nothing.

(Lights change.)

Scene 26

Matt *addresses the audience.*

Matt: Bette goes to the hospital for the fourth time, et cetera, et cetera.

*(***Matt** *exits.* **Karl**, **Soot**, **Boo** *in their hospital "waiting" positions.)*

Boo: Pop. Eventually there's menopause, right? I mean, something happens, and then it stops, and . . .

Karl: Where are the Brennans? Have they lost the playing spirit?

Boo: Bette wasn't that way when I married her, was she?

Soot: Karl, is there still a space between my eyes?

Karl: What did you say, Soot?

Soot: Nothing. I'll wait till I get home. *(Smiles, feels between her eyebrows.)* Lottie always said when your eyebrows start to kiss, you better watch it.

Karl: Your mother's eyebrows are kissing, Bore.

Soot: You make everything sound so dirty, Karl. I wish I hadn't said that.

Karl: You want to hear a dirty story? Bore, are you listening? Once there was a traveling salesman, Soot, who met a girl in a barn who was more stupid than you.

Soot: I don't know this one.

Karl: The girl was an albino. Bore, you listening? She was an albino humpback with a harelip.

Boo: I'm going to get a drink. *(Exits.)*

Karl: And this albino humpback saw the traveling salesman with his dickey hanging out . . .

Soot: Karl, I have heard this one.

Karl: And she saw his dickey, and she said, "What's that?" and he said, "That's my dickey."

Soot: Karl, you told this story to Lottie, and she didn't like it.

Karl: And she said, "Why does it swing around like that?" and he said . . . Soot, what's the end of the story?

Soot: Karl, I never listen to your stories.

Karl: WHAT'S THE ANSWER TO THE JOKE?

Soot (*cries*)**:** Karl, I don't know. Something about a dickey. Maybe Bore knows. Booey? I have to go home and take a bath. I feel awful. (*Enter the* **doctor**. *He drops the baby on the floor, exits.* **Karl** *and* **Soot** *stare at it a moment.*) Catholics can't use birth control, can they? (*Laughs.*) That's a joke on someone. (*Enter* **Boo**.)

Karl: You missed it, Boo.

Boo: Did it live?

Karl: Not unless they redefined the term.

Soot: Don't tease Booey, Karl. Let's distract him, see if he remembers the joke.

Karl: You tell it, Soot.

Soot: No, I don't like the joke. I just thought maybe he'd remember it.

Boo: It didn't live.

Karl: Tell the joke, Soot.

Boo: Pop, I don't feel like hearing a joke.

Soot: Poor Booey.

Boo: I should probably see Bette, but I don't think I can face her.

Soot: Why don't you go get a drink, Booey, you look awful. I've got to go home and check my forehead.

Karl: Tell the damn joke, Soot.

Boo: Pop, I don't want to hear a joke.

Soot: It's all right, Booey. I'll tell it. Your father seems obsessed with it.

Karl *(rams his cigar in her mouth)*: Here, you'll need this.

Soot: Oh, Karl. *(Laughs.)* All right, Booey, you ready?

Boo: I don't want to hear a joke.

Karl: You'll like it, Bore.

Soot: Now, Booey . . . (**Boo** *starts to exit; they follow.)* . . . it seems there was this poor unfortunate, stupid crippled girl, and she met this salesman . . .

Boo: Will you two shut up? I don't want to hear a joke. *(Exits.)*

Soot: He doesn't want to hear the joke.

Karl: You told it wrong, Soot.

Soot: I'm sorry, Karl. I'm really not myself today. *(Touches between her eyes.)* I'm sorry, Booey. Booey!

(They exit.)

Scene 27

Bette, *playing rope or some such thing.*

Bette:

> What is the matter with Mary Jane?
> It isn't a cramp, and it isn't a pain,
> And lovely rice pudding's for dinner again,
> What is the *matter* with Mary Jane?

> Christopher Robin had weasles and sneezles,
> They bundled him into his bed.

(Kneels, looks at imaginary gravestones; then to audience, sadly:) The names of the children are: Patrick Michael, February twenty-sixth; Christopher Tigger, March

eighth; and Pooh Bear Eeyore, March twenty-fifth. Bonnie Wilson and I were, were . . . (Calls:) Father Donnally! Father Donnally . . . (**Father Donnally** *enters into* **Bette**'s *space.*) Father Donnally, can you help me?

Father Donnally: I'll try. What's on your mind, Bette?

Bette: I know sometimes one can misunderstand the will of God. But sex is for having babies, right? I mean, it's not just for marriage. Well, even if it is somewhat, I feel that I should be a mother; and I think it would be a sin for me not to try again. But I don't think Boo wants me to get pregnant again.

Father Donnally: Have you tried the rhythm method?

Bette: But I *want* to get pregnant.

Father Donnally: What does your doctor say?

Bette: The problem is that all the babies die. I don't see why I have to go through all this suffering. And Boo never helps me.

Father Donnally: I give a retreat for young married couples every year in the parish. Why don't you and your husband come to that? I'm sure it will help you if you're having trouble on the marriage couch.

Bette: All right, I'll bring Booey to the retreat. Thank you, Father.

Father Donnally: You're welcome, Bette. (**Father Donnally** *exits.*)

Bette (*crosses away; calls out*)**:** Boo. Boo. Booey. Booey. Booey. (*Enter* **Boo**.)

Boo: What?

Bette: Booey, I'm pregnant again. Do you think I'm going to die?

(*Lights change.*)

Scene 28

The retreat. Present are **Bette**, **Boo**; *also* **Margaret**, **Emily**, **Joan**, *the dead* **Paul** *(with sheet still over him);* **Karl**, **Soot**. *Enter* **Father Donnally**.

Father Donnally: In the name of the Father, of the Son, and of the Holy Ghost, Amen. Good evening, young marrieds. *(Looks about for a moment.)* Am I in the right room?

Emily: I'm not married, Father. I hope you don't mind that I'm here.

Father Donnally: On the contrary. I'm delighted. I'm not married either. *(Laughs.)* The theme of marriage in the Catholic Church and in this retreat is centered around the story of Christ and the wedding feast at Cana. Jesus Christ blessed the young wedding couple at Cana, and when they ran out of expensive wine, He performed His first miracle—He took vats of water and He changed the water into wine. *(Holds up a glass.)* I have some wine right here. *(Sips it.)*

Boo *(to* **Bette***):* He drinks. Why don't you try to get him to stop drinking?

Bette: Be quiet, Boo.

Father Donnally *(laughs, nervously)*: Please don't talk when I'm talking. *(Starts his speech.)* Young marrieds have many problems to get used to. For some of them this is the first person of the opposite sex the other has ever known. The husband may not be used to having a woman in his bathroom. The wife may not be used to a strong masculine odor in her boudoir. Or then the wife may not cook well enough. How many marriages have floundered on the rocks of ill-cooked bacon?

(Pause.) I used to amuse friends by imitating bacon in a saucepan. Would anyone like to see that? *(He looks around.* **Joan**, **Karl**, *and* **Soot** *raise their hands. After a moment,* **Emily**, *rather confused, raises her hand also.* **Father Donnally** *falls to the ground and does a fairly good—or if not good, at least unabashedly peculiar—imitation of bacon, making sizzling noises and contorting his body to represent becoming crisp. Toward the end, he makes sputtering noises into the air. Then he stands up again. All present applaud with varying degrees of approval or incredulity.)* I also do coffee percolating. *(He does this.)* Pt. Pt. Ptptptptptpt-ptptpt. Bacon's better. But things like coffee and bacon are important in a marriage, because they represent things that the wife does to make her husband happy. Or fat. *(Laughs.)* The wife cooks the bacon, and the husband brings home the bacon. This is how St. Paul saw marriage, although they probably didn't really eat pork back then, the curing process was not very well worked out in Christ's time, which is why so many of them followed the Jewish dietary laws even though they were Christians. I know I'm glad to be living now when we have cured pork and plumbing and showers rather than back when Christ lived. Many priests say they wish they had lived in Christ's time so they could have met Him; that would, of course, have been very nice, but I'm glad I live now and that I have a shower. *(***Emily**, *bothered by what he's just said, raises her hand.)* I'm not ready for questions yet, Emily. *(***Emily** *lowers her hand; he sips his wine.)* Man and wife, as St. Paul saw it. Now the woman should obey her husband, but that's not considered a very modern thought, so I don't even want to talk about it. All right, don't obey your husbands, but if chaos follows, don't blame me. The tower of Babel as an image of chaos has always fascinated me—*(***Emily** *raises her hand.)*

Bette: Put your hand down, Emily. *(***Emily** *does.)*

Father Donnally *(to* **Bette***)***: Thank you. Now I don't mean to get off the point. The point is husband and wife, man and woman, Adam and rib. I don't want to dwell on the inequality of the sexes because these vary from couple to couple—sometimes the man is stupid, sometimes the woman is stupid, sometimes both are stupid. The point is man and wife are joined in holy matrimony to complete each other, to populate the earth and to glorify God. That's what it's for. That's what life is for. If you're not a priest or a nun, you normally get married. (**Emily** *raises her hand.*) Yes, I know, you're not married, Emily. Not everyone gets married. But my comments today are geared toward the *married* people here. (**Emily** *takes down her hand.*) Man and wife are helpmates. She helps him, he helps her. In sickness and in health. Anna Karenina should not have left her husband, nor should she have jumped in front of a train. Marriage is not a step to be taken lightly. The Church does not recognize divorce; it does permit it, if you insist for legal purposes, but in the eyes of the Church you are still married and you can never be unmarried, and that's why you can never remarry after a divorce because that would be bigamy and that's a sin and illegal as well. *(Breathes.)* So, for God's sake, if you're going to get married, pay attention to what you're doing, have conversations with the person, figure out if you *really* want to live with that person for years and years and years, because you can't change it. Priests have it easier. If I don't like my pastor, I can apply for a transfer. If I don't like a housekeeper, I can get her fired. *(Looks disgruntled.)* But a husband and wife are *stuck* together. So know what you're doing when you get married. I get so *sick* of these people coming to me after they're married, and they've just gotten to know one another *after* the ceremony, and they've discovered they have nothing in common and they hate one another. And they want me to come up with a solution. (*Throws up his hands.*) What can I do? There is no solution to a problem like that. I can't help them! It puts me in a terrible position. I can't say get a divorce, that's against God's law. I can't say go get some on the side, that's against God's law. I can't say just pretend you're happy and maybe after a while you won't know the difference because, though that's not against God's law, not that many people know how to do that, and if I suggested it to people, they'd write to the Bishop complaining about me and then he'd transfer me to some godforsaken place in Latin America without a shower, and all because these people don't know what they're doing when they get married. (*Shakes his head.*) So I mumble platitudes to these people who come to me with these insoluble problems, and I think to myself, "Why didn't they *think* before they got married?" Why does no one ever *think?* Why did God make people stupid?" (*Pause.*) Are there any questions?

(**Bette** *raises her hand, as does* **Emily**. **Father Donnally** *acknowledges* **Bette**.)

Bette: Father, if I have a little girl rather than a boy, do you think it might live? Should I pray for this?

Father Donnally: You mean . . . a little girl to clean house?

Bette (*irritated*): No. I don't mean a little girl to clean house. I mean that the doctors say that sometimes a little girl baby fights infection better than a little boy baby, and that maybe if I have a little girl baby, the fighting between the Rh positive blood in her body and the Rh negative blood in my body would not destroy her, and she might live. (*Pause.*) Should I pray for this?

Father Donnally: By all means, pray for it. Just don't get your hopes up too high, though, maybe God doesn't want you to have any more babies. It certainly doesn't sound like it to me.

Bette: But I *can* pray?

Father Donnally: Yes. You can. No one can stop you.

Bette: That's what I thought.

(**Emily** *raises her hand.*)

Father Donnally (*dreading whatever she's going to say*): Yes, Emily?

Emily: Do you think maybe it's my fault that all of Bette's babies die? Because I left the convent?

Father Donnally: Yes, I do.

Emily (*stricken*): Oh my God.

Father Donnally: I'm sorry, Emily, I was just kidding. Are there any questions about newly married couples? (*Pause; no one stirs.*) Well, I don't have time for any more questions anyway. We'll take a short break for refreshments, and then Father McNulty will talk to you about sexual problems, which I'm not very good at, and then you can all go home. Thank you for your attention. In the name of the Father, and of the Son, and of the Holy Ghost. Amen. (*Starts to exit.*)

Emily: Father . . .

Father Donnally: I was just kidding, Emily, I am sorry. Excuse me, I have to go to the bathroom. (*Exits in a hurry.*)

Joan: You know, he makes a better piece of bacon than he does a priest.

Emily: I don't think he should joke about something like that.

Margaret: He's a priest, Emily.

Emily: I know you're right, Mom, but everyone should want to meet Our Savior, that's more important than having a shower . . .

Margaret: Don't talk anymore, Emily.

Bette: Did that make you feel better, Boo? Are you going to be easier to live with?

Boo (*sarcastic*)**:** Yes, it's all better now.

Bette: Why won't you let anyone help us?

Boo: What help? He just said that we shouldn't get married, and that if we did, not to bother him with our problems.

Bette: That's not what he said at all.

Margaret: Bette, don't talk anymore. Hello, Mrs. Hudlocke. Did you enjoy the talk?

Soot: I'm sorry, what?

Margaret: Did you enjoy Father's talk?

Soot: You know, I can't hear you. I think I'm going deaf. God, I hope so.

Margaret: What do you mean?

Soot: I'm sorry, I really can't hear you. (*Laughs.*) I haven't been able to hear Karl for about three days. (*Laughs.*) It's wonderful.

Bette: You should see an ear specialist.

Soot: What?

Bette: Oh, never mind.

Emily: Mom, don't you think . . .

Margaret: Emily, I said not to talk.

Bette: Well, if you don't want us to talk, what do you want us to do?

Margaret: Don't be cranky, Betsy. We'll just all wait for Father McNulty. Maybe he'll have something useful to say.

(They all wait. **Soot** *smiles.)*

Soot *(to audience)*: Little blessings. *(Laughs.)*

(Lights change.)

Scene 29

Matt *addresses the audience.* **Bette**, **Boo**, *and the dead* **Paul** *stay onstage.*

Matt: Twenty years later, or perhaps only fifteen, Bette files for a divorce from Boo. They have been separated for several years, since shortly after the death of the final child; and at the suggestion of a therapist Bette has been seeing, Bette decides to make the separation legal in order to formalize the breakup psychologically, and also to get better, and more regular, support payments. Boo, for some reason, decides to contest the divorce; and so there has to be testimony. Margaret and Joanie decide that Catholics can't testify in divorce cases, even though Bette had eventually testified in Joanie's divorce; and so they refuse to testify, frightening Emily into agreeing with them also. Blah blah blah, et cetera. So in lieu of other witnesses, I find myself sort of having to testify against Boo during my sophomore year at college. I am trying to work on a paper on Thomas Hardy, but find it difficult to concentrate. I fly home for the divorce proceedings. My mother's lawyer reminds me of my grandfather Paul.

(**Bette** *and* **Boo** *on opposite sides.* **Matt** *center, testifies, questioned by* **Paul** *who comes to life with no to-do. He still speaks in* **Paul's** *incomprehensible speech, but otherwise is quite lawyerly.)*

Paul: Ehl ee att, oo## oou ing orr agh## er uz acgh acgha@ @ lehc? [Tell me, Matt, do you think your father was an alcoholic?]

Matt: What?

Paul *(irritated he can't be understood, as Paul used to be)*: Oo## oou ing, orr agh# # er uz acgh acgha @ @ lehc? [Do you think your father was an alcoholic?]

Matt: Yes, I do feel he drank a fair amount.

Paul: Uht us ee acgh acgha @ @ lehc? [But was he an alcoholic?]

Matt: I'm really not in the position to say if anyone is actually an alcoholic or not.

Bette: I have a calendar here from the twelve years of our marriage. Every time it says "HD," that stands for "half-drunk." And everytime it says "DD," that stands for "dead drunk." I offer this as Exhibit A.

Paul *(telling her it's not her turn)*: Eeez own awk enn oo aht ahn uh ann. [Please don't talk when you're not on the stand.]

Bette: What?

Boo: I was never dead drunk. She has this thing about drunks.

Matt *(to **Bette**)*: He said you shouldn't talk when you're not on the stand.

Bette: I didn't.

Paul *(to **Bette**)*: Sssh. *(Long question to **Matt**:)* Ehl ee att, ihd oo# # eheh ee or ah # er ah ehey ohazsn, itt or uher? [Tell me, Matt, did you ever see your father, on any occasion, hit your mother?]

Matt: Yes. Hardy wrote *Tess of the d'Urbervilles* in 1891.

Paul *(irritated)*: As ott ut uh ass. [That's not what I asked.]

Matt: Oh, I'm sorry. I misheard the question.

Paul: Ihd ee itt er? [Did he hit her?] *(Makes hitting motion.)*

Matt: Yes, I did see him hit her.

Paul: Ah!

Matt: Of course, she hit him too. They both hit each other. Especially when they were driving. It was fairly harrowing from the back seat.

Bette: He started it.

Boo: She'd talk and talk like it was a sickness. There was no way of shutting her up.

Matt: Well, I would have appreciated your not arguing when you were driving a car.

Paul *(to **Bette** and **Boo**)*: Ee i# # #et! [Be quiet!]

Matt: Or at least left me home.

Paul: Shhh! *(Back to questioning **Matt**:)* Ehl ee att, oo oo# ih or ohn lhahf eher agh uh ink? [Tell me, Matt, do you in your own life ever have a drink?]

Matt: No, I don't know any happily married couples. Certainly not relatives.

Paul *(irritated)*: As ott ut uh ass. [That's not what I asked.]

Matt: Oh, I'm sorry. I thought that's what you asked.

Paul: Oo oo# ih or ohn lhahf eher agh uh ink? [Do you in your own life ever have a drink?]

Matt: No, my paper is on whether Eustacia Vye in *The Return of the Native* is neurotic or psychotic, and how she compares to Emily. That isn't what you asked either, is it? I'm sorry. What?

Paul: *Oo oo# ink?* [Do you drink?]

Matt: Ink?

Paul *(gesturing as if drinking)*: Ink! Ink!

Matt: No, I don't drink, actually.

Paul: Ehl ee att, urr oo uhaagee ehn or errens epyrateted? [Tell me, Matt, were you unhappy when your parents separated?]

*(**Matt** is at a loss. **Paul** must repeat the word "separated" several times, with hand gestures, before **Matt** understands.)*

Matt: No, I was glad when they separated. The arguing got on my nerves a lot. *(Pause.)* I'd hear it in my ear even when they weren't talking. When I was a child, anyway.

Paul: Ehl ee att, oo oo# ink or aher uz uh goooh aher? [Tell me, Matt, do you think your father was a good father?]

Matt: Yes, I am against the war in Vietnam. I'm sorry, is that what you asked?

Paul: Doo oo# ink ee uz a goooh ahzer? [Do you think he was a good father?]

Matt: Oh. Yes. I guess he's been a good father. (*Looks embarrassed.*)

Paul (*pointing at* **Boo**, *pushing for some point*): Buh dyoo oo# ink ee ad ohme or uh inkng bahblim? [But do you think he had some sort of drinking problem?] (*Makes drinking gesture.*)

Matt: Yes, I guess he probably does have some sort of drinking problem. (*Becoming worked up.*) I mean it became such an issue it seems suspicious to me that he didn't just stop, he kept saying there was no . . . (*Pulls back.*) Well, it was odd he didn't stop. It's really not my place to be saying this. I would prefer I wasn't here.

(*Pause.* **Matt** *is uncomfortable, has been uncomfortable relating to* **Boo** *for the whole scene.*)

Paul: Orr ehcoooz, att. [You're excused, Matt.]

Matt: What?

Bette: He said you were excused.

Matt: Oh good.

(**Paul** *exits, or goes back under sheet.*)

Bette: Thank you, Skippy. (*Kisses him.*)

Boo: Well, son. Have a good time back at school.

Matt: Thank you. I'm behind in this paper I'm doing. (*Pause.*) I have to get the plane.

Boo: Well, have a good trip. (*Looks embarrassed, exits.*)

Matt: Thank you. (**Bette** *exits.* **Matt** *addresses the audience:*) Eustacia Vye is definitely neurotic. Whether

she is psychotic as well is . . . In *Return of the Native*,
Hardy is dealing with some of the emotional, as well
as physical, dangers in the . . . One has to be very
careful in order to protect oneself from the physical
and emotional dangers in the world. One must always
be careful crossing streets in traffic. One should try not
to live anywhere near a nuclear power plant. One
should never walk past a building that may have a
sniper on top of it. In the summer one should be on
the alert against bees and wasps.

As to emotional dangers, one should always try to
avoid crazy people, especially in marriage or live-in situations, but in everyday life as well. Although crazy
people often mean well, meaning well is not enough.
On some level Attila the Hun may have meant well.

Sometimes it is hard to decide if a person is crazy,
like Eustacia Vye in *The Return of the Native*, which is
the topic of this paper. Some people may seem sane at
first, and then at some later point turn out to be totally
crazy. If you are at dinner with someone who suddenly seems insane, make up some excuse why you
must leave the dinner immediately. If they don't know
you well, you can say you're a doctor and pretend that
you just heard your beeper. If the crazy person should
call you later, either to express anger at your abrupt
leave-taking or to ask for medical advice, claim the
connection is bad and hang up. If they call back, I'm
afraid you'll have to have your phone number changed
again. When you call the phone company to arrange
this, if the person on the line seems stupid, hostile, or
crazy, simply hang up and call the phone company
back again. This may be done as many times as necessary *until you get someone sane*. As the phone company
has many employees. *(Breathes.)* It is difficult to totally
protect oneself, of course, and there are many precautions that one thinks of only when it's too late. But, as
Virginia Woolf pointed out in *To the Lighthouse*, admit-

tedly in a different context, the attempt is all.

Sometime after the divorce, five years or fifteen or something, Skippy has dinner with Karl and Soot and Margaret and Paul. Karl is near eighty, Margaret is senile, and Paul and Soot are dead.

Scene 30

Matt *sits at a table with all four.* **Paul** *and* **Soot** *have their heads on the table, dead.* **Karl** *seems fairly normal and himself;* **Margaret** *is distracted and vague.*

Matt: Hello. Nice to see you all.

Margaret: Emily! Huh-huh-huh. Tom! Nurse! Huh-huh-huh.

(NOTE: *the "huh-huh-huh" sound is not like laughter, but is a nervous tic, said softly and rather continuously throughout the scene. Technically speaking, it's like a mild vocal exercise using the diaphragm, like an ongoing cough reflex with no real cough behind it. A tic.*)

Karl: You're Skip, aren't you?

Matt: Yes. You remember me?

Karl: Yes, I remember you.

Margaret: Doctor. Mama. Huh-huh-huh. Huh-huh-huh.

Karl (*to* **Margaret**): Shut up.

Matt (*to* **Karl** *with seriousness*): What do you think I should do with my life?

Karl: Well, don't marry Soot.

Matt: Yes, but you know—

Margaret: Emily! Huh-huh-huh.

Matt: Everyone I know is divorced except for you and Soot, and Margaret and Paul. Of course, Soot and Paul are dead, but you all stayed married right up until death. And I wondered what mistakes you thought I could avoid based on all your experience.

Karl: Don't expect much, that's for starters. Look at Bette and Bore. She kept trying to change Bore. That's idiotic. Don't try to change anybody. If you don't like them, be mean to them if you want; try to get them committed if that amuses you, but don't ever expect to *change* them.

(**Matt** *considers this.*)

Matt: Do you agree with that, Grandma?

Margaret (*seeing* **Matt** *for the first time, leaning over to him*): Go to the baperdy sun ride zone a bat.

Matt: Baperdy?

Margaret: Lamin fortris trexin home. Emily!

Karl: It's too bad Paul's not still alive. It would be interesting to hear them talk together now.

(**Matt** *laughs at this.*)

Matt: Grandma, try to be lucid. I think Karl's advice makes sense, sort of, if you're in a bad marriage. But what if you're not in a bad marriage?

Margaret: When the bob?

Matt: I said, do you agree with Karl? Or do you see something more optimistic?

Margaret: I want Emily to clean the mirrors with milk of magnesia. I see people in the mirrors and they don't go away.

Karl: At least that was a complete sentence.

Matt: Emily's not here right now.

Margaret: Everyone's so late. Dabble morning hunting back, Emily. Huh-huh-huh.

Matt (*gives up on* **Margaret**; *back to* **Karl**): You know, I didn't know you and Soot back when you were young, or Margaret and Paul either, for that matter. Maybe your marriages *were* happy. I have no way of knowing.

Karl: I never expected much from life. I wanted to get my way in everything, and that's about all. What did you ask?

Margaret: Huh-huh-huh. Joan. Emily.

Matt: Why did you marry Soot?

Karl: No reason. She was much prettier when she was younger.

Matt: But surely you didn't marry her because she was pretty.

Karl: Don't tell me what I did.

Matt: And why did everyone call her Soot? How did she get the name "Soot"?

Karl: I don't remember. Was her name Soot? I thought it was something else.

Matt: I think her name was Soot. Do you think I misheard it all these years?

Karl: I couldn't say.

Matt: Why were you so mean to Soot?

Karl: Why do you want to know?

Matt: Because I see all of you do the same thing over and over, for years and years, and you never change. And my fear is that I can see all of you but not see myself, and maybe I'm doing something similar, but I just can't see it. What I mean to say is: did you all *intend* to live your lives the way you did?

Karl: Go away. I don't like talking to you. You're an irritating young man.

(**Matt** *leaves the scene.* **Karl**, **Margaret**, **Soot**, *and* **Paul** *exit or fade into darkness.*)

Scene 31

Matt (*trying to find his place, to audience*): Back into chronology again. Bette had the first baby, that is, the first dead baby, in 1951 or something. And then the second one in 1953 or 4 or something, and then . . . (*Enter* **Emily.**)

Emily: Hello, Skippy, dear. How does this sound to you? (*Reads from a note:*) "Please forgive my annoying qualities. I know that I talk too much about a thing and that I make people nervous that I do so. I am praying that I improve that fault and bet that you be patient with me."

Matt: Who is that to, Emily?

Emily: I don't know. Who do you think it should be to?

Matt: I don't know. It would be up to you.

Emily: Do you think it's all right?

Matt: I don't think you should be so hard on yourself, but otherwise I think it's fine.

Emily: Oh, thank you. *(Exits.)*

Matt: Okay. Just as dreams must be analyzed, so must the endless details of waking life be considered.

Having intelligence allows one to analyze problems and to make sense of one's life. This is difficult to achieve, but with perseverance and persistence it is possible not even to get up in the morning. To sleep. "To sleep, perchance to dream," to take the phone off the hook and simply be unreachable. This is less *dramatic* than suicide, but more *reversible*.

I can't make sense out of these things anymore. Um, Bette goes to the hospital for the third time, and there's the second dead baby, and then the fourth time, and the third dead baby, and then sometime after Father Donnally's marriage retreat, Bette goes to the hospital for the fifth time. The *last* child of Bette and Boo.

Scene 32

Enter **Boo**. *He and* **Matt** *are in their "waiting" positions back in the hospital.*

Boo: You don't have to wait here, Skip, if you don't want.

Matt: It's all right.

Boo: Who knows, maybe it will live. The doctors say if it's a girl, girls sometimes fight harder for life. Or something. *(Pause.)* You doing well in school?

Matt: Uh huh.

(The **doctor** *throws the baby, in a pink blanket, in from off-stage.)*

Doctor *(offstage)*: It was a girl.

Boo: You have any problems you want to talk over, son? Your old man could help you out.

Matt: I'll be outside a minute. *(Exits. Enter* **Bette**.*)*

Boo: Bette, let's not have any more. *(Mournfully:)* I've had enough babies. They get you up in the middle of the night, dead. They dirty their cribs, dead. They need constant attention, dead. No more babies.

Bette: I don't love you anymore, Boo.

Boo: What?

Bette: Why do you say what? Can't you hear?

Boo: Why do they never have a bar in this hospital? Maybe there's one on another floor.

Bette: I'm tired of feeling alone talking to you.

Boo: Maybe I'll take the elevator to another floor and check.

Bette: They don't have bars in hospitals, Boo.

Boo: I think I'll walk down. See you later. *(Exits.)*

Bette: I feel alone, Boo. Skippy, are you there? Skippy?

(Enter **Matt**.*)*

Matt: Yes.

Bette: Would you move this for me? *(She indicates the dead baby on floor. He gingerly places it offstage.)* Your father's gone away. All the babies are dead. You're the only thing of value left in my life, Skippy.

Matt: Why do you call me "Skippy"? Why don't you call me "Matt"?

Bette: It's my favorite movie.

Matt (*with growing anger*): My favorite movie is *Citizen Kane*. I don't call you "Citizen Kane."

Bette: Why are you being fresh?

Matt: I don't know.

Bette: I don't want to put any pressure on you, Skippy, dear, but you're the only reason I have left for living now.

Matt: Ah.

Bette: You're so unresponsive.

Matt: I'm sorry. I don't know what to say.

Bette: You're a typical Capricorn, cold and ungiving. I'm an Aries, we like fun, we do three things at once. We make life decisions by writing our options on little pieces of paper and then throwing them up in the air and going "Wheeee!" Wee wee wee, all the way home. I should have had more babies, I'm very good with babies. Babies *give* to you, then they grow up and they don't give. If I'd had more, I wouldn't mind as much. I don't mean to be critical, it's just that I'm so very . . . (*Looks sad, shakes her head.*) I need to go to bed. Come and read to me from A. A. Milne until I fall asleep, would you?

Matt: All right.

(**Bette** *starts to leave.*)

Bette (*suddenly tearful*): I don't want to call you "Matt."

Matt: That's all right. It's fine. I'll be in to read to you in a minute, okay?

Bette: Okay. (**Bette** *exits.*)

Matt: So I read her to sleep from *The House at Pooh Corner*. And then I entered high school, and then I went to college, and then they got divorced, and then I went to graduate school. I stopped studying Thomas Hardy for a while and tried Joseph Conrad. Oh, the horror, the horror. I'm afraid what happened next will sound rather exaggerated, but after she divorced Boo, Bette felt very lonely and unhappy for several years, and then she married another alcoholic, and then after two years that broke up, and then she got cancer. By this time I'm thirty, and I visit her once more in the hospital.

Scene 33

Emily *pushes* **Bette** *on in a wheelchair.* **Bette** *doesn't look well.*

Emily: Doesn't Bette look well today?

Matt: Very well.

Emily: Let's join hands. *(Holds* **Matt's** *and* **Bette's** *hands.)* In the name of the Father, and of the Son, and of the Holy Ghost, Amen. Heavenly Father, please lift this sickness from our beloved Bette. We place ourselves in Your hands. Amen. *(To* **Bette:***)* Do you feel any better?

Bette: The pain is a little duller.

Emily: Well, maybe I better go to the hospital chapel and pray some more.

Bette: That would be nice, Emily. Thank you. *(***Emily** *exits.)* I've spent a lot of time in hospitals.

Matt: Yes.

Bette: I sometimes wonder if God is punishing me for making a second marriage outside the Church. But Father Ehrhart says that God forgives me, and besides the second marriage is over now anyway.

Matt: I don't think God punishes people for specific things.

Bette: That's good.

Matt: I think He punishes people in general, for no reason.

Bette *(laughs)*: You always had a good sense of humor, Skippy. The chemotherapy hasn't been making my hair fall out after all. So I haven't needed those two wigs I bought. The woman at Lord and Taylor's looked at me so funny when I said I needed them because my hair was going to fall out. Now *she* didn't have a good sense of humor. Emily brought me this book on healing, all about these cases of people who are very ill and then someone prays over them and places their hand on the place where the tumor is, and there's this feeling of heat where the tumor is, and then the patient gets completely cured. Would you pray over me, and place your hand on my hip?

Matt: I'm afraid I don't believe in any of that.

Bette: It won't kill you to try to please me.

Matt: All right. *(Puts his hand on her hip.)*

Bette: Now say a prayer.

Matt *(said quickly as befits a parochial school childhood)*: Hail Mary, full of grace, the Lord is with thee. Blessed art thou amongst women, and blessed is the fruit of thy womb, Jesus. Holy Mary, mother of God, pray for us sinners, now and at the hour of our death, amen.

Bette: I think I feel a warmth there.

Bette: You're too old for her.

Boo: What?

Matt: Maybe he's gone deaf.

Boo: No, I can hear. I think it's my brain.

Bette: Do you remember when you tried to vacuum the gravy?

Boo: No.

Bette: Well, you did. It was very funny. Not at the time, of course. And how you used to keep bottles hidden in the cellar. And all the dead babies.

Boo (*smiles, happy*)**:** Yes. We had some good times.

Bette: Yes, we did. And do you remember that time after we got divorced when I came by your office because Mrs. Wright died?

Matt: Mrs. Wright?

Bette: You were at college, and I didn't have her very long. She was a parakeet. (**Matt** *suddenly comprehends with an "ah" or "oh" sound.*) And I called her Mrs. Wright because she lived in a Frank Lloyd Wright birdcage, I think. Actually it was a male parakeet but I liked the name better. Anyway, I kept Mrs. Wright free on the screen porch, out of the cage, because she liked it that way, but she'd always try to follow me to the kitchen, so I'd have to get to the porch door before Mrs. Wright, and I always did. Except this one time, we had a tie, and I squashed Mrs. Wright in the door. Mary Roberts Rinehart wrote a novel called *The Door*, but I like her *Tish* stories better. Well, I was very upset, and it almost made me wish I was still married to Boo so he could pick it up. So I went to Boo's office and I said, "Mrs. Wright is lying on the rug, squashed, come help," and he did. (*To* **Boo**, *with great affection:*) You

were very good. *(To* **Matt:***)* But then I think he went
out and got drunk.

Boo: I remember that parakeet.

Matt *(to* **Boo***)*: Why did you drink? *(To* **Bette:***)* Why did
you keep trying to have babies? Why didn't Soot leave
Karl? Why was her name "Soot"?

Bette: I don't know why her name was "Soot." I never
had a parakeet that talked. I even bought one of those
records that say "Pretty blue boy, pretty blue boy," but
it never picked it up. Boo picked Mrs. Wright up. As a
joke, I called people up and I played the record over
the phone, pretty blue boy, pretty blue boy; and people kept saying, "Who is this?" Except Emily, she tried
to have a conversation with the record.

Boo: I remember that parakeet. You shut the door on
it.

Bette: We moved past that part of the story, Boo. Anyway, then I called Bonnie Wilson and I played the record for her, and she knew it was me right away, she
didn't even have to ask. It's nice seeing your parents
together again, isn't it, Skippy?

Matt *(taken aback, but then it is nice)*: Yes, very nice.

Boo *(to* **Matt***)*: I was just remembering when you were
a little boy, Skip, and how very thrilled your mother
and I were to have you. You had all this hair on your
head, a lot of hair for a baby; we thought, "We have a
little monkey here," but we were very happy to have
you, and I said to your mother . . . *(Pause; he has another blackout; stares . . .)*

Bette: Ooops, there he goes again. Boo? Boo? *(Feels
pain.)* I better ring for the nurse. I need a shot for pain.

Matt: Should I go?

Bette: No. Wait till the nurse comes.

Boo (coming back): . . . to your mother, "Where do you think this little imp of a baby came from?"

Bette: We finished that story, Boo.

Boo: Oh.

Matt: I do need to catch my train.

Bette: Stay a minute. I feel pain. It'll go in a minute.

(**Matt** smiles, looks away, maybe for the nurse. **Bette** closes her eyes, and is motionless.)

Boo: Bette? Bette?

Matt: Is she sleeping?

(**Matt**, with some hesitation, feels for a pulse in her neck. Enter **Emily**.)

Emily: Oh, hello, Boo. It's nice to see you. Are you all right, Skippy?

Matt: She died, Emily.

Emily: Then she's with God. Let's say a prayer over her.

(**Emily** and **Boo** pray by **Bette's** body. Music to "Bette and Boo" theme is heard softly. **Matt** speaks to the audience.)

Matt: Bette passed into death, and is with God. She is in heaven, where she has been reunited with the four dead babies, and where she waits for Boo, and for Bonnie Wilson, and Emily, and Pooh Bear and Eeyore, and Kanga and Roo; and for me.

(Lights dim. End of play.)

AUTHOR'S NOTES

I feel particularly close to *The Marriage of Bette and Boo*, and to the excellent production the play received this past spring at Joseph Papp's New York Shakespeare Festival.

The play itself has a rather long history. I wrote the first draft of the play—a forty-five-minute, one-act version—when I was still a student at Yale School of Drama, and it was produced there my final year (1974).

The play had the same characters and the same number of stillborn children, but otherwise was much more sketchlike, and its emotional impact was far more elliptical. For instance, the scene at Thanksgiving, Bette's phone call, Matt's dinner with the dead grandparents, the divorce scene, the final hospital scene—all these were not in this early version.

The one-act version received a very good student production, directed by Bill Ludel, and featured (among others) Kate McGregor-Stewart as Bette, John Rothman as Boo, Franchelle Stewart Dorn as Emily, Walton Jones as Father Donnally, and Sigourney Weaver as Soot.

At Yale my work had been controversial up to this point, especially *Better Dead Than Sorry*, which featured Sigourney Weaver singing the title song while receiving shock treatments. *Bette and Boo*, though, seemed to win over a far larger audience to my work (at Yale, that is), and was said to have more of a sense of compassion in the midst of the dark humor.

There were subsequently four other productions (that I know of) of the one-act version. The first was at Williamstown Theatre's Second Company, directed by

Peter Schifter. I didn't see this production, but heard positive reports, and was especially gratified to hear it was a big success when presented at a women's prison where the inmates apparently got into cheering on Bette and, well, booing Boo.

Then there was a summer Yale cabaret version, directed by Walton Jones, and featuring Christine Estabrook as Bette, Charles Levin as Boo, and (ah-hem) Meryl Streep as bitter sister Joan. Then a workshop at Chicago's St. Nicholas Theatre Company (now closed, and lamented). And finally a Princeton College undergraduate production, directed by Mitchell Ivers, and with actress-writer Winnie Holzman as a memorable, giggling Soot.

Around 1976, I decided not to let the one-act version be performed anymore, because I felt that the material could be expanded to full-length, and I wanted to hold off wider exposure of the work until I did that.

The play "feels" autobiographical, I rather assume; and it would be disingenuous to pretend that the characters of Bette and Boo did not in many significant ways reflect my parents' lives. Many of the surrounding characters and events are indeed fictionalized, but there is a core to the play that is pretty much rooted in my past.

I wrote the first "expansion" of the play sometime in 1980, and had a reading of it at the Actors Studio. Having met Joseph Papp a few times by then, I called him up and asked him if I could arrange a reading of the play for him—which I did. From that reading, I did various rewrites, especially relating to Father Donnally, and to the character of Matt, which was almost nonexistent in the one-act version.

For complicated reasons, the play kept not being scheduled over the next couple years, though it never died at the Public, thanks to Papp's interest, and to the support of Gail Merrifield and Bill Hart in the play department, and of others there was well (Robert Blacker, Lynn Holst, John Ferraro, Morgan Jenness).

In the summer of 1984, Papp and I agreed upon Jerry Zaks as director, and the play was scheduled for the 1984-5 season. Zaks, as original director of *Sister Mary Ignatius*, *Beyond Therapy* (off-Broadway), and *Baby with the Bathwater*, had clearly become somewhat of a specialist in doing my work, and our familiarity with one another has made for that wonderful ease and shorthand that sometimes happens with a long-term collaboration.

Mr. Papp (I do call him Joe, but Catholic schoolboy manners are hard to break) was very much of the opinion that I should play the part of Matt myself. Just as Tom in *The Glass Menagerie* "feels" like an author surrogate, so does the part of Matt; and Papp, who had seen me perform a few times, felt that my doing the role was a head-on way of dealing with the "author's voice" nature of the part that might pay off.

I was fearful that it might seem self-indulgent or self-pitying to have me play Matt; but conversely I also thought it might work fine, and I had had success sometimes acting in my own plays at Yale (though never in parts that had any biographical reverberations). Plus, I thought that if I were to turn down the chance, I would always wonder what it might have been like. So, particularly since Zaks was to be at the helm, I chose to chance it. (I did tell Jerry before rehearsals that I wouldn't hate him if he decided it wasn't working and I should be replaced.)

Performing the role, particularly in previews when it was very new, sometimes struck me as a preposterously public manner in which to reveal some rather personal thoughts and feelings. Since I don't feel I'm easily open about emotions to begin with, it seemed terribly odd to me that I had gotten myself into this position.

Most of the feedback I got on my doing the part was extremely positive; and I know that the last scene in particular, as experienced from inside it (and shared with actors Joan Allen, Graham Beckel, and Kathryn Grody), seemed suffused with a sense of letting go and finishing that acknowledged anger but ended, basically, with—well, I was going to say with acceptance and love, but that sounds glib and rhythmically convenient. But then that probably is what I mean. I know that acting the last scene did feel extremely positive and not at all despairing (though certainly sadness was there).

Some people, I'm told, dismiss this play as too angry; I don't agree with them and feel they may be denying something I've found to be true: that unless you go through all the genuine angers you feel, both justified and unjustified, the feelings of love that you do have will not have any legitimate base and will be at least partially false. Plus, eventually you will go crazy. Well, anyway, I'm glad I wrote the expanded version and that I played Matt.

The production of *The Marriage of Bette and Boo* at the Public Theatre was the most positive and joyful experience I have had in professional theater up to this point (and I say that having liked most of my theatrical experiences). The pleasure of working with Jerry Zaks again, total agreement with all three designers, the support of all the departments in Papp's excellent New York Shakespeare Festival—this made for a production experience with no drawbacks. I may sound gaga with praise, but it would be pointless not to acknowledge it.

As for the actors, I've usually felt fondness and admiration for all the casts I've worked with, but the *Bette and Boo* company grew to be an especially close and loving one.

The ten parts are of varying size, of course, but each part is rather meaty in its way; and a few days after our opening in early May, all ten of us shared in an Obie award for Ensemble Acting. The "Ensemble," as we grew fond of grandly calling ourselves, consisted of Joan Allen, Graham Beckel, Olympia Dukakis, Patricia Falkenhain, Kathryn Grody, Bill McCutcheon, Bill Moor, Mercedes Ruehl, Richard B. Shull, and myself. God bless us, each and every one.

I also won an Obie for playwriting, Jerry Zaks for direction (and for his direction of Larry Shue's *The Foreigner*), and Loren Sherman for his set designs over the past couple of seasons, including *Bette and Boo*. One wants to limit how important awards and critical praise seem for all the times one doesn't receive them, and for the instances when fine work of others doesn't get acknowledgment. But, that said, we were pretty happy about the Obies.

Well, anyway, it was a terrific experience.

Specific Notes for Actors and Directors

I am in the habit of writing notes to the acting editions of my plays in an attempt to offer what I would say to the director and actors of a future production if I were able to be present during their rehearsals. The notes are not meant to inhibit the creative impulses of either director or actor, but to help clarify any confusing aspects in the play or in its production, and to offer my ideas on what acting tone best serves my work. Words are only precise up to a point, so your common sense and aesthetic judgment will have to be your chief guide. But I hope you will read these notes as you might have a conversation with me at a preproduction meeting.

Bette's Name

I intend the name "Bette" to be pronounced as "Bet"—one syllable, which better contrasts with her nickname of Betsy.

Another pronunciation thing: please pronounce "Nikkos" as Nee-kos. Margaret may Americanize it as Nick-os, perhaps, but the others should get it right.

Music

Please use Richard Peaslee's music. (He is the distinguished composer of *Marat/Sade*.) The music box melodiousness of his "Bette and Boo" theme seems to set just the right tone for the play's opening; and yet the melody has an underlying poignance to it when it comes back later.

Jerry Zaks used a repeat of the theme played on piano (on tape) at the end of Act I, and again at the end of the play. The music helps the acts to end, and the theme's poignance is worth adding to those two moments as well. (I'm always upset when an audience doesn't know an act—or a play—is over; in this case, I know that the endings do play as endings with the proper directorial skill.)

Zaks started the music at the end of Act I somewhere around Bette saying, "Are you awake, Boo? Boo?"; and at the end of the play, right after Emily's "Let's say a prayer over her," and before Matt's final speech. I recommend the use of the music at the end of Act I, and request it at the end of Act II.

Zaks also used a recurring musical intro for the entrance of the characters into each of the hospital scenes (except the last one, Scene 32), which I also recommend. (It's actually a jaunty fragment of the "Bette and Boo" theme, and is in Peaslee's packet of music.)

The Opening

The "Bette and Boo" theme at the opening of the play is sung through once, sweetly and simply, and then is sung again, more up-tempo, as a two-part round.

The opening moments are very nonrealistic. In Zaks's version, the wedding couple and the relatives and Father Donnally all stood close together on a group of steps in front of stained-glass windows, and sang looking straight out. (They were not specifically performing "for" the audience, they just sang straight out, that's all.)

When the characters call out to one another, it's as if they are all in isolation, calling out to their significant others, uncertain where the other is. They are not upset particularly, just desirous that they get a response—though Joan may be annoyed about Nikkos, and Emily may be somewhat worried as she usually is, and so on as is logical for the other characters. It will seem a little enigmatic to the audience, but it's meant to be so, and the enigmatic quality is a good setup for Matt's opening comments about looking for order.

In Zaks's version, Matt was able to be hidden behind the people on the steps, and make his first entrance coming from behind them (which was nice thematically, as Matt indeed has "come from" this group of people). If that didn't work in terms of your sightlines, just have Matt enter from offstage after the calling out, I would think.

The Setting

I mentioned stained-glass windows above, so perhaps this is a good time to discuss the set.

Loren Sherman is a brilliant stage designer who,
judging from his work on *Bette and Boo*, *Baby with the
Bathwater*, and Peter Parnell's *Romance Language*, seems
especially gifted in solving the problems presented by
plays with many different settings that need to move
quickly and fluidly.

In describing what he did, I do not mean to imply
that his is the only solution or one you should try to
copy, just that it should be of interest how his set ad-
dressed problems inherent in the script.

Sherman's set was a series of sliding maroon-colored
panels that slid on a track recessed into a carpet that
covered the stage. These panels were operated by
stagehands who stood behind them, but it could be
done mechanically as well.

The panels were used to change the stage space in
numerous ways, to suggest all the various locales; importantly, they were designed and rehearsed so that
the changes were just about instantaneous. With
thirty-three scenes, eliminating "waits" between the
scenes is of the highest importance.

There were three sets of panels: an upstage set,
which created the back wall of the setting; a midstage
set of panels; and a downstage set of panels.

The upstage, or back wall, panels were designed to
be any of three things: first, a solid maroon background with three stained-glass windows, obviously
suggesting a church; second, a solid background with
one or more windows with venetian blinds and curtains on them, suggesting any of the home settings;
and third, a solid maroon background with nothing on
it, allowing for an "anyplace" setting.

The midstage and downstage sets of panels were also solid-colored with nothing on them, and were used to change and limit the stage space (and to allow stagehands to set up for the next scene behind them).

The "bigger" scenes were performed on the full playing space, using the upstage panels for the appropriate back wall, and with a few chosen furniture pieces. "Big" scenes included the wedding, Thanksgiving at Bette and Boo's house, the retreat, etc.—usually a scene with a lot of people or that "felt" big.

The "smaller" scenes took place in playing areas defined and limited by configurations of the panels.

In any case, these three rows of panels were used in an extremely complicated way to change the shape and size of the playing space in a split second. The logistics of how the furniture pieces were set up behind the closed panels so that when they opened the next set was already in place—these logistics are too complicated for me to articulate for the purposes of this essay.

However, I don't intend for you to copy this system, just to be aware how this panel system allowed for the stage space and setting to be changed instantaneously as far as the audience was concerned—which is my main concern. With thirty-three scenes, speed in going from scene to scene is of the essence.

In terms of other setting ideas, full realistic settings for any of the scenes would probably be wrong; there are just too many changes for "full" settings not to seem laborious. I'm pretty sure you want a "suggestive" setting for this play, one that changes its implications and looks easily.

One single setting (an all-purpose living room, perhaps) that with lighting and staging kept suggesting different locales would be fine with me, and a logical way to solve the problems in designing this play.

Or a totally nonrealistic space that had modulelike blocks that stood in for furniture (as is used in all plays at the O'Neill National Playwrights Conference, for instance), is also fine with me. I even suggested to Zaks and Sherman the rather crackpot notion of setting the play on a great big enormous wedding cake (with the characters able to sit or stand on the different "edges" of the cake); though that might be an extreme setting, it would have the benefit of standing in easily for all the different scene changes, without any waits for the audience, and that's my major concern. (I wouldn't want an all-purpose church setting, though, as that would overstate the Catholic influence in the play. With our use of the stained-glass windows, it was extremely important to me that they could also disappear when we wanted them to.)

One additional comment about Sherman's solution, though. Aside from the ability to keep the action moving with no stops, the sliding panels sometimes acted as punctuation to the end of a scene. (You could try to get a similar effect with lighting, or doors closing, I imagine.)

A Brief Harangue

A stray note about the set. Please don't set the play "where Matt lives," wherever that may be. I saw a production of the full-length version that seemed to be in some depressing lower-class tenement, with a cheap kitchen table and a window center stage overlooking a brick wall and a fire escape. This was a "one-setting solution" (which I certainly don't object to), so all the scenes took place in this set. Aside from finding the set, though, extremely demoralizing to look at, I wondered why the director had decided that the Brennan and Hudlocke families were so poor; I thought of them as firmly in the middle class, even (especially the Hudlockes) upper-middle class.

I was flabbergasted when the director told me that the set didn't reflect the Brennans or Hudlockes at all but was "where Matt lived." Since there are no scenes where Matt lives, the audience (I am convinced) had no more idea than I did that this depressing abode represented Matt's apartment. So this bad idea was not even effectively communicated. But, more importantly, it is a very bad idea. Yes, the play in many ways *is* Matt's memory play, but to set the play "where Matt lives" makes as little sense as looking at Tom's last speech in *The Glass Menagerie* and then setting the whole play in Amsterdam.

This same production staged Scene 30 (Matt has dinner with Karl, Soot, Margaret, and Paul) with Karl and Margaret *not* at the table (though Soot and Paul were), and with Matt not at the table, but *lying on his back*, downstage, staring at the ceiling. His opening line, "Hello. Nice to see you all," was very confusing, as one didn't know to whom he was speaking. And since most of the time he didn't get to look at Karl (he finally got up off his back, after a while), the content of the scene never really took place.

The director explained this staging by saying he feared that the audience would think the scene "real" if Matt actually sat at the table; I pointed out to him that since there were two dead people at the table, it was not highly likely that the audience would think the scene "real."

Furthermore, his belief that he had to somehow specially address what was or wasn't "real," due to the fact that Matt is remembering some scenes and presumably imagining and/or exaggerating others—this belief was, I feel, an incorrect and dangerous side path he had wandered down. The director basically didn't trust the audience to make sense of this issue *as communicated by the script itself*, and felt he had to run around "interpreting" it for them with little signals. (The set and this scene were not the only examples. The last scene of the play, a rather realistic piece of writing, was staged Beckett-style, with all three characters sitting in chairs, staring straight ahead, never looking at one another. I don't know what that was supposed to do—perhaps remove the scene's natural warmth, which it certainly did.) What made it worse, he was talented, and he meant well. (I sound like Matt.) But it was not a happy meeting of play and director.

Some people, I'm told, bristle at the fact that I write these notes. As an actor, I can sympathize to some degree, and I don't want to straitjacket creativity. But seeing tenements "where Matt lives" and a dinner scene staged with none of the participants at dinner is an extremely painful experience for an author. If a director puts Hamlet on roller skates, or even if a director sets *Endgame* in a subway station—the plays are so famous one knows that it is a directorial interpretation, for good or bad. (And the subway setting, for instance, which Joanne Akalitis tried at American Repertory Theatre, even sounds interesting to me.) But if a director does a strange interpretation of a new play, the audience quite logically assumes that that is how the author wrote it. And I don't think that's fair.

And that's why I write these notes—probably not for the directors who would stage Matt lying on his back no matter what I said, but for people who might genuinely want to capture the tone I had in mind, and who don't mind some pointers in getting there.

Well, enough of that. But please don't set this play "where Matt lives," or in Matt's mind, or in Amsterdam. Please do not have people lie on their backs on the floor every time a director says "at table." Thank you.

The Costumes

Thirty-three scenes spanning thirty years seems a nightmare in terms of changing costumes to keep up with the time span; plus, many of the scenes are so short, it's probably not even possible. Luckily, I don't think it's desirable either.

Costume designer William Ivey Long, in agreement with me and Zaks, chose to leave everyone in their wedding clothes, more or less, for the whole play. This was thematically appealing to me as well—we are always reminded of how the characters started out.

Though the characters' "core costumes" did indeed remain the same throughout, there were tiny changes for all that made for variety (and a rather significant change for Bette).

As the play went on, the removal of suit coats for the men, or of hats and veils and lace jackets for the women, made for a sense of variety, as well as let the characters look more relaxed for some scenes (when they're at home), and more formal for others (Soot and Margaret putting their hats back on for Thanksgiving, say, or for the early hospital scenes).

Further, there were certain small logical additions— Paul, usually a bit downtrodden, added to his costume a dumpy-looking cardigan sweater once he was rid of his wedding jacket. Likewise a loose, rather gloomy-looking sweater was eventually worn by the non-fashion-conscious Emily.

In designing the wedding clothes, Long made a conscious decision to give the characters good taste, with which I concur. I would be unhappy with cheap shots making fun of any corny clothing choices, or making any comments about vulgar 1950s garb (like those awful wide skirts that flair out at the sides, which made me think of 1955 movies). Indeed, since the wedding takes place in the late 1940s (judging from the chronology that Matt sputters out in Scene 31), Long pointed out to me that it would be a 1940s look that the wedding apparel would have, not a mid-50s Doris Day look.

The core costume used at the wedding should, though, not be distracting later in the play. For instance, if one dressed Emily and Joan in full-length bridesmaids' outfits, it would be problematic in the later scenes. So Long didn't give Emily and Joan floor-length gowns, but nonmatching (though pastel coordinated) normal-length dresses, with corsages and little lace jackets; the corsages and jackets were removed for later scenes.

Boo wore tails for the wedding itself, but by Scene 4, had removed his tailcoat to remain in just his vest and tie, then later removed the tie, then later, as his life disintegrated more, removed the vest and was put in his shirt sleeves. (He though, rather touchingly, dressed back up in his wedding garb for his final visit to Bette in the hospital.)

Bette's wedding dress was the larger problem. Long wanted a full-length full bridal gown look for Bette at the top of the play. I concurred, but felt that it would be too distracting in later scenes. (Imagine Bette striding around yelling, "You don't vacuum gravy" in a floor-length wedding gown. It *could* work, actually, I suppose, as a thematic statement, but the dangers for pretentiousness and ludicrousness are high.)

Long told me—as I didn't know—that particularly in the 1950s, women's magazines encouraged their readers to re-do their wedding gowns into cocktail dresses, so he decided to build Bette a dress that was normal length but otherwise copied her wedding dress. (For Act II, he gave her a light blue version of the same dress, as if she had dyed it somewhere along the way; Long added this just for variety.)

In dress rehearsals, I found the look of Bette's cocktail dress rather more formal-looking than I expected, and I felt that its relation to the wedding dress was not as obvious as I thought it would be. So on the night of the first preview, I asked Zaks and Long if I could add a line for Matt to say about Bette having refashioned her wedding gown at the suggestion of *Redbook*. I did this only for the sake of clarity, but discovered that the line played also as one of the biggest and most consistent laughs of the evening. Such are the joys of collaboration.

For the hospital scene at the end, Long designed a nightgown for Bette that was from the same cream-colored material as her wedding gown and had a similar neckline. Since Bette had been in light blue for all of Act II, the sudden return to wedding white coupled with Boo's return to his tails was very touching. (At the final dress, when Graham Beckel as Boo entered the hospital carrying a bouquet of flowers and dressed again in his tails, Joan Allen as Bette, seeing this costume choice for the first time, had to fight back tears in order to continue the scene.)

Another costume issue—the pregnancies of Joan and Bette. I think they should be noticeably pregnant when indicated in the script, but not overdone so as to be grotesque. (Whether Joan should look pregnant in the wedding scene I leave to your discretion. In Scene 6, Bette should not look pregnant yet; she has probably just learned she's expecting.)

For the Christmas at the Hudlockes' scene, the second pledge, and Joan's birthday party, it is important that Bette look pregnant. Unfortunately, Scene 23

("Twenty years later, Bette has dinner with her son") comes in the middle of this, and Bette clearly must not look pregnant in the twenty years later scene. Our solution was to make a little pillow that fit under Bette's dress, attached around her waist with Velcro, and which was removable and replaceable quickly, offstage. If, for some reason, you had trouble with this, dispense with the pregnancy look for Christmas and the second pledge, and just use it for the birthday party, which is after Scene 23.

A final Bette costume issue, Karl must pour his drink on her at the end of Christmas. At the Public, her dress was Scotchgarded so that water literally ran off it, without damaging the dress. (She actually had two identical Act II dresses, one not Scotchgarded, so that she was not stuck in a wet dress if any of the water should fall onto the non-Scotchgarded part.)

The final costume issues are the doctor, the priest, and Matt.

The doctor is a small part, doubled by the actor who plays Father Donnally (for purposes of convenience, as well as a slight thematic tie of the doctor and priest being outside authorities who deal with Bette and Boo). The doctor's costume should be whatever says "doctor" quickly to the audience and makes it clear that it's not Father Donnally dressed differently.

Father Donnally is a parish priest, and as such has the normal black cassock that Bing Crosby wore in so many films (and so many priests wore in life, I suppose I should add). Zaks and I felt that the black cassock was a little drab for the opening, and so for that one he wore nice white-and-silver priest's wedding robes.

Matt is not dressed for the wedding, as he was not born at that point. Although if you wanted to dress him up out of "respect" for the event, that's okay. I rather prefer Long's solution, which was to dress him as "student," with clothes that clearly wouldn't fit in with the wedding picture.

Though Matt would have been in college in the 1960s, a full-out radical student look for him would not be a correct match with his personality. Long went for preppy casual—a nice sports jacket, a loosened tie over a blue workshirt, jeans. Long liked that the jeans in particular clashed visually with the wedding party, more than a dressier casual choice (khaki, corduroy) would have. Matt needn't—and shouldn't—change clothes for the duration of the play.

If you set the play in Amsterdam, Matt should wear a sailor suit and have tattoos saying MOTHER on his forearms. (Just kidding, just kidding!)

Another Harangue

No, false alarm.

From here on in, I'm going to offer comments on miscellaneous issues, and will skip around rather.

The Honeymoon

Zaks staged Scene 4 (the honeymoon, continued) with Bette and Boo in a bed, unlike how I had it in the script, which was Bette and Boo standing together wrapped in a sheet. I've left it the latter way in the script because I think it's easier to stage without a bed, but I have no objection to the scene taking place in a bed, if that works out for you.

However, either way (sheet or bed), I like the stylization of keeping Bette and Boo more or less still dressed in their wedding clothes. If you have them either in their underwear or, worse, with their shirts off,

I find that that distracts from the content of the scene itself, and for the comedy in it as well. (It can turn it sniggering, which is unpleasant. The scene certainly has a flirtatious feel to some of it, but it's really not *about* sex or "first time" at all. It's primarily about the workings of Bette's mind (charming but somewhat infantile).

The Hospital Scenes

I envisioned the hospital "lineup" for every scene to be all the characters standing in a straight line, facing out to the audience, as if their backs were against a hospital hallway. This isn't a very realistic pose, but the stylization of it seems right for the scene, and the fact that we can always see their faces at the top of the scene waiting is also important. (I don't mean they stay frozen, staring out; they look at each other when they speak, and turn to the doctor when he comes out. I just mean they start out that way.)

The doctor, the script says, "drops the baby." He does not "throw" the baby down in anger, or disgust; or conversely, he does not toss it onto the ground with some fake cheeriness. He either shows no emotion or, maybe as time goes by, a little normal fatigue over doing the same thing over and over (but subtly). He announces the fact: "It's dead. The baby's dead." Then he lets go of the bundle that has been in his arms, and it drops to the floor. Let the action make the moment; don't color it in any particular way.

The Baby Prop

The original student production and Zaks's production did the baby prop as a believably shaped "bundle" that made a thud when dropped. It was constructed as a beanbag (I think), more or less in a baby's form, but *totally* wrapped in a blanket, so that one could not see any "baby" or beanbag. I'm sorry to be didactic, but I think that is the one way to design the baby.

If you use a real doll that you can see through an opening in the blanket (as I've seen), the first thing that happens is that the audience gasps because the image for a split second becomes too real—you think about the horror of dropping a real baby on the ground; then a second later, the audience reminds itself that the doll is, of course, fake and not a baby at all, and by then they're outside the play and not thinking about Bette or the dead baby or any of the characters onstage.

Using the visible doll made the audience react in two stages (within a few seconds), which is not good. When it is only the bundle that is dropped, the audience is able to react together at the same time on the same issue: they are shocked the baby is dead, they are shocked it has been dropped, they laugh that it has been dropped, they question whether it is appropriate to laugh that it has been dropped.

And using any very nonrealistic representation—like a basketball or something—is also not good: it will take us too far out of reality and be too jokey. For all the oddness of my representing the babies' deaths the way I have, it does still communicate that Bette has lost a child. A bouncing basketball would not do that well. (Plus, it should make a small thud sound when it hits—which will help trigger the audience's conflicted laughter; if it bounces, it's too farcical, too unreal.)

The Fake Scene

Scene 22 (twenty years later, Bette also has dinner with his son) starts realistically enough, but starting with "You're right, it's not fair to bring up the children that died," it starts to shift to Matt's fantasy of a scene where his mother suddenly becomes super-reasonable and undemanding. Don't tip this to the audience too early. Let Bette play her first two long speeches as convincingly and as logically as possible. If she overdoes any of the comments, the audience will realize it's false too soon. I love instead the sort of cumulative doubt that creeps into the audience—you can feel them thinking, "This scene sounds a little false."

What's the Matter With You?

The end of Scene 23 when Bette and Boo's quarrel disintegrates into "What's the matter with you?", "What's the matter with you?", etc. When the actors convincingly are fighting, but just find themselves stuck making the same point back and forth, their genuine amusement seems a very good way to end the scene. Because it was hard to totally set that (faking the amusement seemed hard), Zaks and I let the actors keep adding "What's the matter with you?" (up to a reasonable point, three or four more than the script says) if that helps them. I also like it when Boo starts the laughter.

The Characters

Matt: I'm pretty sure Matt should be onstage only when indicated in the script. If he's on for scenes where he's not written in—like his birth, for instance

—it overdoes the "this is Matt's memory play" stuff.

It also fights against the unusual shape of the play. I think in Act I, it should feel like Bette's play; in Act II, it begins to feel like Bette *and* Matt's play; for a little while (from the divorce through the final baby), it starts to feel like Matt's play; and from Bette's entrance in Scene 32 on to the end, it feels like Bette and Matt's play again. (Boo is certainly terribly important, and part of the ending; but something more central seems to happen between Matt and Bette, I think.)

Matt starts the play believing he can make sense of things through analyzing them. As time goes on, this works less and less well for him, culminating in his "I can't make sense out of these things anymore" (a speech I wrote triggered by Joe Papp's comment that Matt should somehow "finish" with his Thomas Hardy stuff, a good comment).

Matt should have a sense of humor—if he seems only sensitive, I find the material becomes pleading and embarrassing (to me, at least). And much of the humor is in the deadpan delivery of comments, I believe.

And though I don't want Matt's position to become pathetic, still, from Thanksgiving on, there's no getting around that he suffers in the situations. Edith Oliver's description (in *The New Yorker*) of Matt watching— "sometimes visibly suffering, sometimes numb"—is appropriate, I think.

And the "sometimes numb" image is useful to keep in mind, to avoid any obvious pleading for sympathy; it's accurate as well—children in alcoholic homes often become quite stoic; everyone else around them is in such a mess, they don't want to be any bother, and so they become little adults. And speaking of little adults, it's also good to avoid actually *playing* Matt as a little boy; just keep it simple for the "arts and crafts" scene, and by the time we're to Thanksgiving he's already a little adult.

Zaks encouraged me and Joan Allen as Bette not to shrink away from rather full-anger choices in the Bette-Matt arguments (especially in Scenes 22, 32, and the brief disagreement about healing and prayer in 33).

I resisted this direction at first, due to fear that full out anger might seem too "Oh pity poor Matt"; in playing it, I decided Zaks was very right, and that the full anger made the play not sentimental, just honest. (Damn it, though, it's so tricky passing this sort of advice on. I saw two Matts who did "My favorite movie is *Citizen Kane*, I don't call you 'Citizen Kane'" with genuine anger, and the line still got the appropriate laugh I think it should get; I saw another Matt do the same line with similar anger, and yet due to some overseriousness that the actor communicated, the line was not at all funny, and, alas, I think that's wrong. And I can't prove that to you, or tell you exactly how to do it right.)

One last thing about Matt. His final speech ("Bette passed into death and is with God") has *no* irony in it. The impulse behind it is to share with the audience the only comfort human beings have found to cope with death—the belief in an afterlife. Matt has made clear that he doesn't seem to believe in all that, *but the fact doesn't belong in this moment*. The moment is about sharing with the audience the sense of loss; perhaps for the moment, Matt decides to believe in heaven—or to speak as if he believes because it's the only comfort available, the only thing he can think to say. Any sense of "Matt looks down or separates himself from those who believe" (which appeared in guess which favorite production) is totally at odds with what I mean by the moment.

Bette: Before starting to cast Bette, Zaks and I agreed we were looking for someone who seemed like a "winner." (And Joan Allen, a fabulous actress, is very much a winner.) Part of Bette's story is that she is someone for whom things basically should have and could have gone right. She is thus genuinely charming, very vivacious, etc.; it just all goes very wrong. But, for all her chatter, she is not stupid. She comes from a background where the chatter is considered part of a woman's charm, and where no one is expected to have to make thoughtful decisions as nothing problematic is supposed to happen.

If she's not stupid, though, she is also not wise. Karl is partially right in Scene 30—she keeps trying for far too long to change things she can't change (Boo's drinking, having another child against medical likelihood). But unlike the other characters, she is in there trying, and that's something.

We should, of course, feel for her. She can act like a bitch often, but that's not, at core, what she is. Joan Allen can yell with the best of them when the script calls for that, but she also had an extraordinary vulnerability somewhere within Bette's iron will that made Bette's plight extremely moving.

Boo: Boo is at core very sweet, and he probably loves Bette very much (Graham Beckel was terrific looking at Bette with infatuation in the honeymoon scene). However, his personality never confronts anything—he seems totally inured to watching his father insult his mother, for instance (though, of course, he would have had many years getting used to it).

He drinks, presumably, to escape, and Bette keeps on and on at him trying to keep him from escaping; and in that way, they are deeply incompatible.

I was grateful that Beckel as an actor never made a fuss about how passive Boo is, particularly in the

Hudlocke scenes; he took it as a given of Boo's character, which I think it is. His mother laughs when awful things are said; Boo either doesn't listen, or takes a drink.

Beckel also was very painful to watch in the divorce scene and in the final baby scene; his Boo, when circumstances *forced* him to see something irrevocable, had hurt eyes.

Zaks made a terrific point about the last scene. For all the fact that Boo keeps staring off suddenly, most of the time he and Bette have a lovely ease between them in this final scene that, in Zaks's words, made you wish that they had found a way to get that ease earlier. His seeing that ease was important for this scene— because for all the sadness in the situation, the sadness isn't what to play (except for the occasional inescapable moments). Bette has given up trying to change Boo, and that has allowed her to enjoy his affection for the first time in ages. It's a scene that shows that a reconciliation among all three has sort of happened— not a triumphant one, because everyone has lowered their stakes and expectations, but a reconciliation nonetheless.

Some of the Other Characters

Soot: Soot's laugh is terribly important, and an integral part of her character. Don't cast an actress who can't or won't do the laugh. Also, please have Soot do the "Oh, Karl" (laughs) lines as written—that is, she says "Oh, Karl," and *then* laughs; the laugh and the line should be separated.

Soot is one of my favorite characters (and usually one of the audience's as well).

Many of us would gather offstage nightly to watch certain of Olympia Dukakis's scenes, she was so remarkable. I was particularly enamored of how she would look over at Karl every time he began to speak with this expression of pleased expectation, as if she knew that whatever was about to come out of his mouth was, without question, certain to be the most delightful and charming remark imaginable. She would then listen with rapt attention as he said his usually horrible or insulting comment, and then she would laugh delightedly *as if* her pleased expectation had been totally correct. Occasionally, if her line was a slight reproach of Karl—such as "You shouldn't tease everyone so"—her attitude seemed to be that Karl had just said something slightly naughty but still vastly amusing, while what any sane person would have heard was that Karl had just been shocking and cruel.

This extremely crazy disparity between what Karl says and how she responds is the core of Soot's character. It's hilarious and, without the actress having to push it, sort of heartbreaking.

Karl: A major thing about Karl—cast him as intelligent and upper-class. (Soot should be upper-class as well.) He is *not* meant to be a lower-class Archie Bunker, uncouth and stupid. He is mean to his wife and to others because he is a misanthrope; I think he looked at the world early in life, didn't like what he saw, and out of that perception began to watch everything around him like a scientist looking at bugs through a microscope. But he *is* smart.

Along these lines, I recall Bill Moor listening to Bette rattle on about having more children and about Jackie Cooper's cuteness versus Shirley Temple's (Scene 14), and seeing on his face, subtly, the thought that Bette was very stupid for making these decisions about having children. You saw the opinion on his face—and this opinion was a more genuine response to what was going on in the room than anything that was coming from anyone else in the scene: Boo is drinking and trying not to listen, and Soot, who can't stand any problems of any sort, is smiling at Bette as if everything she was saying was delightful. Of course, Karl follows this silent reaction by being very insulting to Bette, which doesn't particularly help anyone; but the insult comes from a genuine opinion about how foolishly she is running her life.

Another choice Bill Moor made that was useful, I think, was that he decided that Karl was, most times, amused by Soot. This helped explain what kept them together, probably. Karl is a realist and sees things, he just doesn't believe anything can be done about anything, and so he has chosen to be nasty. Soot can't stand reality because most things frighten her, and so she pretends to herself (so successfully that she doesn't even know she's pretending) that everything is fine with everything. In a strange way, they certainly "go" together.

The characters of the Brennan family and Father Donnally are seemingly less open to misunderstanding, and so I'll spend less time on them.

Paul is a kind father, and most of the lines I've given him are actually rather sensible, it's just nobody can undertand him. Bill McCutcheon seemed sweet and fond of his girls. He also always looked very irritated whenever Margaret told him not to speak, and would mutter to himself, which was a funny choice.

A stray thing about Paul's speech. I describe how I envision it in the script, in terms of Paul's dropping most of his consonants so that it is mostly impossible to understand him. I have seen some actors do that but then add to it a staccato, jerky rhythm to how Paul speaks. I would prefer your Paul not do this—it sounds slightly retarded to me, which is wrong (Paul's mind is absolutely fine), or else like an actor's choice that I just don't "get." Plus, the staccato rhythms very much hurt the divorce scene where Paul's rhythms should be very much like an old-time lawyer—conversational, making points, talking to the judge, etc.; it's just he's incomprehensible. (McCutcheon was hilarious as this frustrated lawyer; if we all watched Olympia's scenes, I noted that she always stood offstage to watch that scene.)

So, if you would, I prefer normal speaking rhythms (just lose most of the consonants.)

Joan is a smallish part, and, judging by auditions, a little hard to get a handle on. However, the actresses we called back all had in common an extremely dry delivery and the ability to make the force of Joan's unhappiness and edgy bitterness *funny*. Probably Joan liked somebody in the world once, but it's not shown in this play. Mercedes Ruehl gave an indelible performance, and it's a tribute to her gifts how much she was noticed in this part. Also, early laughs in a play are important to cue the audience "what kind of play this is going to be," and Joan's character (and Margaret's) have a lot of lines that are laugh lines *depending* on how you say them. ("She does. You look lovely, Bette" is funny when said with the proper, flat, semihostile disinterest. Oh God, he's giving line readings now.)

Margaret says, "Let's not talk about it" many times in the play, whenever anyone brings up a problem. Soot pretends (or has convinced herself) the problems aren't there. Margaret does see them, it's just that she is of the old school who feels you shouldn't talk about unpleasant things. Patricia Falkenhain was hilariously on the nose when, for instance, in Thanksgiving she'd tell Bette that she and Skippy might stay with her to avoid Boo's drunkenness, and then a moment later says with utter cheeriness as if nothing has happened, "Good-bye, Boo!"

As Margaret lets drop in her longest speech (Scene 24), she *likes* her children to have problems, it makes her feel needed. That speech is one of the meannest I've ever written, I think, but it *does* happen that way; and Patricia Falkenhain's charm was the absolute appropriate interpretation of it—Margaret *is* charming, she *is* a caring mother, she just wants to be the queen bee, so she likes all the bickering that goes on around her.

Emily: Audiences love Emily. She is dear, and doesn't seem to have a mean bone in her body. But her mind sure is mucked-up, and writing her I was reminded of a comment a friend once made about a poignant character in a movie (Shirley Knight in *Petulia*, mistreated by her husband George C. Scott): I was saying how touching I found her vulnerability, and my friend (a woman) said, yes, she supposed so but one also felt the satisfaction of seeing a sensitive person "get it." I thought this remark was rather shocking, but also rather true.

Emily obviously works out of guilt, very misplaced and deeply rooted. She's also rather childlike—her mind seems to move slower than other people's, and she has a child's belief that everything is connected to her (and, in her case, is her fault). I adored watching Kathryn Grody as Emily trying desperately to make sense of what Father Donnally was saying, and always presuming that if she didn't follow it, it must be her fault (ergo, all her hand raisings).

Zaks and Kathryn also made Emily strong in the last scene; she knows about prayer, and about offering comfort, and so there was no apologetic quality to any of her behavior in the last scene; she was (in a nice way) in her element.

Father Donnally was Richard B. Shull. Shull is like one of the marvelous character actors in films from the 1930s and 40s; though this priest was often kindly to Bette (and others), irritation is always not too far below the surface; the last third of Shull's marriage retreat was a hilarious explosion of built-up irritation at his intolerable position, being asked to solve impossible problems. If he joined Karl at dinner in Scene 30, they would have had some points of agreement about not being able to change some things (although Donnally is basically kindly).

And Now the End

I really must apologize. I have gone on too long, and though I've tried to edit this (and have cut some stuff, believe it or not), I have fussed and fussed with this for too long, and so I've decided to leave it lengthy so you can choose what to make use of, and what to reject.

I really do know that there is rarely only one way to do something in acting and directing—but within that range of possibilities, there really are, I think, choices that hit the right tone for my stuff, and choices that make it fall flat, or go nasty or go silly. That's what I'm trying to control. Children of alcoholics, I have read, often have trouble in later life trying to overcontrol things, and I guess this essay is a bit of an example of that. But at least I'm not coming to your house directly, to bother you; and at least I got to praise the actors who worked with such commitment on the play at the Public, and to whom I offer much affection and gratitude.

Christopher Durang
November 1985

THE MANUAL OF
INDOOR
PHOTOGRAPHY

Michael Freeman

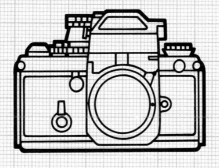

ZIFF-DAVIS PUBLISHING COMPANY
NEW YORK

An Adkinson Parrish Book

Published by
Ziff-Davis Publishing Company
One Park Avenue,
New York, NY 10016.

ISBN 0-87165-111-4

First printing 1981

Library of Congress Catalog Card Number 80-54315

Designed and produced by Adkinson Parrish Limited, London

Managing Editor   Clare Howell
Design Manager   Christopher White
Editor   John Roberts
Designers   Mike Rose Robert Lamb
                       Rose & Lamb Design Partnership
Illustrators   Richard Blakeley Phil Holmes
                       Dave Pugh Rob Shone Ken Stott

Contents

Phototypeset by Servis Filmsetting Limited, Manchester

Colour illustrations originated by Siviter Smith Limited, Birmingham

Printed and bound in Spain by Printer industria gráfica sa,
Sant Vicenç dels Horts, Barcelona
DLB 22754 - 1980

Introduction

As a working companion to *The Manual of Outdoor Photography*, this book is both complementary and independent. It covers different subjects and occasions, and is complete in itself.

Because both manuals have been designed to be highly practical, the subject matter has been divided so that each covers a major group of picture-taking situations. In other words, the division is practical rather than theoretical. In keeping with the principles behind the outdoor manual, the intention has been to give you, the photographer, rapid access to all the essential information and advice you might need while shooting. Philosophy is kept to a minimum and the armchair appreciation of photography has been eschewed in favour of hard information and concrete examples.

If your photography is essentially limited to studio work and other indoor situations, then this manual is clearly more useful than the companion volume. If on the other hand, your interests are broader, then the two books will together cover all practical aspects of photography, making a comprehensive pair. Because of the differences between the subjects, there are inevitably some structural differences between the two manuals. As a general rule, indoor photography involves more planning and more control than location work, particularly in the studio. Portraits, still-lifes, and room interiors all lend themselves, on most occasions, to a considered approach. As a result, a large part of this book is taken up with specific examples of lighting situations and types of subject. Fine control over lighting is more frequently possible indoors, but naturally calls for a more technical approach than when working with daylight. To ease the problems of working with artificial lighting, individual situations are described as thoroughly as possible, many of them with clear lighting diagrams.

While there is probably as great a degree of specialization in outdoor photography, the actual techniques of indoor work have become more

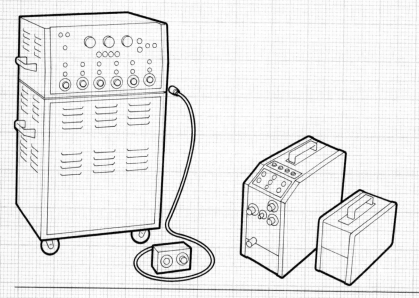

exact and more highly developed. Over decades the methods of, say, portrait lighting and still-life lighting have been refined to the point where they now bear only a passing resemblance to each other. Although there is inevitably a danger that set approaches to particular subjects can stifle originality, the highly developed and often esoteric techniques used by professional studio photographers offer valuable solutions to a whole variety of problems. Because of the way it can be used either to complement or to counteract the effect of different lamps, beauty make-up is in some ways a lighting technique. In still-life photography, shiny surfaces such as polished silver or mirrors may seem to pose insurmountable problems, yet there are a number of more or less sophisticated ways of dealing with them. Some of the techniques may even appear to verge on outright trickery, but have been developed as the only of handling difficult situations. Using ice-cubes that will not melt, suspending objects in mid-air, making a common brick loom as large as a high-rise building — these and other intricate solutions to particular problems are explained clearly and precisely.

Until quite recently, indoor photography virtually demanded additional artificial lighting, or at least the use of tripods and time-exposure. Now, however, with the latest fast films and fast lenses, candid photography is possible in many indoor situations. While relatively low light levels prohibit the freedom possible outdoors, hand-held shooting is now an important and distinct area of indoor photography.

People, room interiors, and the wide range of studio subjects are the main types of photography dealt with in the manual. In addition, all the basic techniques, including exposure measurement, the handling and care of equipment, and the variety of post-production methods available, are fully dealt with.

MICHAEL FREEMAN

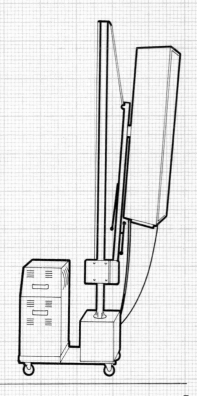

1. LIGHTING
Lighting and studios

There is such a great variety of lighting equipment now available, covering a wide range of intensity, colour temperature and diffusion, that very great subtlety of illumination is possible. Even types of lighting that are not designed specifically for cameras and film can be used, with simple precautions. The following pages describe comprehensively the lighting that you can expect to find or can introduce for indoor photography. The term *available light* covers all non-photographic light sources, such as domestic tungsten, fluorescent and vapour discharge lamps, as well as daylight from windows, which is largely uncontrollable.

Available interior lighting has an increased importance now that fast films, including colour, and wide aperture lenses have helped develop hand-held and candid indoor work into a relatively new area of photography. An oper-
ational threshold has been crossed, and it is often possible to work indoors without additional lighting.

This new freedom, formerly possible only with black-and-white film, is one of two major new trends in indoor photography. The other is the growing use of high-powered electronic flash. In size and cost these are no longer restricted to professional studios and the extra power they provide over camera-mounted flash guns makes it possible to use them with many different types of diffusing head. For convenience and consistency, they also have considerable advantages over the traditional tungsten lamps.

Although studios are normally associated with professional photography, and particularly with such specialized subjects as still-life, portraits or fashion, studio work is not really dis-

Available light Fast films and fast lenses have extended the range of indoor photography to include hand-held shots, without the addition of any photographic lighting. Despite the problems involved when working with the limited daylight from windows or electric lighting, with its low levels and colour imbalances, excellent and varied results can be achieved – far superior to the unnatural and unattractive appearance of most shots using portable flash.

tinguished by the physical trappings of complex lighting equipment, backgrounds, props and changing rooms so much as one very general and simple principle – photographic control. The single purpose of a studio is to give the photographer the maximum amount of control over the image. Whether the studio is beautifully appointed, has a large array of facilities or even whether it is permanent is irrelevant. The only important consideration is that it provides a controlled environment which makes it possible to mould the subject – people, objects or sets – into the desired photographic image.

To this end, a small living-room or a large warehouse can be converted with minimal alteration for just a few hours, or as long as it takes to create the photograph. Makeshift studios can even be put together out of doors. Naturally, the more sophisticated and comfortable the premises, the easier the studio will be to work in, but good permanent studios carry two burdens from which temporary ones are free – inflexibility and

cost. The more precisely suited a studio is to a particular kind of photography, the more difficult it is to adapt to another purpose. Even professional photographers should bear in mind that an expensive lease and fittings are overheads that will have to be paid for, requiring a substantial turnover.

The idea of a studio as a controlled area for photography carries with it two implications: first, studio photography is rarely haphazard because the fine degree of control virtually obliges the photographer to plan shots in advance. Second, lighting has to be provided, which gives the opportunity to build up a picture from scratch, with each tone and colour recorded precisely as desired. It is therefore important to have a good working knowledge of all the possible types of lighting – available, portable flash and professional systems. The control and use of light is probably the single most important factor in achieving success with indoor photography.

The studio The particular advantage of indoor photography is the ability to introduce and control lighting to a precise degree. The result is the highly polished and deliberate effect of studio lighting, producing photographs in which every element has been placed and lit according to the photographer's intentions. But the 'studio' is a broad term – it can be taken to include any environment in which the lighting is introduced by the photographer, from a complex motion picture studio to the amateur's living room.

Daylight and tungsten lighting

Daylight and tungsten lighting both have a measurable *colour temperature*. This quality, expressed in kelvins (K), consists of a scale from bluish (high colour temperature) to reddish (low colour temperature), and is based on the colours that an inert substance would glow if heated to various temperatures. Colour temperature is particularly critical in interior photography, as light sources vary considerably. The eye, which quite quickly adjusts to differences in colour temperature, is a poor judge – after being in a room lit by domestic tungsten lamps for a short time, the illumination usually seems normal, yet when compared with daylight tungsten light is distinctly yellowish. Use the table right as a yardstick. Mean noon sunlight (5,400K, but often rounded out for convenience to 5,500K) is standard 'white', and the blue or yellow/red bias of other light sources is measured against this.

To make calculations more convenient, another measurement of colour temperature is the mired scale, which is equivalent to one million divided by Kelvins. This can be used more easily to select colour balancing filters for correcting a particular light source so that it will record as 'white' on film. A full list of colour balancing filters appears on page 37. Bluish filters raise colour temperature and have negative mired values, whilst yellowish filters lower the colour temperature, and have positive mired values. As an example, the difference between the light from a 2,900K domestic lamp (344 mireds) and film balanced for 3,200K (312 mireds) is 32 mireds. To make the light appear 'white' when using this film requires a bluish filter with a mired value of 32 mireds – in other words, an 82B.

Daylight The most common available lighting found in interiors is daylight. Because most windows receive their light from just a small angle of sky, the colour temperature can vary widely, depending on the time of day and whether the sky is cloudy or clear. Direct sunlight streaming into the room has a colour temperature of about 5,400K, although this may be altered slightly by reflection from the surrounding carpet, wallpaper and furniture. An overcast sky is usually slightly colder – around 6,000K, while light from a clear blue sky can be as high as 10,000K to 18,000K. In addition, if some of the light is reflected from surfaces outside the window, such as a garden wall, this will also affect the colour temperature. All these variables make it difficult to ensure colour accuracy. Where perfect colour balance is critical, make a range of exposures with different strengths of colour balancing filter (see pages 36–37) or use a colour temperature meter.

Tungsten Most domestic tungsten lighting has a colour temperature of 2,900K, although this may vary, particularly if there are fluctuations in the voltage (see pages 14–15). So, when used as the main light source, it is too warm even for tungsten-balanced film (type A is designed for use at 3,400K and Type B at 3,200K), and a corrective filter should be used. In many interior shots, however, table and other small lamps are included only for effect, and in this case it rarely matters that they appear yellowish in the photograph. In fact, the extra warmth in a small area of the picture is often attractive.

The typical lighting situations shown on pages 106–115 and 124–137 show in detail how the permutations of daylight and tungsten in interiors should be handled.

Colour temperature meters

By taking separate light readings through a blue and a red filter, a colour temperature meter can give the exact kelvin measurement for any light source. Some colour temperature meters also incorporate a calculator to show the filter or filters needed to correct the light to the film you are using. The range covered is normally from about 2,000K to 30,000K. Strictly speaking, colour temperature only applies to incandescent light sources (the sun or tungsten lamps), but two-way meters that measure not only blue against red but also red against green can be used to measure the filtration needed by fluorescent lamps (see next page).

Colour temperature of light sources in interiors	Kelvins	Mired value
Candle	1,930 K	518
Domestic tungsten lamp	about 2,900 K	344
Photographic lamp	3,200 K	312
Photoflood lamp	3,400 K	294
Clear flashbulb	3,800 K	263
Direct noon sunlight	5,400 K	185
Blue flashbulb	6,000 K	167
Electronic flash tube	6,000 K	167
Daylight: cloudy sky	6,000 K	167
Daylight: partly cloudy sky	about 7,500 K	133
Daylight: clear blue sky	over 10,000 K	100

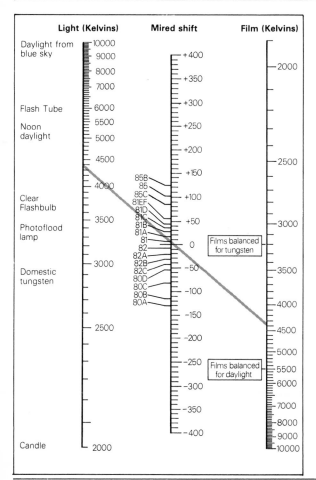

Colour balancing filters To balance the film you are using to the light, hold a straight edge from the colour temperature of the light source on the left to the film type on the right. Where the edge crosses the central scale, the correct filter is indicated, together with the mired shift value.

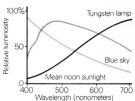

Spectrum characteristics of light sources The graphs above and on the following pages show the different colour components of the various types of light likely to be encountered.

11

Discharge lighting

Discharge lighting, including fluorescent, mercury vapour, sodium vapour and metal halide lamps, is both unpredictable and difficult to control in colour interior photography. Increasingly common, particularly in large interiors such as offices and factories, discharge lamps are efficient and cheap to run, but tend to be unsuited to photography. Although they may appear 'white' to the eye, film picks out their deficiencies with unwanted accuracy. These lights work by means of an electrical discharge which vaporizes a metal such as mercury. This glows but the light produced covers only very narrow bands of the spectrum. The light from a sodium vapour lamp, for example, is almost entirely in one yellow wavelength. This makes it impossible to achieve correction with filters, as with a tungsten lamp, because there are no other colours present. A blue filter would merely produce a darker yellow.

In an attempt to give some resemblance to a full spectrum, some lamps have a fluorescent coating or additional metals in the tube. This often makes it possible to use filters to achieve lighting with a normal appearance.

Mercury vapour lamps These powerful and efficient lamps are often used for lighting very large interiors, such as factories, warehouses and sports stadiums. A basic mercury vapour lamp emits light strong in blue and green wavelengths, without any orange or red – no amount of red filtration will help. However, and this is what makes these lamps so unpredictable unless you can identify the particular type, some fill in the missing red with higher pressure, added metals or a fluorescent coating. Some mercury vapour lamps are thus quite well corrected for daylight-balanced film. Prior testing is the safest solution, with a range of red filters from about CC50R to none.

Fluorescent lamps Fluorescent lamps are essentially mercury vapour lamps with a fluorescent coating on the inside of the glass tube. Depending on the composition of this coating, an almost complete spectrum can be produced, but most appear greenish on film. The precise colour varies from make to make, and if you can identify the particular tube (ask the resident electrician if any one type is used) the table on this page will allow you to work out the corrective filters you need. Making a test beforehand is still the safest method, but if you do not have that opportunity make a range of exposures with different filters. Daylight film is almost always

Fluorescent lighting: filters and exposure increase

Type of lamp	Daylight	White	Warm white	Warm white delux	Cool white	Cool white delux
Daylight-balanced film	40M+30Y 1 stop	20C+30M 1 stop	40C+40M 1⅓ stops	60C+30M 1⅔ stops	30M ⅔ stop	30C+20M 1 stop
Tungsten-balanced film	85B+30M +10Y 1 stop	40M+40Y 1 stop	30M+20Y 1 stop	10Y ⅓ stop	50M+60Y 1⅓ stop	10M+30Y ⅔ stop

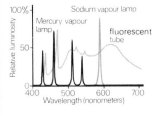

Sodium vapour lights Sodium vapour lights are sometimes found in industrial interiors – here, in a California winery. Unfiltered, the result is a yellowish cast. Note that the small area of daylight appears white on the film.

more closely balanced for fluorescent lights than Type B film, and the most typical filtration is CC30 Magenta or CC30 Red. A two-way colour temperature meter, that reads blue against red and red against green, can also be used. An alternative to placing a filter over the lens is to tape a large sheet of the magenta film available from theatrical suppliers for use in spotlights over the fluorescent tubes. This can be useful when you have to cope with mixed lighting in a room.

Sodium vapour lamps Using sodium instead of the more usual mercury, these lamps are particularly difficult to use, as about 95 per cent of their output is in the yellow part of the spectrum. Fortunately, they are not very common in interiors and their principal use is in street lighting.

Mercury vapour lamps Used for large interiors such as sports stadiums, mercury vapour gives a strong green light which may benefit from the use of red filters. Trial and error is the best method of achieving a correctly balanced result.

Fluorescent lights The common forms of strip light have different colour imbalances, but tend to produce greenish results. Note that the tungsten light in the control window appears reddish on the daylight film.

Photographic lights

There are two basic types of light designed for still photography: tungsten and flash. The wide variety of light fittings is shown on pages 20 to 27, but the actual light sources are fewer in type. The higher light output and greater consistency of electronic flash have helped it to supersede the traditional tungsten lamps used in studios, and in most respects flash has the advantages. Nevertheless, tungsten still has some important uses, notably in lighting large interiors, where the total quantity of light needed for the exposure may be more than a single flash discharge can provide. In such cases, a time exposure with a continuous light may be more convenient.

Tungsten lamps Photographic lamps are similar to regular tungsten lights, except that they give a higher output. Colour temperature is either 3,200 K for use with Type B film, or 3,400 K for Type A. An 81A filter (yellowish) or 82A (bluish) can be used to match these two types of lamp to the two films.

Straightforward tungsten lamps become less efficient with age, due to blackening caused by the vaporized filament depositing on the glass, and have lower colour temperatures. More efficient are tungsten-halogen lamps, which have the same colour temperature as a new tungsten lamp throughout their lives. They operate at a higher temperature, which causes the vaporized filament to deposit on the filament itself rather than the envelope. Never touch the special quartz-like envelope with bare skin even when it is cold, as the greasy finger marks begin a chemical reaction that will shorten the life of the lamp. If you touch them by mistake, clean immediately with alcohol.

Voltage fluctuations cause differences in colour temperature as well as in light output. A 10 per cent change in the voltage causes a difference of about 100K. For example, a drop from 240 to 220 volts in the supply (or 120 to 110 volts) will lower the colour temperature of a 3,200K lamp to 3,100K.

Flash bulbs Much less common now, in the face of inexpensive electronic flash, flash bulbs are nevertheless useful for providing a high light intensity with the minimum of equipment. The flash duration is relatively long (about 50 milliseconds with the highest output over 15 milliseconds) and the flash synchronization should be set at 'M' on the camera.

Tungsten-halogen lamps

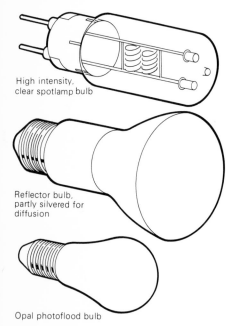

High intensity, clear spotlamp bulb

Reflector bulb, partly silvered for diffusion

Opal photoflood bulb

Flash bulbs

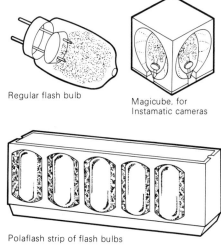

Regular flash bulb

Magicube, for Instamatic cameras

Polaflash strip of flash bulbs

Electronic flash All flash tubes, whether powered by battery or mains electricity, operate on the same principle, with an electrical discharge passing through a gas-filled tube. Small flash units used at minimum power have extremely short durations – around 1/50,000 sec – whilst the discharge in a powerful studio flash head may be as long as 1/1,000 sec. Colour temperature is about 6,000K, although it is as well to test this with a new unit. If your camera has both 'X' and 'M' synchronizations, use 'X'. Also, while leaf shutters can synchronize with flash at any speed, focal plane shutters are limited to a maximum shutter speed with flash of around 1/60 sec to 1/80 sec.

The load of the electrical input to the head from the capacitor is stated in joules (watt-seconds). This is a useful measure when comparing line powered studio units but is not a measure of light output. The standard measure of illumination from a flash unit is BCPS (beam candlepower-seconds). This is independent of film speed but can be compared with the guide number (see the table below). The guide number, which is particularly useful when portable flash units are to be used in a variety of locations, is a quick method of calculating exposure. Dividing it by the distance to the subject gives the aperture.

Checking the guide number of electronic flash

Set the unit at full power and use colour transparency film which has less latitude and so gives a more precise test. Stand a test subject, such as a person, at a known distance from the flash and make a wide range of exposures in half-stop increments. Then, with the film processed, choose the most satisfactory exposure and multiply the aperture number by the distance. For example, if the best exposure at 10 feet with ASA 64 film is f8, then the guide number in feet is (f)8×10 (ft)=80.

All flash units need time to recycle. Many units have optimistic ready lights that function before the capacitor is fully charged. Typically, they have only 80 per cent of the full charge when the light first appears and it is better to wait a few more seconds for consistent results.

Ringflash A special flash unit, fitting round the front of the lens, for all-round frontal illumination with close-up and macro photography (see pages 196–203).

For studio flash, see pages 20–21.

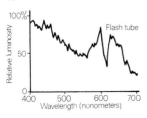

Guide numbers for electronic flash										
ASA film speed	BCPS output of electronic flash unit									
	350	500	700	1000	1400	2000	2800	4000	5600	8000
20	18	22	26	32	35	45	55	65	75	90
25	20	24	30	35	40	50	60	70	85	100
32	24	28	32	40	50	55	65	80	95	110
40	26	32	35	45	55	65	75	90	110	130
50	30	35	40	50	60	70	85	100	120	140
64	32	40	45	55	65	80	95	110	130	160
80	35	45	55	65	75	90	110	130	150	180
100	40	50	60	70	85	100	120	140	170	200
125	45	55	65	80	95	110	130	160	190	220
160	55	65	75	90	110	130	150	180	210	250
200	60	70	85	100	120	140	170	200	240	280
250	65	80	95	110	130	160	190	220	260	320
320	75	90	110	130	150	180	210	250	300	360
400	85	100	120	140	170	200	240	280	340	400
500	95	110	130	160	190	220	260	320	370	450
650	110	130	150	180	210	260	300	360	430	510
800	120	140	170	200	240	280	330	400	470	560
1000	130	160	190	220	260	320	380	450	530	630
1250	150	180	210	250	300	350	420	500	600	700
1600	170	200	240	280	340	400	480	560	670	800

100%

Relative luminosity

Flash tube

50

0
400   500   600   700
Wavelength (nonometers)

Exposure basics

Light levels in interiors are less predictable than in outdoor situations and it is not possible to suggest settings that apply generally. This is particularly true of available light conditions, where rigorously accurate measurement is essential. In the studio, using lights that you are familiar with under standardized conditions, exposures become easy to calculate through experience. But exactly because studio work is so controllable, greater precision is normally expected.

In the majority of indoor situations, an exposure meter can and should be used. In addition, however, use the exposure information given for the examples included later in this manual as a guide to the levels you can expect in different situations.

Latitude The exposure latitude of a film is the measure of its ability to record images acceptably at exposures less than or greater than the ideal. This built-in safety margin varies with the type of film – negative films have more latitude than reversal films, black-and-white has more than colour, and faster emulsions more than slower ones. This means that you need to be accurate to within half a stop when using a slow colour transparency film, whereas a two stop error on a fast black-and-white negative film may be tolerable.

Bracketing A valuable insurance against exposure mistakes is to shoot each image over a range of exposures. Bracketing, as this is known, is widely used by professional photographers, and for any important shot is a worthwhile safeguard. It is usual to vary the exposure in half-stop increments – a range of three (half a stop under/normal/half a stop over) if you are fairly certain of the setting, or a range of five (from one stop under to one stop over) in more difficult situations. In effect, this delays some of the decision about exposure setting until the film has been processed.

Exposure meters There are three main types of exposure meter: through-the-lens (TTL), hand-held and spot meters. Because of the distances involved, spot meters are less useful in interior work than outdoor.

TTL meters are incorporated in the majority of cameras and are the most common method of exposure measurement. Because of the great variety of lighting found in interiors, however, TTL meters need to be used with caution, particularly when only available light is used. They are best with average scenes, whereas many interiors are lit unevenly, with pools of light

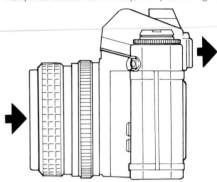

TTL meter Most modern 35mm SLR cameras have through the lens metering, actually measuring the light entering rhe camera. Care must be taken to compensate for backlighting or light sources in the picture frame which will influence the reading. The meter usually takes a greater proportion of the reading from the bottom half of the picture area to correspond to an 'average' photographic subject

Bracketing Particularly with films with little latitude, such as colour transparencies, bracketing helps ensure correct exposure. Depending on the level of difficulty, bracket three or five exposures, one or two half stops on each side of the meter's indicated setting.

from individual lamps and a rapid fall-off in illumination from windows. TTL metering systems use very sensitive cells, such as cadmium sulphide, silicon and gallium (the latter is particularly useful in dimly lit interiors). The viewfinder display varies from a moving needle to red light-emitting diodes (LEDs) and liquid crystal displays (LCDs).

Hand-held meters are better in many interior situations because of their versatility. They can be used for direct, reflected light readings or, by covering the sensor with a translucent plastic dome, for incident light readings. In the incident light setting, the meter is usually aimed at the camera from the position of the subject and measures the light falling on the subject. In studio work this is the normal metering method, partly because of its accuracy and partly because the lighting is generally consistent, while settings and backgrounds often vary greatly. Some hand-held meters use self-powered selenium cells, which need no batteries but are less sensitive than CdS cells.

Flash meters function in the same way as hand-held continuous light meters except that they measure the flash discharge rather than the ambient lighting. That is, they do not respond to the normal room lighting. Because flash meters have traditionally been used in studio work, they are normally operated as incident meters, but some have the ability to take reflected flash readings.

Hand-held meter A versatile and essential item in the serious photographer's equipment bag. The better versions can be fitted with a translucent dome and used for both reflected and incident light readings (see pages 18–19). Incident readings are particularly useful in studio photography.

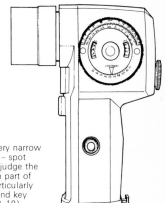

Spot meter With a very narrow angle of view – just 1° – spot meters can be used to judge the ideal exposure for each part of the scene. They are particularly suitable for high-low and key readings (see pages 18–19).

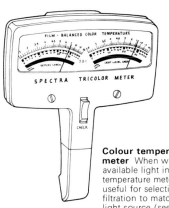

SPECTRA TRICOLOR METER

Flash meter Capable of registering the light of short flash durations, as well as continuous light, the flash meter is essential equipment for studio work with flash lighting. Some can also be used with portable flash. The Calcu-flash (right) gives a precise f-stop reading for flash as main light, fill-in and when bounced.

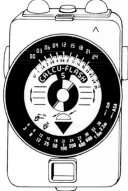

Colour temperature meter When working by available light indoors, a colour temperature meter can be very useful for selecting the correct filtration to match the film to the light source (see pages 10–11).

Exposure techniques

Exposure measurements can be made either from the brightness of the subject or from the amount of light falling on it. Most meters can be adapted to take either kind of reading, although some are more adaptable than others. Because of the great variety of lighting conditions found in indoor photography, it is particularly important to be able to use different exposure methods to suit differnent situations. There are three basic exposure methods, the first measuring the subject, the other two measuring the light itself.

Reflected light readings TTL meters, hand-held meters used directly, and spot meters all operate on this principle, measuring, in effect, the light that is reflected from the subject – the brightness that the camera sees.

Incident light readings Hand-held meters fitted with a cone or dome of translucent plastic over the sensor are used for this method. Pointed towards the camera position, they give a measurement of the amount of light, irrespective of the subject. Because they are uninfluenced by the subject or its background, they can be used

very accurately, and this method is the most common in studio work. Most flash meters are used like this.

Substitute readings By placing a surface of known reflectance in the same lighting as the subject, the light can be measured with a direct reading. An 18 per cent grey card, used for this purpose, is an average tone, halfway between white and black. A reflected light reading taken of this using the camera's TTL meter, for example, will give exactly the same exposure figure as an incident reading. Substitute readings and incident readings are in fact interchangeable.

If you do not have an 18 per cent grey card, other surfaces can be used as long as you make the appropriate allowances. A piece of white card or paper is three stops lighter than average grey. Make a substitute reading from it and then reduce the exposure setting by three stops from that indicated. Alternatively, use your own hand, having made a comparative measurement first so that you know its reflectance. Average

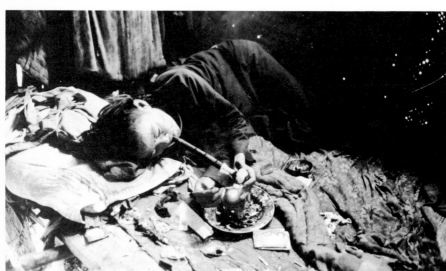

Taking an exposure reading
Many hand-held meters can be used for reflected light readings, where the meter is pointed at the subject to measure the light coming from it (left), or incident light readings, where a translucent dome is fitted and the light source is measured as it falls on the subject (right).

Average reading With a scene that is fairly evenly lit, with a variety of tones of equal importance, an average reading is sufficient. Use a TTL or hand-held meter in a normal way, pointing it at the subject as a whole. Remember the TTL meter's probable loading towards the bottom half of the frame.

Caucasian skin is about one stop lighter than average grey.

Techniques to suit the subject Apart from choosing the most convenient of the three exposure methods, it is important to decide which part of the scene in front of the camera to measure for. In indoor photography in particular, where contrast is often high and there can be a mixture of deep shadows and pools of light, this is not as straightforward as it may seem at first. An average reading is just that – the mean of all highlights, shadows and mid-tones – and may not suit a subject that is lit very differently from its background. The following techniques are the most useful.

Average reading When there are no great differences in tone across the scene, then use a TTL meter or hand-held meter normally. Although many TTL metering systems have a built-in bias towards the lower centre of the frame, corresponding to the most common type of composition, they read the scene in front of them more or less indiscriminately. Hand-held meters also make average readings over a fairly wide angle – approximately that of a standard lens.

High-low reading When there is high contrast in a scene, with two dominant areas of tone, one brightly lit, the other shadowed, the exposure latitude of the film will be stretched to the full. If both areas are equally important to the picture, the exposure must be a compromise between the two. Using any exposure method or metering system, take a reading for both areas and set the exposure halfway between.

Key reading When the subject contrasts in tone with its background and particularly when it is fairly small in the picture frame, make the exposure measurement for it alone, ignoring the background. In other words, decide where the important interest in your photograph lies. For example, an average reading, taken from a distance, of a spotlit actor on a dark stage would be so influenced by the background, that the actor would be seriously over-exposed. In such a case, of course, the actor is the key subject – the darkness is irrelevant to the exposure measurement. Spot meters, which have a 1° angle of view, are well suited to this technique. Otherwise, approach close to the key subject when using a TTL or hand-held meter. Alternatively, use a TTL meter with a long-focus lens fitted temporarily to narrow down the angle of view.

High-low reading To handle subjects with a high degree of contrast or light fall-off, as here, take a reading from two areas of the scene including detail you want recorded – one bright, the other dark. Set the exposure midway between the two readings.

Key reading High contrast is a common feature of studio shots and room interiors, largely because small light sources are used. In this studio portrait, the contrast is intentionally extreme, and any average measurement of exposure would be unreliable. Here, the best method is to decide which area of the image is the most important (the lit part of the face) and take the meter reading for that alone.

Lighting equipment 1

The choice between electronic flash and continuous tungsten lighting rests on both cost and the type of photography intended. For most subjects, the advantages of flash prevail, although large power units are very expensive. Flash freezes most movement, is unaffected by other, ambient lighting, and does not overheat the set. The amount of power needed depends on the smallest aperture you intend to work with. Units of 500 or 1,000 Joules (watt-seconds) are normally sufficient for most small and medium format cameras, but view cameras, which often need to be used at f45 or even f64, generally need large power units.

Tungsten lighting, which has been largely superseded in still photography studios by flash,

still has advantages in some situations. Where a large interior has to be lit strongly, multiple flash technique may take longer than continuous lighting, and risks damage to the flash heads. Continuous lighting also lets you see exactly how the final image will appear.

There is a very wide range of equipment available to alter the quality of light — reflectors, diffusers, masks and shades of different types. Most can be used on either flash or tungsten heads, but enclosed diffusers, such as opal-fronted windows and fish-fryers, are unsatisfactory with strong tungsten lamps, as the heat quickly builds up to a dangerous level. Even electronic flash heads can overheat if enclosed and used heavily.

Power units Two basic kinds of power source are available — free-standing, separate units, and those that are integrated with the head. The former are more traditional, can be linked together in series, can operate different heads at the same time, and are usually more powerful. A booster can be added to speed up the recycling time. Integrated units, on the other hand, are uncomplicated and very portable and are well suited to location work.

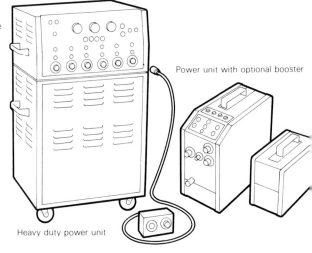

Power unit with optional booster

Heavy duty power unit

Flash tubes The basic quality of light is first determined by the shape of the flash tube — ring, coil or linear. Ring tubes are the most common and are generally shaped around a tungsten modelling lamp. For handling the greater output of a large power pack — say 5,000 Joules (watt-seconds) — a coiled tube is needed. For strip lights and large area lights, such as those illustrated opposite, a linear tube is more effective. These generally have fluorescent tubes as modelling lights.

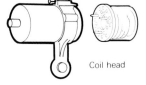

Coil head

Bowens Monolight (integrated power pack and head)

Slave trigger

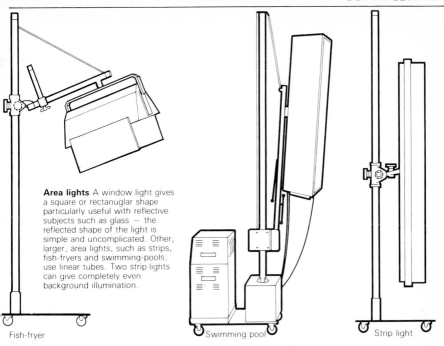

Area lights A window light gives a square or rectanuglar shape particularly useful with reflective subjects such as glass — the reflected shape of the light is simple and uncomplicated. Other, larger, area lights, such as strips, fish-fryers and swimming-pools, use linear tubes. Two strip lights can give completely even background illumination.

Fish-fryer

Swimming pool

Strip light

Tungsten lamps A 1,000 watt quartz light is a useful basic lamp. It should be fitted with shaped barn doors to control the light spill. In most situations, it is used in conjunction with diffusers or reflectors. The deep, white reflector dish of a Softlight and its central bar to shade the lamp give a broader illumination with softer shadow edges. One of the most portable lights for its level of output is the 1,000 watt Lowell Totalite, which folds away when not in use. Among the more sophisticated tungsten lights, used principally in the motion picture industry, is the Fresnel Luminaire. Both the reflector behind the filament and the Fresnel lens in front can be adjusted, giving precise control over the shape and quality of the light.

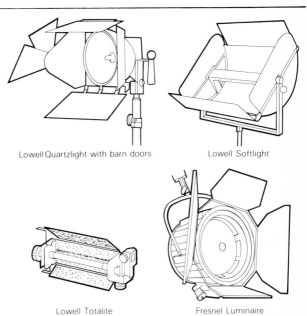

Lowell Quartzlight with barn doors

Lowell Softlight

Lowell Totalite

Fresnel Luminaire

Head attachments The purpose of head attachments is to modify the light — to concentrate, diffuse or shape it.

A condenser lens focuses the light into a small spot. A black tube without this lens is known as a snoot, and also concentrates the beam, but less precisely.

Diffusion increases the area of the light source, reduces shadow intensity, and softens shadow edges, but to accomplish this, light intensity is reduced. A silver or white painted bowl broadens the light source in proportion to its depth and diameter — small deep bowls give little diffusion and illuminate a small angle, large shallow bowls give a softer light over a larger area. A spiller cap shields the subject from the direct beam. Screens of different materials increase diffusion (opal perspex (plexiglass) is the most effective), and adjustable barn doors alter shape.

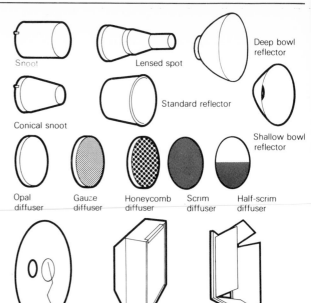

Snoot

Lensed spot

Deep bowl reflector

Standard reflector

Conical snoot

Shallow bowl reflector

Opal diffuser

Gauze diffuser

Honeycomb diffuser

Scrim diffuser

Half-scrim diffuser

Dished bowl with spiller cap

Opal diffused window light

Barn doors

Shading devices Various shades can be suspended in front of a light to control the way it falls on the subject. A French flag is a small mask, usually fitted to an articulated arm, attached on or near the camera to shade the lens. A gobo is a large flag, normally attached to a light stand.

A yashmak, as its name implies, is a large 'veil', generally of gauze, to reduce a part of the light reaching the subject. A cookie gives a mottled distribution of light.

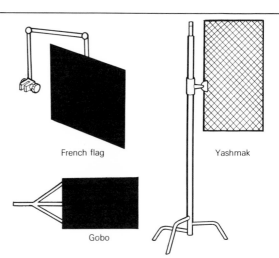

French flag

Yashmak

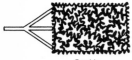

Cookie

Gobo

Trace frames and flats A trace frame is a simply constructed large area diffuser. Covered with tracing paper or thin cloth, it can be used in the same way as a swimming pool (see previous page), although it is less adjustable.

A flat, generally painted white, is a large, rigid screen that can be used either for shading or as a fill-in reflector.

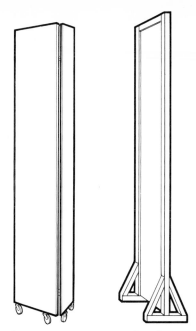

Folding flat   Trace frame

Umbrellas Umbrellas give very broad, diffuse but unshaped lighting. White, silver or gold lined umbrellas are less diffuse than translucent ones, which can also be used in front of the light.

Apart from these standard fittings a variety of specially shaped diffusers can be custom-built. An example is the all-enveloping light tent used for reflective subjects (see pages 174-177).

Translucent umbrella   Silvered umbrella

Gold umbrella   Square umbrellas

Portable flash

Although some of the smaller units are manual, most portable flash is now automatic, with light-sensitive cells that measure the quantity of light reflected back from the subject and thyristors that terminate the flash discharge as soon as the correct exposure is reached. In other words, the exposure is reduced by shortening the duration of the flash. For consistent, average results, all that is necessary with automatic units is to set the film speed on the unit and adjust the lens aperture as indicated. Many automatic flash units have a range of levels of output – useful if you want to choose between different aperture settings to vary the depth of field.

Integrated flash units (also sometimes known as 'dedicated' units) have an even more advanced method of automation, although in practically all situations the effect is the same. Integrated units are designed to be used with just one camera model, and extra contacts on the hot-shoe connect the flash with the camera's electronic shutter and the viewfinder display. The shutter is then automatically synchronized and the flash ready light appears in the viewfinder. In some models, the camera's own TTL metering system is used to control the flash output.

In order to use a very small aperture, when bouncing the flash off a ceiling or when the subject is distant, you will need as much light as possible. In these circumstances, it is usually better to switch an automatic unit to its manual setting and select the aperture according to one of the methods described on pages 14–15. The BCPS and guide number of a flash unit is normally calculated by the manufacturer for use in a typical domestic interior with close reflecting surfaces, and in this typical situation there is no need to make any elaborate tests. With a new flash unit, however, it is worth shooting a roll of film of subjects at varying distances with the unit at different power levels as a basic check for accuracy.

Flash position Although camera and flash manufacturers intend the units to be fired from the camera position, attached either to the camera's hot-shoe or to a short bracket, this is rarely the best position to achieve effective lighting. The result will be flat, with little modelling. An additional danger with portraits is the direct reflection from the subject's retina descriptively known as 'red-eye'. For these reasons, it is often better to hold the flash to one side of the camera or even to mount it onto a stand positioned well to the side.

A second, related problem is that the flash tube and reflector on a typical portable unit is so small that it will cause extremely hard shadows and small bright highlights. There are occasions when you might deliberately seek this effect, but for most situations it is better to diffuse the light. This can be done either by aiming the flash through a translucent screen or by reflecting it from a broad white surface (see opposite).

Small flash units Limited in power and versatility, these attach to the camera's hot-shoe. Manual units (left) have a fixed output. Automatic units (right), here with a tilting head for bounce flash, have a sensor which measures the light reflecting from the subject, controlling the duration of the flash for automatic exposure correction.

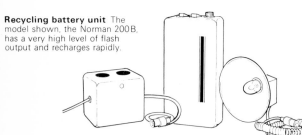

Recycling battery unit The model shown, the Norman 200B, has a very high level of flash output and recharges rapidly.

Wet cell units With a larger, rechargeable battery carried on a shoulder strap, these give greater power and more rapid recharging between flashes. They can be directed at will and even positioned at some distance from the camera.

Diffusing the light

The basic principle for softening shadows and making the illumination more even is to broaden the light source. These four standard methods employ either a diffusing material or a reflector.

1. Wrap a white handkerchief or thin cloth around the flash head. This gives only moderate diffusion but is uncomplicated. With an automatic unit, be careful not to cover the sensor with the handkerchief. With a manual unit, the exposure reduction is about one stop. Some flash units have fittings for plastic screens that do the same job.

2. Bounce the light off a white ceiling or wall by tilting the head of the flash unit.

In a normal domestic interior, with a ceiling 10 feet (3 metres) high, this reduces the illumination by about two stops. If the head of th automatic unit can be tilted independently of the sensor, you need make no adjustments.

3. Use a small studio umbrella on a light stand as a reflector to create low powered studio lighting. Unless the sensor of an automatic unit can be directed independently towards the subject, measure the exposure with a flash meter.

4. Bounce the light off a white card clipped to a small stand. The same exposure considerations apply as for an umbrella.

White handkerchief used as diffuser.

White card reflector on stand for bounce flash.

Tilting head for bounce flash.

Studio umbrella as reflector with portable flash.

Light stands and supports

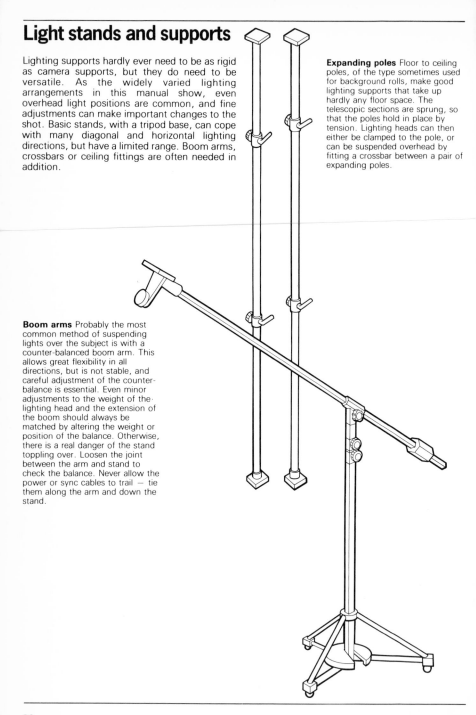

Lighting supports hardly ever need to be as rigid as camera supports, but they do need to be versatile. As the widely varied lighting arrangements in this manual show, even overhead light positions are common, and fine adjustments can make important changes to the shot. Basic stands, with a tripod base, can cope with many diagonal and horizontal lighting directions, but have a limited range. Boom arms, crossbars or ceiling fittings are often needed in addition.

Expanding poles Floor to ceiling poles, of the type sometimes used for background rolls, make good lighting supports that take up hardly any floor space. The telescopic sections are sprung, so that the poles hold in place by tension. Lighting heads can then either be clamped to the pole, or can be suspended overhead by fitting a crossbar between a pair of expanding poles.

Boom arms Probably the most common method of suspending lights over the subject is with a counter-balanced boom arm. This allows great flexibility in all directions, but is not stable, and careful adjustment of the counter-balance is essential. Even minor adjustments to the weight of the· lighting head and the extension of the boom should always be matched by altering the weight or position of the balance. Otherwise, there is a real danger of the stand toppling over. Loosen the joint between the arm and stand to check the balance. Never allow the power or sync cables to trail — tie them along the arm and down the stand.

Tripod stands These are the work horses of lighting support and are available in many sizes, heights and degrees of stability. They are best for lighting directions that are either horizontal or diagonal from above. They do not allow overhead positions.

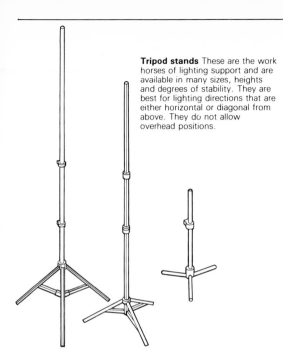

Pantograph A professional support borrowed from motion picture studios, the pantograph allows variable overhead and diagonal positions without occupying any floor space. Pantographs are normally fitted to tracks set in the ceiling so that the lights can be moved horizontally.

Mobile stands Dollies are sometimes fitted to the larger stands and are useful in permanent studios for heavy lighting heads. Large tungsten lights, such as luminaires, are difficult to move by lifting.

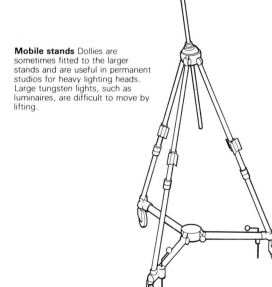

Clamps Lighting heads can be fitted to a variety of clamps, and then attached to bars, poles, or even furniture, such as desk tops and chair backs. Most clamps rely either on a screw lock or, as here, the tension of a spring.

Studio layout 1

When planning the layout of a studio, follow the same principles whether you are designing a permanent, professional workplace or a make-shift adaptation of a living room or garage. First consider the type of shot you will need the studio for and then sketch a floor plan. By laying down the camera angles, the likely size of the subjects and the area of background, you can decide what size of room will be needed or whether a shot will be possible with a particular lens in the space available. Use a protractor or, alternatively, the set of angles drawn on pages 216–217.

The floor plan This is the first essential stage in designing a studio layout. The camera angle is the key – use the coverage across the edges of the picture frame rather than the diagonal angle normally quoted by lens manufacturers (see pages 62–63). This, together with the scale of the subject, determines the working camera to subject distance. Alternatively, if you have to work within an existing room space, the working distance and size of subject will determine the camera angle. Remember to allow space behind the camera and space between the subject and background. Also, if you are likely to place equipment behind the subject, such as a spotlight, allow even more room.

Portrait studio The complex lighting for portraits will require a fair amount of space out of the shot. Depending on the type of work, however, it may be possible to establish one or two basic arrangements and stick to them in accordance with the space available.
Suggested dimensions:
30 x 20ft (9 x 6m)
Height: 10ft (3m)

Large portrait studio For groups, portraits in a studio set, and beauty or glamour shots, a larger studio is a great advantage. A longer focal length can be used and also a wider background. The example here is a well appointed professional studio, requiring considerable income to be economical. Professional photographers sometimes share large studios.
Suggested dimensions:
26 x 41ft (8 x 12m)
Height: 12ft (3.5m)

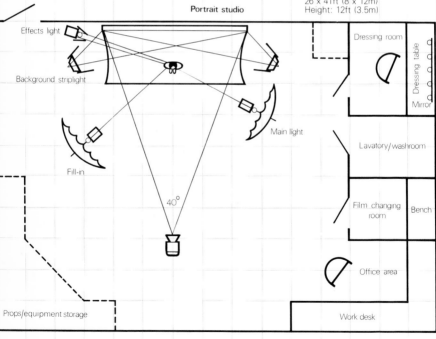

Portrait studio

Effects light

Background striplight

Main light

Fill-in

40°

Dressing room

Dressing table

Mirror

Lavatory/washroom

Film changing room

Bench

Office area

Props/equipment storage

Work desk

2ft
(.6m)

Large portrait studio

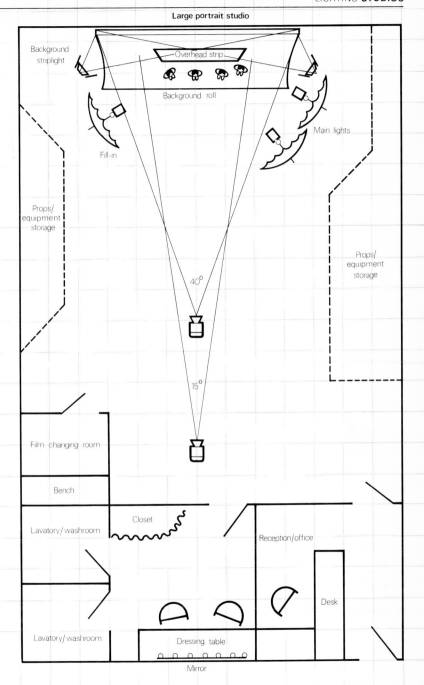

Background
striplight

Overhead strip

Background roll

Main lights

Fill-in

Props/
equipment
storage

Props/
equipment
storage

40°

15°

Film changing room

Bench

Closet

Lavatory/washroom

Reception/office

Desk

Lavatory/washroom

Dressing table

Mirror

Food studio

Work desk

Props/equipment
storage

Oven 1   Oven 2

Hob

Kitchen

worktop

Shelving

Central
worktop

Refrigerator/freezer

Sink

Calor gas

Fish-fryer
on stand

Portable cooker

40°

Power pack

Window light
on boom stand

Double
sliding door

40°

6' wide scoop

Work desk

Office

Food studio For regular
photographic work with food,
considerable space should be
given over to the kitchen.
Efficient and tidy preparation of
the food will allow for more time
and energy to be spent on the
photography itself. A portable
cooker for keeping food hot right
up to or in the shot can be very
useful.
Suggested dimensions:
26 x 19ft (8 x 5.5m)
Height: 10ft (3m)

Basic facilities Beyond a basic, workable
floor plan, most other considerations are simply
refinements. For specific subjects, certain facilities are essential (for example, convenient
plumbing for food photography), but if you are
prepared to accept some inconvenience you can
operate a studio in a surprising variety of
conditions.

The ability to black out the studio is fairly
important, but if you use flash rather than
tungsten lamps it is possible to work with some
ambient lighting. Special access is important if
the subjects you are photographing are likely to
be too large for a normal doorway or too heavy to
carry up a staircase.

Small still-life studio

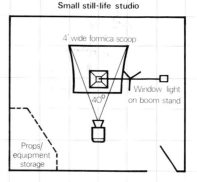

4' wide formica scoop

Window light
on boom stand

40°

Props/
equipment
storage

Large still-life studio

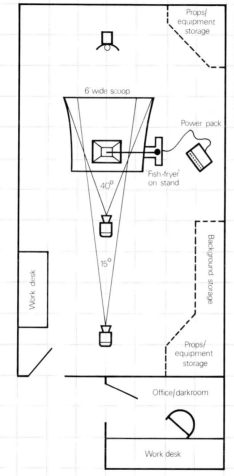

6' wide scoop

40°

'Fish-fryer'
on stand

Power pack

15°

Work desk

Background storage

Props/
equipment
storage

Props/
equipment
storage

Office/darkroom

Work desk

Large still-life studio More
space will allow you to use
lenses of longer focal lengths and
also to place lights behind the
subject. Storage space is essential
if you expect to do much still-life
work as a bank of props can
make the setting up of a shot
much quicker.
Suggested dimensions:
24 x 14ft (6.5 x 4m)
Height: 10ft (3m)

Small still-life studio Because
you will be working on a fairly
small scale, close to the subject,
a large floor area will not be
necessary. The lighting also tends
to be relatively simple.
Suggested dimensions:
12 x 10ft (3.5 x 3m)
Height: 8ft (2.5m)

Room set studio With plenty of space and the type of commission that calls for perfectly controlled lighting, a large studio can be arranged for specially constructed room settings. As with a movie studio, this approach enables the photographer to remove the walls of the 'room' at will to achieve the desired angle of view. The lighting can also be arranged to achieve very subtle effects as desired. An especially high ceiling is needed.
Suggested dimensions:
47½ x 40ft (14 x 12m)
Height: 16ft (5m)

Room set studio

Props/equipment storage

Painted backdrop

Trace frame

Set

65°

Office

Building area

5ft
(1.5m)

Studio fitting checklist Although not all of the items below may be needed, check through them to make sure that nothing important is missed.
1. Smooth, durable floor covering, such as parquet, tiles.
2. Blacking out. Either paint over windows, fit shutters, or install a customized light-tight blind.
3. Electricity. Check that the existing circuits will take all your lighting equipment. If, for example, you use a heavy duty 5,000 Joule (watt-second) power pack, you should have high-amp protected outlets.
4. Gas. For stoves, gas gives more rapid control than electricity. If there are no gas mains, use portable tanks.
5. Plumbing. A sink or wash-basin is generally useful, and for food photography is essential. Keep high voltage equipment in another part of the studio.
6. Storage. Make sure that there is sufficient room for background materials such as rolls, sheets or boards, as well as props and equipment. Shelving keeps things off the floor. Tools can be hung on a large peg-board for accessibility. Film is best stored in a refrigerator.
7. Heating/air-conditioning.
8. Ventilation. If the room is sealed in order to exclude light, an extractor may be necessary.
9. Film changing. A small light-tight closet for changing sheet film and dealing with miscellaneous emergencies can be converted from a walk-in cupboard or even built inside the main studio space.
10. Dressing room. For regular portrait work, provide changing and make-up facilities in a separate room or in a curtained-off area. A dressing table and wall mirror framed with naked lamps as in theatrical dressing rooms are the basic fittings.
11. Work desk. With a light box for viewing transparencies.

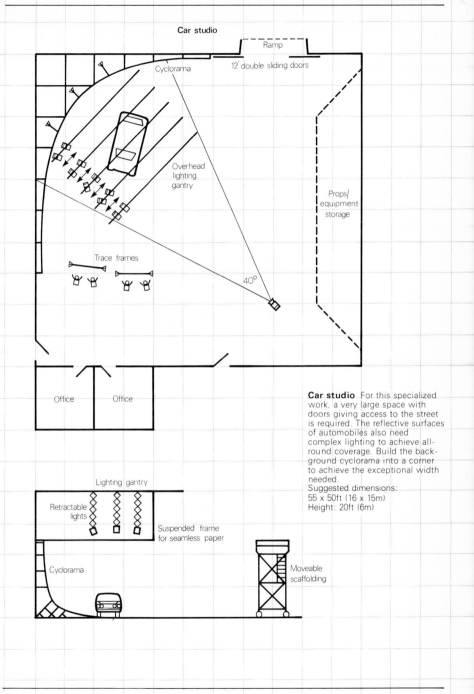

Car studio

Ramp

12 double sliding doors

Cyclorama

Overhead
lighting
gantry

Props/
equipment
storage

Trace frames

40°

Office

Office

Lighting gantry

Retractable
lights

Suspended frame
for seamless paper

Cyclorama

Moveable
scaffolding

Car studio For this specialized
work, a very large space with
doors giving access to the street
is required. The reflective surfaces
of automobiles also need
complex lighting to achieve all-
round coverage. Build the background cyclorama into a corner
to achieve the exceptional width
needed.
Suggested dimensions:
55 x 50ft (16 x 15m)
Height: 20ft (6m)

2. FILM
Colour film types

Choose film to suit the type of photography and make your selection based on the main qualities listed below. Some major differences such as the graininess of a fast film compared with that of a slow one are easily noticed, but most are quite subtle. Between competing makes of the same category of film, the differences may be so small that it is only a question of personal preference. Apart from the obvious difference between negative and reversal film, depending on whether prints or transparencies are desired, the two fundamental choices are between daylight-balanced and tungsten-balanced film, and between slow and fast.

Where tungsten lighting is predominant in an interior, use Type B (tungsten-balanced) film, although a daylight-balanced emulsion can be used with a bluish colour-balancing filter such

Colour transparencies: daylight

Kodachrome 25 ASA 25. An extremely fine grain, very sharp film, with high resolving power. A very good film for general photography when detail is important.

Agfachrome 50S ASA 50. A fine grain film (although Ektachrome 64 is finer). It is sharp and has high resolving power. Blacks are dense and pale colours are faithfully reproduced, but it has higher contrast and less latitude than Ektachrome 64.

Agfachrome CT18 ASA 50. The non-professional version of Agfachrome 50S. Its coarse graininess compares unfavourably with competitive types of film with similar speeds. Reds and yellows are well saturated, but other colours less so.

Kodachrome 64 ASA 64. A very fine grain, very sharp film with high resolving power. An excellent general purpose film with fine grain used extensively by professionals, although designed for amateur use.

Ektachrome 64 ASA 64. Fine grain, very sharp, very high resolving power. Intended for general use, it is slightly grainier than Kodachrome 64. It is available in sheet film form as Ektachrome 64 Professional 6117

Agfachrome CT21 ASA 100. Agfa's non-professional, medium speed film. As CT18, it has coarser grain and poorer resolution than competitive types. Even the faster Ektachrome 200 is better in these respects.

Fujichrome 100 ASA 100. A medium speed film using the same E-6 process as Ektachrome It is comparable with Ektachrome 200 in resolving power and graininess, and has fairly high contrast. An acceptable general purpose film.

Ektachrome 200 ASA 200. A general purpose film with high speed. It has slightly higher contrast than Ektachrome 64 but the same high resolving power. Colours are slightly less saturated, but the graininess is only a little coarser.

Ektachrome 400 ASA 400. An excellent high speed film for low light conditions or action shots calling for fast shutter speeds. Extremely versatile, even giving acceptable results in tungsten lighting.

Fujichrome 400 ASA 400. Competitive with Ektachrome 400, it has similar contrast and graininess, but with a generally warmer cast. Greens are reproduced particularly well. It cannot be push-processed very successfully.

Colour transparencies: tungsten lighting

Ektachrome 50 ASA 50 (used with 3,200 lighting). The tungsten light version of Ektachrome 64. It is designed for fairly long exposures and at shutter speeds from 1/100 sec to just over 1 sec needs no correction for reciprocity failure.

Agfachrome 50L ASA 50 (used with 3,200K lighting). Its characteristics are in most respects similar to the daylight version, Agfachrome 50S.

as an 80B. Otherwise, where the available lighting is daylight, fluorescent or vapour discharge, or with flash, use daylight-balanced film.

Fast films, with speeds up to ASA 400, are a natural choice for hand-held shooting in available light, whereas the fine grain of a slow emulsion is better where detail is important, as in still-life work.

Colour fidelity Most films are fairly accurate across a wide range of colours, but for specific hues, some makes and types may be better than others. The information on these pages may help you choose.

Speed and graininess These two qualities are linked, so that for fine grain the film must have low sensitivity and therefore a slow speed, whereas strong graininess inevitably accompanies high speed.

Sharpness This is a subjective quality, and depends on acutance, resolution and contrast.

Colour saturation Modern films have stronger colour saturation than previous emulsions due to improvements in the dyes.

Ektachrome 160 ASA 160 (used with 3,200K lighting). The tungsten light version of Ektachrome 200, with the same high resolving power and similar graininess.

Vericolor II Professional Type S ASA 125. A professional film, particularly good for portrait work, designed for short exposures by flash or daylight. It has slightly lower contrast than Kodacolor II. Neutral and flesh tones reproduce well together.

Ektachrome Professional 6118 The speed is rated by batches, but is generally around ASA 32 when used with 3,200K lighting. It is designed for use from 1/100 sec to 100 secs, but optimally at 5 secs exposure. It suffers from very little reciprocity failure.

Colour negatives: daylight

Agfacolor 80S ASA 80. Fine grain, very sharp and high resolving power. A general purpose film, comparable to and competitive with Kodacolor II.

Kodacolor 400 ASA 400. A high speed film for low light conditions demanding fast shutter speeds. It is slightly grainier and has less resolving power than Kodacolor II but is very versatile. It works well without filters even with tungsten and fluorescent light. It also has wide exposure latitude.

Agfacolor CNS 400 ASA 400. Similar to Kodacolor 400.

Kodacolor II ASA 100. Ultrafine grain, very sharp, high resolving power, and good colour saturation. This is a good general purpose film designed for amateur use.

Fujicolor 400 ASA 400. Competitive with Kodacolor 400, with very similar characteristics but with less graininess.

Fujicolor FII ASA 100. Similar in all practical respects to Kodacolor II.

Sakuracolor 400 ASA 400. Competitive with and similar to Kodacolor 400 and Fujicolor 400.

Sakuracolor II ASA 100. Similar to Kodacolor II and Fujicolor II.

Colour negatives: tungsten lighting

Vericolor II Professional Type L ASA 100 (used with 3,200K lighting). The tungsten light version of Vericolor Type S. A professional film designed for exposures from 1/50 sec to 60 secs. At 1/50 sec the rating is ASA 80.

Colour: filters

A variety of filters are available which modify the effect of light reaching colour film. Indoor photography, particularly studio work, frequently demands great precision and the use of filters has an important part to play – whether to correct colour casts resulting from the deficiencies in artificial light sources or to achieve desired effects in carefully prepared shots.

Colour balancing filters These are used to alter the colour temperature of light reaching the film, as described on pages 10–11. The 81 and 85 series are bluish, the 82 and 80 series yellowish. The stronger the filter, the greater the exposure compensation required, as the table shows. Exposure compensation is not necessary with TTL metering.

Colour compensating filters These are in the six primary and secondary colours, allowing correction of deficiencies in the film or light source. They also counteract reciprocity failure. Unless you are using a TTL meter, exposure compensation will be necessary.

Ultraviolet filters These are useful both as protection for the front element of the lens, and to absorb the ultraviolet output of some flash tubes which can give a slight bluish cast to colour photographs.

Polarizing filters Some daylight, such as reflections from non-metallic surfaces, is naturally polarized. By rotating a polarizing filter fitted to the lens, this light can be absorbed. This is particularly useful in controlling reflections from glass. To do the same with artificial lighting, which is rarely polarized, fit a polarizing screen

Matching film to light source This bowl of fruit was shot on daylight film (Kodachrome 64). Because of the tungsten lighting, an orange cast results. A type of film balanced for tungsten should have been used.

Colour balancing filters Here, the same film and lighting produce an acceptable result because of the use of a colour balancing filter. To correct daylight film to the 3,400K lighting, an 80B filter was required, with an extra one and a half stops exposure (see pages 10–11).

in front of the lights and a polarizing filter over the lens (see pages 206 to 207). Polarizing filters reduce exposure by one and a third stops. Compensate for this when setting the aperture and shutter speed.

Neutral density filters Being neutral grey, these filters cause no colour shift. They can be used to reduce exposure with bright light and fast film.

Graduated filters One half of this type of filter is toned, either neutral density or coloured. The edge of the toned area is graduated so as to disappear smoothly, without hard transitions. Graduated filters can be used when only part of the image needs filtration.

Effects filters A wide variety of optical changes is possible with the many different types of effects filters available. Because most have such obvious results, they are easy to over-use and frequently produce nothing more than clichés.

Diffusers Used to conceal wrinkles and blemishes in portraiture, and to give a luminous edge with backlighting.
Fog filters Reduce contrast and de-saturate colours for a misty effect.
Star filters Turn points of light into small stars.
Prism filters Give repetitive images, the number and pattern depending on the way it is cut.
Diffraction filters Give a multi-hued effect in different patterns.
Colour effect filters Give an overall colour cast.

Auxiliary lenses Some lenses fit over the front of a lens and are used similarly to effects filters.
Split-diopter lenses Bi-focal auxiliary lenses that allow two planes of focus in one shot – one at a distance, the other close to the lens.
Anamorphic lenses Cylindrical attachments that stretch the image.
Fish-eye attachments These attach to a normal lens to give the effect of a fish-eye lens.

Exposure increase with colour balancing filters

Filter	Exposure increase
85B	$\frac{2}{3}$ stop
85	$\frac{2}{3}$ stop
85C	$\frac{2}{3}$ stop
85EF	$\frac{2}{3}$ stop
81D	$\frac{2}{3}$ stop
81C	$\frac{1}{3}$ stop
81B	$\frac{1}{3}$ stop
81A	$\frac{1}{3}$ stop
81	$\frac{1}{3}$ stop
82	$\frac{1}{3}$ stop
82A	$\frac{1}{3}$ stop
82B	$\frac{2}{3}$ stop
82C	$\frac{2}{3}$ stop
80D	$\frac{2}{3}$ stop
80C	1 stop
80B	$1\frac{2}{3}$ stops
80A	2 stops

Exposure increase with neutral density filters

ND filter	Exposure increase	Light transmitted
0.1	$\frac{1}{3}$ stop	80%
0.2	$\frac{2}{3}$ stop	63%
0.3	1 stop	50%
0.4	$1\frac{1}{3}$ stops	40%
0.5	$1\frac{2}{3}$ stops	32%
0.6	2 stops	25%
0.7	$2\frac{1}{3}$ stops	20%
0.8	$2\frac{2}{3}$ stops	16%
0.9	3 stops	13%
1.0	$3\frac{1}{3}$ stops	10%
2.0	$6\frac{2}{3}$ stops	1%
3.0	10 stops	0.1%
4.0	$13\frac{1}{3}$ stops	0.01%

Colour cast to be corrected	Select
Red	Cyan
Magenta	Green
Blue	Yellow
Cyan	Red
Green	Magenta
Yellow	Blue

Exposure increase with Colour Compensating filters

No increase	$\frac{1}{3}$ stop	$\frac{2}{3}$ stop	1 stop	$1\frac{1}{3}$ stops
CC05 Yellow	CC05–CC20 Cyan	CC30–CC40 Cyan	CC50 Cyan	CC50 Blue
	CC05–CC20 Magenta	CC30–CC50 Magenta	CC50 Red	
	CC10–CC40 Yellow	CC50 Yellow	CC50 Green	
	CC05–CC20 Red	CC30–CC40 Red	CC40 Blue	
	CC05–CC20 Green	CC30–CC40 Green		
	CC05–CC10 Blue	CC20–CC30 Blue		

Colour balance and processing

Obtaining the results you want from colour film depends on more than choosing the right type and make of emulsion. When buying film, take account of manufacturing tolerances, then store it carefully and have it processed under conditions you are familiar with. By using colour compensating filters and altering development, you can exercise even more control over the behaviour of film.

Colour balance The colour balance between different batches of the same manufacturer's film can vary widely. When possible, buy a large quantity of one batch that has a satisfactory balance, and store it in a refrigerator or freezer. The storage procedures described for black-and-white film on pages 52 to 53 apply equally here.

Some makes of film are available in 'professional' and 'amateur' versions. The former are

designed to give their best results immediately, whilst 'amateur' films are intended to age slightly – by up to three months on a dealer's shelf at room temperature. 'Professional' films have a more accurate colour balance, but 'amateur' films need less care.

Processing Colour processing is straightforward, but needs strict quality control for consistently good results. Consistency is rarely possible with home processing unless you handle large quantities, and it is usually better to try a number of different professional processing labs until you find one that satisfies you, and then stay with that one. Remember that processing variations can affect colour balance.

Altering the development of film changes some of its characteristics, and although this is most commonly .done to correct under-exposure, it is also used by many professional

---

The effects of decreased or 'cut' development
1 *Loss of film speed*
2 *Reduced contrast* Highlight areas are most strongly affected. Cut development can be used as a method for compressing a wide tonal range to within the film's recording capability.
3 *Colour shift* Varies between films. Shifts towards blue or magenta are most common.

The effects of increased development ('push-processing')
1 *Increased film speed* Push-processing is most commonly used for this purpose.
2 *Increased contrast* This can be useful with low-contrast subjects.
3 *Weaker maximum density* A disadvantage – shadow areas tend to become thin and fogged.
4 *Increased graininess* A major drawback with push-processing, although it can be used for effect if desired.
5 *Colour shift* This varies between films. The shift is generally towards yellow.

Reciprocity failure These two pictures show reciprocity failure, uncorrected and corrected. Long exposures frequently cause a colour cast and wrong exposure because, beyond a certain point, film will not respond to the extra light falling on it in the same way as at normal exposures. It is simply not being used in a way allowed for in its original design specification. Frequently, colour correction filters and increased exposure time can restore balanced colour (see the table opposite).

photographers to achieve subtle differences in colour and contrast. Contrast control is particularly important in still-life work, where technical standards are very high – pushing film half a stop, for instance, can brighten highlights and generally clean up the appearance of, say, a food shot. All good processing labs will 'push' (increase development) or 'cut' (reduce development) as requested, and most will not charge extra for alterations of up to one stop. Kodachrome, however, does not respond well to this treatment, and only a few independent labs will attempt it. The effects of altered development are described opposite.

Reciprocity failure Under normal conditions, film reacts proportionately to changes in exposure time. In other words, changing the shutter speed from 1/125 sec to 1/60 sec doubles the exposure. At very long exposure times, and in some cases with extremely short ones, this stops being true, and film reacts less and less to each increase in exposure time. Doubling the exposure time from 10 seconds to 20 seconds has only a very small effect on most films. This is known as reciprocity failure, and its effect is even more serious with colour film, as the three layers of emulsion react differently, causing a colour shift, usually towards green or yellow. The table below gives the compensation needed for the major film types.

How to compensate for reciprocity failure
add filtration and increase exposure as follows: NR=not recommended

Exposure time	1/1,000 sec	1/100 sec	1/10 sec	1 sec	10 secs	100 secs
Kodachrome 25	—	—	—	+1 stop CC10M	+1½ stops CC10M	+2½ stops CC10M
Kodachrome 40 (tungsten)	—	—	—	+½ stop No filter	+1 stop No filter	NR
Kodachrome 64	—	—	+1 stop	CC10R	NR	NR
Ektachrome 50 (tungsten)	+½ stop CC10G	—	—	—	+1 stop CC20B	NR
Ektachrome 64/	—	—	—	+1 stop CC15B	+1½ stops CC20B	NR
Ektachrome 6117						
Ektachrome 6118 (tungsten)	See film instructions. Intended range 1/10 sec to 1/100 secs; normally no filtration needed at these speeds.					
Agfachrome 50S	—	—	—	+½ stop	NR	NR
Agfachrome 50L (tungsten)	CC05Y	CC05Y	—	—	+⅓ stop No filter	+⅔ stop CC10R or CC10Y
Fujichrome 100	—	—	—	—	+½ stop CC05C	+1½ stops CC10C
Ektachrome 160 (tungsten)	—	—	—	+½ stop CC10R	+1 stop CC15R	NR
Ektachrome 200	—	—	—	+½ stop CC10R	NR	NR
Ektachrome 400	—	—	—	+½ stop No filter	+1½ stops No filter	+2½ stops CC10C
Colour Negative Films						
Kodacolor II	—	—	—	+½ stop No filter	+1½ stops CC10C	+2½ stops CC10C+10G
Vericolor II Type S	—	—	—	NR	NR	NR
Vericolor II Type L	NR	NR	See film instructions			
Kodacolor 400	—	—	—	+½ stop No filter	+1 stop No filter	+2 stops No filter

Colour: faults

Use these examples of common faults to help identify others as they occur. If a particular fault is difficult to pin down, eliminate the possibilities progressively trying at first to establish whether the problem lies in the film stock, when taking the photograph, or during processing. Identifying a fault is important because, if you cannot find the cause, it may continue to occur.

	In the film stock	Manufacturing defect Poor storage Wrong film
Fault	During Picture-taking	Poor camera handling Defect in camera body Wrong camera setting Lens defect Wrong lens setting
	During processing	Wrong procedure Accident Carelessness

Colour imbalance Two factors affect the fine degrees of colour balance: manufacturing tolerances and the lighting. Although most modern films are accurate to within CC05 of neutral, some batches are more accurate than others. In the studio, an additional complication is the colour temperature of the lamps and the colour of any diffusers or reflectors. Opal perspex (plexiglass) diffusers, for example, can cause unexpected tints.

Filter flare In studio work, one of the dangers of fitting a gelatin filter in front of the lens is that, if the filter buckles, it may catch the reflection of the light. Always make a last minute visual check before shooting.

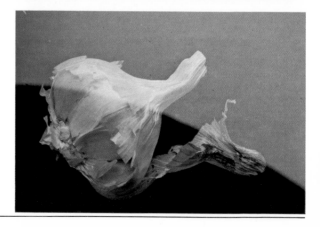

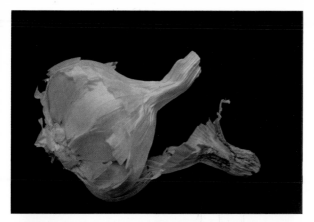

Daylight film used with tungsten light Daylight film is balanced for 5,500 Kelvins. When used by mistake with studio tungsten lamps, the result is a pronounced orange cast, too strong to be corrected by duplicating.

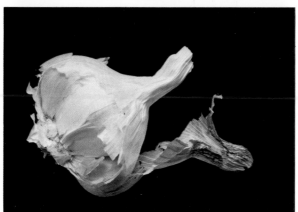

Tungsten film used with flash The reverse mismatching is tungsten balanced film (Type A or Type B) used with studio flash. Again the resulting transparency cannot be corrected by duplicating.

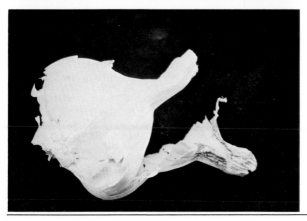

Gross overexposure When using lenses that do not have a fully automatic diaphragm (FAD), remember to stop down to the working aperture after viewing and composing at full aperture. This is particularly important in studio work, where very small apertures are usually needed for great depth of field.

Instant film types 1

In indoor photography, and particularly in the studio, the value of instant film lies not only in being able to have finished photographs immediately, but also in being able to test composition, colour and other qualities before shooting on regular film.

Instant film contain their own developing and fixing chemicals in a sealed pod, which is squeezed out over the film after exposure by rollers. 'Peel-apart' instant films use a negative that is discarded after the image has formed, whilst in the newer 'integral' films the chemicals remain sealed inside, under the final image.

Compared with regular films, instant films have these characteristics:
- High resolution, because they are contact-printed
- Narrow contrast range (therefore high contrast)
- Little latitude, not normally a problem because a wrong exposure can be corrected instantly by making a second one
- A diffuse silver haze, particularly noticeable in integral films. The effect has some slight similarities with that of a light diffusing filter

Polaroid Type 52

Polaroid Type 51   Polaroid Type 55 (Positive)

Polaroid Type 57

Polaroid Type 55 (Negative)

Polaroid Type 52 ASA 400. Available in 4×5in sheets only, Type 52 gives subtly graded, high resolution prints with a contrast range that covers about six stops. With moderately high contrast, it is best suited to low contrast scenes. Print quality is extremely fine.

Polaroid Types 57, 87 and 107 ASA 3,000. These fast films are useful for available light photography at small apertures and high shutter speeds. They have higher contrast than Type 52, covering a range of about five stops only, and are also grainier. They are useful for adding life to low contrast scenes.

Polaroid Type 51 ASA 320 in daylight, ASA 125 in tungsten light. This is a specialized film giving extremely high-contrast prints. It is blue-sensitive rather than panchromatic, hence its slower speed in artificial light. It is useful for graphic effects, and for giving a bright, lively result with very flat lighting.

Polaroid Type 55 P/N ASA 50 for prints, ASA 25 for negatives. Polaroid 55 P/N (in 4×5in sheets) gives not only a high-resolution, finely-graded print, but also an instantly usable negative with the very high resolving power of 150–160 lines per millimetre. To clear residual chemicals from the negative, dip it in a sodium sulphite solution at room temperature within three minutes, and leave it for at least a minute. Alternatively, put it in water until you have access to the sodium sulphite solution. Polaroid supply a plastic tub for storing negatives in solution while on location. Finally, remove the metal tab and the black perforated strip, which can cause staining if left in contact with another negative. Then wash the negative in running water for five minutes. An acid hardening bath is optional, but not really necessary. Hang to dry. Note the different ratings for print and negative. This means that a properly exposed print will give a thin negative, whereas a good negative accompanies an over-exposed print.

Polaroid Type 665 P/N ASA 75 for prints, ASA 35 for negatives. The medium format version of Type 55 P/N, with similar performance and procedures for use.

Polacolor 2 ASA 75. Available in five different Polaroid film sizes (Types 58, 108, 668, 88 and 808). Like all instant films, Polacolor 2 has rather high contrast, and cannot handle bright light and deep shadows together. Frontal, frontal to side, or diffused lighting gives the best results. The film has little latitude, and exposures need to be correct to within half a stop.

Polacolor 3 (Polacolor ER) ASA 125. Polaroid's most recently announced peel-apart film shows considerable improvement over previous instant colour films and has been very well received by the photographic press. Its colour separation and saturation are extremely good, and it can be used successfully in a wider variety of lighting conditions than Polacolor 2. It also has greatly increased exposure latitude. Initially, it will be available in 4×5in format (Type 59) and 8×10in (Type 809).

Polaroid SX-70 (no rating, but effectively somewhere around ASA 150). This is a self-timing, integral film for use only in special Polaroid cameras. Roller ejection is automatic, using an electric motor in the camera and batteries in the film pack, reducing the risk of uneven processing. The plastic and polymer layers that seal the print help to give the image a special quality that is quite different from other instant prints. The most recent version, 'Time-Zero', takes only one minute to complete its integrated processing.

Kodak Instant Picture Print Film PR10 (no rating, but effectively somewhere around ASA 150). Also a self-timing integral film, this is essentially similar to Polaroid SX-70 except for a rectangular format and a textured front surface.

Polacolor 2

Polaroid SX-70

Polaroid SX-70 Time Zero

Instant film in indoor photography

With the right equipment and film types, instant film has uses that go far beyond straightforward snapshots. In studio work and in interiors generally, instant film is widely used to make tests and to check compositional and lighting aspect in order to improve the image.

As a substitute for normal film Instant film has certain specific qualities (see pages 42–43) that set it apart from normal emulsions and it is in no way inferior. Its diffuse silver haze can be particularly attractive with some subjects and the quality of Polaroid Types 52, 55 and 665, especially the tonal gradation, is almost impossible to match with normal black-and-white film and printing. Instant prints can be reproduced in publications without difficulty or loss of quality.

For testing This is a major use for instant film in indoor photography, partly because of the lighting difficulties that often have to be overcome, and partly because of the common requirement with studio work for a perfected image. Viewing an approximation of the finished photograph on the spot is a great aid to evaluation, and possible corrections or opportunities that might be missed through the viewfinder can often be picked up by examining a print.

As a learning technique There are great and largely unexploited opportunities for using the immediacy of instant film as a method of learning the various elements of photography, such as composition. Compare print with subject and experiment with differences in camera position, subject arrangement and lighting.

For single-opportunity shots With fast-moving, unpredictable events, when there might be uncertainty about whether the precise moment had been captured, instant film offers valuable reassurance.

For goodwill Giving people an instant portrait of themselves makes it easier to gain their co-operation as photographic subjects, and is much more effective than promising to send a photograph later.

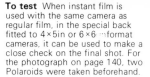

To test When instant film is used with the same camera as regular film, in the special back fitted to 4×5in or 6×6 in format cameras, it can be used to make a close check on the final shot. For the photograph on page 140, two Polaroids were taken beforehand.

In the first test, two things are obviously wrong: the dark carpet at lower left unbalances the composition, and the outstretched left leg is awkwardly exaggerated by the wide-angle lens used to give an overall view In the second test, some papers

are re-arranged on the floor, solving the composition problem. The leg is further back, but still does not look right, even though the camera was raised for a very slightly higher viewpoint. Adjustments were made accordingly for the final shot.

Controlling the instant image

Although the majority of instant film cameras are fully automatic and have only a simple 'darken/lighten' control, further limited adjustments can be made with some film types.

Exposure control With automatic cameras, exposure can be altered by more than the range of the 'darken/lighten' control with the help of a neutral density filter. ND 0.30 reduces the light by one stop. Places over the sensor but not the lens, this gives one stop greater exposure. If it is placed over the lens rather than the sensor, the exposure will be reduced by one stop.

Instant film used in backs that fit onto regular cameras can be treated as normal film – all the camera controls can be used.

Development control: black-and-white With Polaroid black-and-white instant films extended development time gives darker shadows and reduced development lightens them. Light areas, on the other hand, will not be affected by altering development time. So, by adjusting the exposure to control the highlights, it is possible to alter the contrast by changing the development time. Extended development gives more contrast, reduced development gives less.

Development control: colour This can only be done with peel-apart colour film. Development of Polacolor 2, extended to between 75 and 90 seconds instead of the recommended 60 seconds, gives more saturated colours and deeper blacks and, although a slight blue-green colour bias is introduced, this can be corrected by using yellow or red filters according to taste.

Delayed coating Black-and-white Polaroid films must be coated after the image has formed, partly to prevent further bleaching of highlights. By delaying this, contrast is increased.

Pre-exposure This is a method of decreasing contrast wth subjects that have bright highlights and strong shadows. With a camera that allows you to make a double exposure, aim it first at a featureless area of continuous tone, such as a sheet of paper or blank wall, completely out of focus. Make an exposure at three stops less than the meter indicates, and then photograph your subject on the same film. The pre-exposure will lighten the shadow areas slightly without affecting the highlights. With Polacolor 2 and 3, you can use this technique to alter the shadow colours alone by pre-exposing through a coloured filter

---

Instant film faults
Completely black Film incorrectly inserted, lens cap left on or shutter failure.
White corner Pulling too fast.
Light spots Pulling too fast.
Regularly spaced marks Dirt on the rollers.
Partial fogging A light leak, perhaps because the film or holder is incorrectly positioned.
Bars or streaks Pulling unevenly or too fast.

Reciprocity failure with Polacolor 2

Long exposures require the following compensation:

Exposure time	Compensation	Filters
1/1,000–100 sec	–	–
1/10 sec	+$\frac{1}{3}$ stop	CC05R+CC05Y
1 sec	+1$\frac{1}{2}$ stops	CC10R+CC20Y
10 secs	+2$\frac{1}{2}$ stops	CC30R+CC20Y
100 secs	+3 stops	CC30R+CC20Y

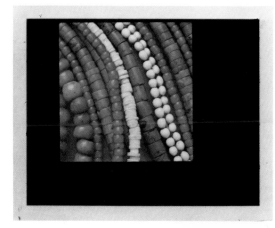

Controlling contrast Apart from the positive/negative films, which remain unaltered, all Polaroid black and white films have greater or lesser contrast according to the length of time they are allowed to develop. In this pair of shots, the print at left was developed for the minimum 30 seconds and as a result lacks contrast. There is also a slight unevenness in the background. The right hand print was developed for two minutes, and has a better tonal range.

Altering colour intensity By increasing development time, Polacolor 2 can be made to yield richer colours. The print of coloured beads above was given normal development, 60 seconds; that at right was developed for 90 seconds. This extra development gives more colour intensity, but also a blue-green cast, which was corrected here by adding CC05 Red and CC05 Yelow filters.

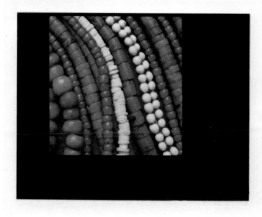

Black-and-white film types

Apart from specialized films, such as high speed infrared and ortho line film, there are three basic types: slow, medium and fast. The finest grain films have slow film speeds – around ASA 32 – whilst coarse grain inevitably accompanies high ASA ratings. Choice of developer can effect grain size, as can altered development, but it is not possible to have fine grain and fast film speed. The two are mutually exclusive.

New film technology, borrowed from colour films, is being introduced which will change the way film is speed rated. Ilford XP1 and Agfapan Vario-XL, which will soon become generally available, can be rated from ASA 125 to 1,600. Effectively ASA 400 films comparable to Kodak Tri-X, they can be used at slower or faster speeds with exceptionally good results – with small grain size and high contrast.

Speed and graininess For carefully set up studio shots, with controlled lighting, long exposures are possible. In these conditions, the fine grain of a film such as Kodak Panatomic-X (right) gives an extremely high quality result. For action shots by available light, however, a fast film such as Kodak Tri-X (far right) will be needed. The level of graininess will be correspondingly high, but this is not necessarily a disadvantage as it can contribute to the dramatic effect.

Agfapan 25 ASA 25. A very slow, very sharp film with extremely fine grain and very high resolution at 185 lines/mm (lines per millimetre). Similar to the Kodak and Ilford slow films.

FOR 36 B/W-PRINTS

Kodak Plus-X Pan ASA 125 Similar in characteristics to Verichrome Pan but available in different formats. It also has a retouchable surface.

Kodak Panatomic-X ASA 32. Extremely fine grain, very sharp and with high resolution. Very good for recording fine detail or when great enlargements are to be made, but it is too slow for many hand-held situations. It can be processed to produce transparencies.

Ilford FP4 ASA 125. The Ilford equivalent to Verichrome Pan and Plus-X, with no significant differences.

Ilford Pan F ASA 50. Similar in characteristics to Panatomic-X, it is very sharp and has extremely fine grain and high resolution. It has the same applications as Panatomic-X, including transparency processing.

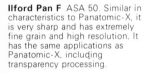

Agfapan 200 ASA 200. A medium speed sheet film, very sharp, with fine grain and high resolving power (110 lines/mm). Can be retouched easily.

FÜR 36 S/W-BILDER

Agfapan 100 ASA 100. A medium speed, very sharp film. It has fine grain and high resolution (145 lines/mm). For general use.

FOR 36 B/W-PRINTS

Ilford HP5 ASA 400. An excellent fast film, with fine grain and high resolving power. It is very sharp and has great latitude. The ASA rating is only nominal, for by choosing the appropriate developer the rating can be set anywhere between ASA 200 and ASA 650 with normal development.

Kodak Verichrome Pan ASA 125. A medium speed film. It has extremely fine grain and high resolution. A very sharp general purpose film, designed for amateur use.

Tri-X Pan ASA 400. Similar to HP5 and equally suitable for situations with low light levels or requiring fast shutter speeds. Its speed can be increased by push-processing, with an inevitable increase in graininess.

Agfapan 400 ASA 400. The Agfa version of HP5 and Tri-X. It has similar characteristics with a high level of resolution (110 lines/mm).

Specialist films

Kodak High Speed Infrared The speed rating varies according to the heat-reflecting properties of the subject, but is generally around ASA 50 with a Wratten 25 Red filter in daylight. It requires special handling.

Kodak Royal Pan 400 ASA 400. The sheet film version of Tri-X.

Kodalith Ortho Type 3 Establish the speed by trial and error, using ASA 12 as a starting point. A very high contrast film. With special development, it produces a solid black image on a clear film base, useful for special effects and masks.

Kodak Recording Film 2475 ASA 1,000. The fastest commercially available film in 35mm format. Its sharpness is low, its resolving power medium and its graininess coarse. It can be push-processed by up to two stops.

Agfaortho 25 Similar to Kodalith. When used with a high contrast subject and high contrast developer, it can reduce the tonal range to just black and white.

Royal-X Pan ASA 1,250. An extremely fast film available in 120 size only. It can even be push-processed by one stop. It is very sharp but its graininess and resolving power are only medium – the price to be paid for the film's great speed.

Agfa Dia-Direct ASA 32. A film specifically designed for black-and-white transparencies, with a clear base. It requires reversal processing.

Black-and-white: filters

By using coloured filters with black-and-white film, the tones in which colours in the subject are reproduced on the print can be altered considerably. Colours record on black-and-white film according to the sensitivity of the film, so that reds, for example, to which film is relatively insensitive, appear very pale in the negative, and therefore dark in the print. Blues, to which film is more sensitive than the human eye, are usually well exposed on the negative, and so pale in the print.

These are the most obvious differences in colour sensitivity between film and human vision, and if uncorrected usually give an unnatural appearance. By using a filter of a complementary colour, however, the tones in the final print can be made to approximate to those perceived by the eye. So, for example, if a glass of red wine is photographed without any filter on normal panchromatic black-and-white film, it will appear much darker in the print than it should – the film is too sensitive to its red colour. But a green filter placed over the lens will block most of the red light, so that it appears much lighter in the print.

Apart from this type of correction, coloured filters can be used to manipulate the tones in any way that you want. For example, a pale red and dark blue that appear together may have such similar tones in a black-and-white print that they are hard to distinguish. By using either a blue or a red filter, contrast can be introduced, making either the red darker than the blue with a red filter, or the blue darker than the red with a blue filter.

Many of the filters already described for use with colour film (see pages 36–37) have the same effects with black-and-white emulsions. Ultraviolet, polarizing and neutral density filters can be used in the same way, as can many effects filters. Graduated filters are rather less useful with black-and-white photography because shading and printing-in during enlargement can give the same results, but with more precision.

Controlling tones with filters
Specific colours can be made to look lighter or darker in black-and-white with the addition of coloured filters. In the examples on these pages, a red pot with a green lid is photographed on a blue background. The lemons are yellow. Use the table opposite to select the filter – it will also show the 'side-effects' with other colours than the one you want to alter.

No filter

Blue filter (Wratten 47)

Red filter (Wratten 25)

Green filter (Wratten 58)

Yellow filter (Wratten 8)

Filters for lightening and darkening specific colours

Colour of subject	To darken (Wratten numbers)	To lighten (Wratten numbers)
Red	58, 47, 44	29, 25, 32, 21, 16, 12
Orange	58, 47, 44	25, 32, 21, 16, 12
Yellow	47, 44	12, 11, 8, 16, 21, 25
Yellow-green	47, 32	11, 12, 8, 16, 58
Green	29, 25, 47, 32	58, 11, 12, 8, 44
Blue-green	29, 25	44, 47, 58
Blue	25, 16, 12, 11, 8, 58	47, 44, 32
Violet	58, 11, 12, 8	32, 47
Magenta	58, 11, 16	32, 47, 25

Black-and-white care and processing

Although black-and-white film has more latitude than colour and is less susceptible to ageing, careful storage and handling are still important for the best results. Treat all film as a perishable product, which it is, and always process it as soon as possible after you have used it. Because there are no colour shifts to worry about, altered development is even more useful for controlling image values than it is with colour film.

Storage and handling The two conditions that do more than anything else to speed up ageing are heat and humidity, and when combined their effect is increased even further. Unexposed film is more stable than film that has been used but still awaits processing.

The best conditions for storing film are in a freezer at −18°C (0°F), sealed in moisture-proof containers. This will virtually halt any ageing, but before use the film must be allowed to warm up gradually for a few hours. Condensation is also a danger, so leave film unopened in the manufacturer's sealed can or pack until you are ready to use it.

For more general use, film can be kept in a refrigerator at 4°C (40°F) for several months without showing signs of deterioration. When travelling, try always to keep film below 16°C (60°F) and at a relative humidity of 40 to 60 per cent, and never leave it in direct sunlight. A picnic box lined with polystyrene (styrofoam) is very good for keeping film at moderate temperatures. If the air is noticeably humid, include porous packets of desiccant, such as silica gel powder or crystals, and fill up the container with film to leave as little room as possible for moisture laden air. Regularly dry out the silica gel by heating it to 200°C (390°F) in an oven.

At airports, do not allow film to pass through X-ray security machines. Although the staff are usually at pains to assure travellers that film will not be affected, X-rays have the same fogging effect as light, and this effect is cumulative. So, although one pass through a low dose machine may have no noticeable effect on the film, several may. There is a 'fog threshold level' beyond which damage is evident, and there is no on the spot way of finding out what is happening to an individual roll of film. The safest method is to ask for a hand inspection, which is readily granted at most airports. Do not rely on lead lined pouches advertised for the purpose as the X-ray machine operator may well increase the dosage until the rays penetrate to the contents.

Altering development Increasing or decreasing the development of black-and-white film is simpler than for colour film, and is widely used as a means of controlling contrast and adjusting the tonal range. So, with a very high contrast subject, deliberately over-expose by one stop, and later have the development reduced by the same amount. Changing the ASA rating on the camera's TTL meter – say, from ASA 400 to ASA 200 – is a simple way of changing the exposure. If, on the other hand, the subject has a flat tonal range and you want to sharpen the differences, reduce the exposure and increase development.

Development can be altered by changing the dilution or temperature of the developing fluid, or the time given. Two stops is the practical limit before image quality suffers noticeably. Specifically, altered development has the following effects:

Increased development ('pushed')
1. Increased film speed
2. Increased contrast
3. Increased graininess

Decreased development ('cut')
1. Loss of film speed
2. Less contrast

Reciprocity failure Black-and-white film, with its greater latitude than colour film and its single layer of emulsion, suffers less from reciprocity failure, and it is by no means as serious a problem. If in doubt, check the manufacturer's instructions. As a rule of thumb, 1 sec will probably require about one stop extra exposure, 10 secs two stops and 100 secs 3 stops.

Altering development changes the behaviour of the film and can be used to adjust the final result, particularly in controlling contrast. With this still-life of an old camera, similar results could also have been achieved at the printing stage.

Cut development To reduce contrast in a harshly lit scene, the film can be over-exposed by, say, one stop (halving the ASA rating would achieve this) and under-developed by the same amount. Contrast will thus be reduced. There is no benefit of reducing grain size, so the effect is not simply the reverse of push-processing.

Normal development By rating the film at the recommended speed and using standard development procedures, film will respond in the manner it is designed for.

Pushed development Up-rating the film by one stop (doubling the ASA number) effectively under-exposes the film by the same amount. Increasing the development time by one stop compensates for this but gives greater contrast. The unwanted side-effect is an increase in grain size.

Black-and-white: faults

Many of the examples shown on pages 40–41 for colour film also apply to black-and-white film. In addition, more common faults are shown on these two pages. When trying to identify a fault, examine the negative directly rather than the contact sheet – remember that light leaks and flare show up as dark patches. Generally, processing errors are more frequent with black-and-white than colour film, due to lower standards at laboratories.

Unsynchronized flash So that the full peak of an electronic flash coincides with an open shutter, SLR's must be synchronized at a speed of less than 1/60 sec or 1/125 sec — the exact speed depends on the camera. By using too fast a shutter speed, part of the focal plane blind obstructs the view when the flash fires, as here.

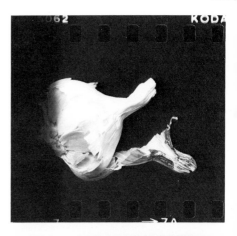

Camera shake With continuous lighting, either day or tungsten, the slow shutter speeds common in indoor photography risk camera shake. This frequently results when the tripod is not secure, or if a cable release is not used.

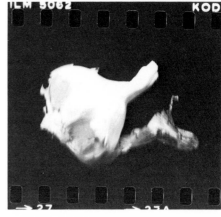

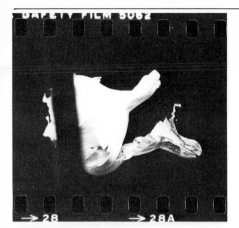

Cable in front of lens Because sync leads and cable releases are used frequently in studios, this fault can easily happen at small apertures, particularly when the image is viewed at full aperture (above) when the obstruction is not obvious.

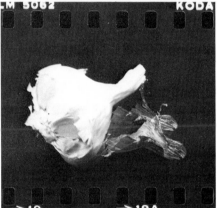

Subject movement
Distinguishable from the soft blur of camera shake by the sharp edges of the image, this fault can occur when several electronic flashes are used on one exposure. In between flashes, objects can move if not supported carefully.

Mismatched chemicals
Pronounced staining on the negative is usually a sign of a chemical processing fault. These circular stains were caused by the use of a wrong anti-foaming agent.

3. CAMERAS AND LENSES
Camera handling

Indoor photography frequently involves the use of the camera supports described on pages 58–61. The low light levels found out of direct sunlight require slower shutter speeds. The hand-held camera is often just not steady enough. On the other hand, with faster films and lenses now available, there are many situations in which hand-held photography can achieve good results indoors. Candid photography, for example, offers excellent opportunities. The camera handling techniques on these pages are of the first importance in this – for the difference between a steady and an unsteady camera grip can be equivalent to two exposure stops.

35mm grip Because of its small size and compact shape, with convenient viewing and focusing, the 35mm SLR is one of the easiest cameras to handle effectively. Camera shake can be reduced to a minimum with the use of the correct grips. The important point is to keep the camera firmly braced against your forehead and cheek, with the elbows using the chest for support. Squeeze rather than jab the shutter release.

Horizontal format The camera body rests on the heel of the left hand, with the thumb and forefinger free to adjust the lens controls. The weight of the camera is spread between the two hands.

Vertical format The best method has the left elbow against the chest for support and the right hand steadies the camera back against the forehead

35mm stance Standing is not particularly stable, but it is often the only available position in a particular shooting situation. Spread your weight evenly and relax, leaning against a wall for support, if one is available. Wide-angle lenses are least prone to camera shake, and long-focus lenses are particularly difficult. Do not expect to be able to use a long-focus lens effectively at slow shutter speeds. Even with practice, 1/125 sec is the working minimum with an unsupported 200mm lens.

Normal stance Place one foot in front of the other to spread your weight. When possible, lean against a wall or other firm object for support (right).

Kneeling and squatting

These are both good shooting positions, offering greater steadiness than standing. The aim should be to use the body as a rigid support, with both elbows resting on the knees when squatting and one when kneeling. These techniques create lines of support from the camera to the ground.

Kneeling Sit back on your right heel and place your elbow on your left knee. The camera is on a tripod consisting of both feet and one knee.

Squatting Uncomfortable at first, with practice this is a steady position. Rest both elbows on the knees for firm support.

Medium format cameras

6 × 6cm or 6 × 7cm cameras are more likely to be used on a tripod, but if you are using one hand-held, remember to use your body to give the camera the greatest support possible.

Waist-level finder Take the weight in your cupped left hand, holding the camera firmly against your body. There is no advantage in holding the camera higher than just above your waist.

Magnifier and 45° viewer These are not particularly steady hand-held. Keep the elbows against your body for support.

Non-reflex 6 × 6cm The direct viewer of the Hasselblad SWC makes it rather like handling a 35mm SLR. This is a good camera for hand-held use.

Long-focus medium format A pistol grip will help when using a long-focus lens on medium format. But do not expect to be able to use slow shutter speeds.

Camera supports 1

For practically every area of indoor photography, a tripod or alternative camera support is essential equipment. It has two functions: to provide a stable platform during long exposures (or when multiple flash is used to increase light output), and to hold the camera in position for a precisely composed image. Although a tripod is easier to use indoors than on location, where wind and uneven ground are frequent problems, it should still be set up with care, and needs to be strong enough for the particular camera being used.

Miniature tripod Not a studio item, this small tripod is nevertheless useful for general work in interiors with a 35mm camera, and is small enough to be carried as a regular item in a shoulder bag.

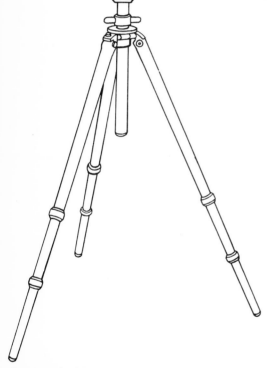

Standard tripod For most small and medium format cameras, a basic tripod like this, weighing not much more than about nine pounds (four kilos), is satisfactory. Three-sectioned telescoping legs allow a reasonable height with stability when fully extended. A centre column is valuable for small height changes without altering the basic attitude of the camera.

Table-top tripod A very light, small tripod with fixed legs, this can be used as an emergency support on level surfaces — table, floor, even a wall if held firmly in one hand.

Heavy duty tripod For view cameras, a large, robust tripod is necessary. Tilting a 4 x 5in (9 x 12cm) view camera downwards, for example, may topple a standard tripod. As with all tripods, always use the thickest leg extensions — in other words, extend the thinner sections last.

Camera stand In a permanent studio, many of the advantages of a tripod are lost — its collapsibility is no longer important, and it is no longer called on to cope with uneven surfaces. The spread of its legs takes up considerable space and it can easily be knocked out of position. The most stable camera platform for a studio is a camera stand, basically a thick column on a rolling base. Its weight and cost make it very much a professional piece of equipment; it is exceedingly easy to use, ideal for large format cameras, and occupies very little floor space.

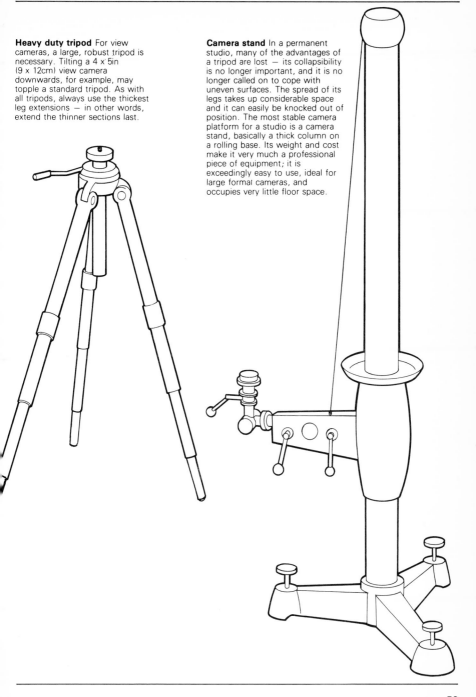

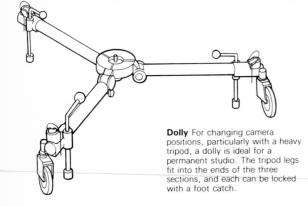

Ground plate For the lowest viewpoint, a tripod head can be screwed directly onto a ground plate, essentially a heavy metal disc.

Ground plate

Dolly For changing camera positions, particularly with a heavy tripod, a dolly is ideal for a permanent studio. The tripod legs fit into the ends of the three sections, and each can be locked with a foot catch.

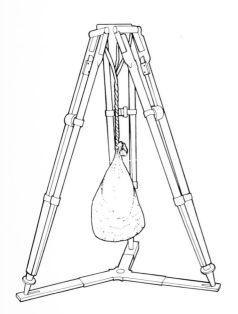

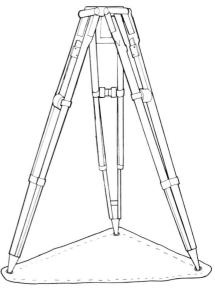

Spreader To prevent movement of the tripod legs, which can be a problem on smooth floors, a spreader holds the feet securely in position.

Canvas spreader A lighter foldable version of the spreader consists of just a triangle of canvas, with a reinforced eyelet in each corner.

Horizontal arm In copying and other types of photography where the camera has to be aimed vertically downwards, one or more tripod legs sometimes appear in shot. One way of avoiding this is to fit a horizontal arm to the tripod. This extends the camera far enough for an unobstructed view.

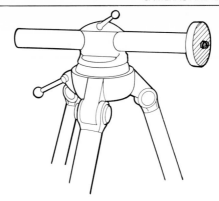

G-clamp A variety of locking clamps can be used as camera supports. They can be attached to furniture, or used in places that would be inaccessible for a tripod.

Vise Similar in function to other clamps, this ordinary hand vise fitted with a small tripod head can be used as an emergency support.

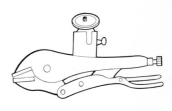

Pan and tilt head The most common type of tripod head has separate movements for forward tilt, sideways tilt and panning. A tripod head should be an integral part of the support, and as stable as the tripod it is attached to.

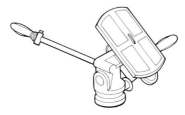

Ball and socket head An alternative to the conventional pan-and-tilt mount is a ball-and-socket. It has the advantage of free movement in all directions, but even slight adjustments involve changing the complete orientation of the camera. A heavy duty head such as this can hold even an 8 x 10in (18 x 24cm) view camera securely.

Tripod foot Some tripods have interchangeable feet. For indoor use, spikes are inappropriate, and rubber pads are more usual.

Angle of view and choice of lens

For any given format, the angle of view is determined by the focal length of the lens. So-called 'standard' lenses give an image that seems normal in its angle of view and perspective to the eye. Long-focus lenses produce a magnified image, and therefore a narrower angle of view. Short lenses have greater coverage than the eye can take in at one glance.

With experience, it is quite easy to judge by eye the lens that would be needed to cover a particular scene, or alternatively the coverage that any focal length would give. As a basic guide, however, the table opposite gives the angles of view for all the common focal lengths for each major film format. In addition, the drawings below show how to reproduce the angles of view of the most popular focal lengths with your hands. Because the ratio of hand size

to arm length varies from person to person, these angles are approximate. Nevertheless, they are a useful aid to visualizing angle of view without resorting to the laborious process of trying out each lens in turn.

Although most lens manufactures quote the angle of view for the diagonal of the film frame, the angle across the longer side is more useful in practical terms, and this is the measurement given here.

With view cameras, in order to make full use of the camera movements (see pages 68-71), it is important that the full coverage of the lens is greater than for just the picture area. As this coverage varies between makes of lens, however, here only the coverage across the picture frame is quoted, and is thus comparable with 35mm and 6 x 6cm coverage.

Angles of view For most people, these hand positions, with the arms fully outstretched in front, give a quick, approximate guide to the angles of view of the most useful focal lengths. If your arms are particularly long or short, or if your hands are large or small, you can work out alternative methods to suit your own dimensions by comparing these hand positions with different lenses.

4–5°
35mm camera: 400/500mm lens
6×6cm camera: 650/800mm lens
9×12cm camera: 1,500mm lens

10–12°
35mm camera: 200mm lens
6×6cm camera: 300mm lens
9×12cm camera: 600mm lens

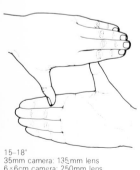

15–18°
35mm camera: 135mm lens
6×6cm camera: 250mm lens
9×12cm camera: 450mm lens

40–50°
35mm camera: 50mm lens
6×6cm camera: 80mm lens
9×12cm camera: 150mm lens

Wide-angle In this case, the thumbs touch the tip of the nose.

90–100°
35mm camera: 20mm lens
6×6cm camera: 30mm lens
9×12cm camera: 60mm lens

Angle of view across longer side	35mm camera	Focal length of lens (in millimetres)			
		6×6cm (2¼×2¼in) camera	9×12cm (4×5in) camera	13×18cm (5×7in) camera	18×24cm (8×10in) camera
220°	6mm circular fish-eye				
180°	8mm circular fish-eye				
137°	16mm circular fish-eye				
112°	30mm full-frame fish-eye				
108°	13				
100°	15				
90°	18		60	90	120
84°	20			100	135
78°			75		150
76°		38			
74°	24	40		120	
72°					165
67°	28		90	135	180
62°		50	100	150	
60°					210
58°				165	
54°	35	60	120	180	240
48°			135		
46°				210	
44°			150		300
41°		80	165	240	
39°	50				
37°	55		180		360
33°		100		300	
32°		105	210		420
30°					450
28°		120	240	360	480
25°		135		420	
23°	90	150	300	450	600
20°	100			480	
19°			360		
17°			400	600	
16°			420		
15°	135		450		
14°		250	480		1,000
12°					
11°	180		600		1,200
10°	200	350		1,000	
8°				1,200	
7°	300		1,000		
6°		500	1,200		
5°	400				
4°	600	1,000			
3°	800				
2°	1,000/1,200				
1°	2,000				

Focus and depth of field

In focusing a lens, the image of the subject is made as sharp as possible, and for every distance there is just one setting of the lens that will focus it most precisely. Nevertheless, sharpness is subjective. It depends on what is acceptable to the individual viewing the image. Beyond the point of sharp focus, and in front of it, the image is increasingly blurred. The points at which it becomes too blurred to be acceptable mark the limits of the *depth of field*. Managing the depth of field is a very basic skill, and is the most usual way of controlling the distribution of sharpness over the picture area. Altering the aperture changes the depth of field, and by stopping down, narrowing the aperture, more of the image is brought into focus.

Depth of field is defined as the zone on either side of the plane of sharp focus in which the image is acceptably sharp. An acceptable degree of sharpness depends on several factors:
The criterion for sharp focus No lens is perfect and even the best records a point as a tiny circle. If the circle is small enough, then it looks like a point to the eye, and therefore seems sharp. The largest circle that appears as a point is called the

'circle of confusion' and is the yardstick by which sharpness is measured. A diameter of 0.033mm is a generally accepted (although severe) standard, although not all lens manufacturers like to put their products to so stringent a test.
Subject distance The closer a subject is to the camera, the less the depth of field. In close-up and macro photography (see pages 196–203) depth of field is extremely limited, even at the smallest apertures.
Focal length Lenses with long focal lengths give less depth of field than wide-angle lenses, which have relatively short focal lengths.
Lens quality Good quality lenses that resolve detail very well actually give less depth of field because their accuracy reveals minute blurring more easily. A poorer lens shows less difference between what is in focus and what is slightly out.
Aperture Reducing the aperture increases the depth of field, and this is the standard way of controlling it in photography.
Lighting In the same way that high-resolution lenses give a more critical image, bright, hard lighting gives sharper images than diffuse lighting, and so appears to give less depth of field.

Near focus, 12 ins (31cm): f3.5

Far focus, 13ins (33cm): f3.5

Depth of field At the close working distances of a still-life setting, depth of field is more of a problem than with large scale outdoor subjects. The closer the subject, the less depth of field. In this series of photographs of a

pen, the lens was first focused on the nib, at full aperture (left). The distance on the lens scale was noted, and then the lens was refocused to the opposite end of the pen (centre). Finally, using the smallest aperture for greatest

depth of field, the lens was set mid-way between these two distances (right). With subjects close to the camera, you can achieve the greatest depth of field by focusing half way between the nearest and farthest points.

Controlling depth of field Choosing the focal length of the lens determines depth of field to some extent. If you want a very shallow depth of field so that the main subject appears sharply focused against a blurred and indistinct background and foreground, use a long-focus lens. Alternatively, front-to-back sharpness over a great distance is only possible with a wide-angle lens.

For precise control, however, vary the aperture. Shooting at the widest possible aperture gives the least depth of field. Stopping down fully makes as much of the image sharp as is possible. For much indoor photography, and in particular for the majority of still-life and interior work, maximum depth of field is the ideal.

Calculating depth of field Lens manufacturers can normally supply depth of field tables. Although an accurate method of calculation, they are cumbersome to use, and the following are more usually employed:

Visual check With reflex cameras, stopping the lens down to the working aperture gives an accurate preview of the sharpness of different parts of the image, although the viewfinder may be so dim that it is difficult to see without additional strong light. In studio still-life work, where very small apertures are commonly used, some professionals use an extra lamp or strong torch especially to check sharpness. Shade the viewing screen from extraneous light, if necessary by covering it and your head with a black cloth, and wait a few seconds for your eye to adjust to the lower light level. Visual checking is only possible with reflex and view cameras.

Lens scale Lenses for small and medium format cameras have a depth of field scale engraved on the mount, showing the limits of the depth of field. This gives an approximate idea of how much of the image will be sharp, but for critical work, make a visual check as well. View cameras focus by moving the front or rear standard, and so cannot have a fixed depth of field scale. Some systems, such as Sinar, have an adjustable scale attached to the rear standard that gives some indication of depth of field.

Rule of thumb This depends very much on the scale of the subject, but between several feet and infinity you can get the greatest depth of field by focusing at a point one third of the way back into the part of the scene you want to be in focus, that is one third of the distance between the far point and the near point of desired focus. With closer subjects, such as a studio still-life, focus halfway between the near and far points. This is only a very approximate method.

Mid focus, 12½ins (32cm): f32

For more distant subjects, focus ⅓ into the area you want to be in focus.

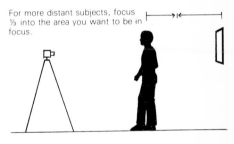

For close-up subjects focus on the mid point of the subject's depth.

Lens controls and fittings

Filters and lens shades are two important ways of controlling the image and achieving high quality. The filters described on pages 36–37 and 50–51 are available in several different materials with different characteristics.

Optical flat This is the highest quality glass and produces the minimum optical error, but is expensive.

Glass Glass filters are less expensive than optical flats and for most photography are quite adequate. They also give protection to the lens.

Plastic Although plastic is less durable than glass and scratches fairly easily, it is less expensive and can be used in the manufacture of complex effects filters more easily.

Gelatin Gelatin filters give very little optical distortion as they are extremely thin. They are very fragile and are easily ruined by moisture or scratching, but are at less risk of damage in the studio than outdoors. Because of their low cost, they are the most useful of all filter types.

Filter mounts Filters may be fitted in a number

Series filters simply slip inside a wide flange and are held in place by a retaining ring.

A bayonet fitting is used on some cameras, notably the Hasselblad 6×6cm SLR.

Most 35mm camera lenses have a screw fitting for attaching filters or lens shades.

Plastic holders are useful for square gelatin and plastic filters.

of ways, some of which are shown here. Because a filter adds another surface to the optical system, there is a greater risk of flare. Ensure that all filters are perfectly clean and shade them so that light does not strike them directly. Even without filters, it is essential to use a lens shade for maximum contrast and colour saturation. Any light from outside the picture area that falls on the lens will degrade the image. Whenever possible, mask down right to the edges of the picture area. In the studio, it may be more convenient to use large pieces of card called flags or gobos close to the light sources rather than use a shade on the lens.

Some professional lens shades, adjustable to suit the focal length, also contain gelatin filter holders.

With a fish-eye lens, cut a gelatin filter to shape and tape it behind the lens.

f-stop fractions

Apertures are measured in f-stops, each f-stop being equivalent to one stop in the scale of shutter speeds. This makes it possible to adjust exposure by altering either shutter speed or aperture or both without complex calculations. For greater precision, particularly when adjusting exposure to compensate for filters, fractions of a stop may have to be used. Many lenses allow for half or one third stop adjustments to the aperture. Below are the f numbers for these fractions. The conventional f-stop scale is included in bold figures.

In steps of one third	In steps of one half
1 1.1 1.3	**1** 1.2
1.4 1.6 1.8	**1.4** 1.7
2 2.2 2.5	**2** 2.4
2.8 3.2 3.6	**2.8** 3.4
4 4.5 5	**4** 4.7
5.6 6.4 7.1	**5.6** 6.8
8 9 10	**8** 9.5
11 13 14	**11** 13.5
16 18 20	**16** 19
22 25 29	**22** 27
32 36 40	**32** 38
45 51 57	**45** 54
64 72 81	**64** 76
91 102 114	**91** 108
128	**128**

Camera movements 1

On large format view cameras, the front standard, which carries the lens panel, and the rear standard, which carries the ground glass screen and film, can both be moved independently. Each can be raised, lowered, shifted sideways or rotated about vertical and horizontal axes. The illustrations here and on the following pages show the full range of movements and how they can be used to control the image.

Image control, in fact, is the real value of camera movements. The plane of focus can be altered and the shape can be changed – all by changing the relative positions of the film plane and lens.

By altering either the film plane or the plane that the lens lies in, the distribution of sharp focus is changed. With no movements, the lens panel and film plane are parallel. As a result, the plane of sharp focus is also parallel. By tilting either the lens or film, however, the plane of sharp focus is also tilted – according to the grandly-named Scheimpflug Principle, the three planes of film, lens, and sharp focus all meet at a common point. Using this technique, rather than relying completely on controlling depth of field, the area of sharpness in a photograph can be increased. Tilting the lens panel changes only the focus, but tilting the film plane has the additional effect of distorting the image. This can be very useful in still-life work – to keep the sides of vertical objects parallel even when the camera is pointing down, for example.

In order to make full use of these camera movements, the lens must produce an image

The Scheimpflug principle

With the planes of the film, lens and subject parallel, the whole subject is in focus.

With the subject plane at an angle, only part is in focus.

With all three planes intersecting, the whole subject is in focus.

that covers a greater area than the film format. The greater the useful area, the more extreme the movements that can be made. Some limited shift movements are possible with a few special lenses for small-format cameras, such as 35mm and rollfilm, and these are useful chiefly in architectural photography where they can be used to correct converging verticals (see pages 102–103).

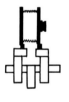

Far focus With no movements, the lens and film plane are parallel. Focus is evenly distributed but, with a wide aperture, the depth of field is shallow. Focusing on the near objects would throw the middle and rear parts of the subject out of focus.

Front standard down or rear standard up Lowering the lens panel or raising the film lifts the subject in the frame. More foreground is included.

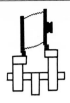

Front standard up or rear standard down Raising the lens panel or lowering the film drops the subject in the frame.

Front standard tilted forward Tilting the lens panel forward brings more of the foreground into focus. Shape and perspective are unaltered.

Front standard tilted back Tilting the lens panel back makes the plane of focus cut across the subject, throwing most of the image out of focus.

Front standard tilted forward, rear standard tilted back With lens and film planes tilted so that they intersect below the camera, both shape and sharpness distribution are altered strongly – here, bringing much of the subject into focus.

Rear standard tilted forward Tilting the film plane forward places the plane of focus counter to the subject, giving very limited focus in the image.

Rear standard tilted back
Tilting the film plane back has the same useful effect on focus as tilting the lens panel forward, bringing more of the subject into focus. It also introduces strong perspective.

Front standard tilted back, rear standard tilted forward
Tilting film and lens planes so they converge above the camera reduces the area in focus and strongly alters shape.

Front standard shifted to the side Moving the lens panel to the left includes more of the right hand part of the subject. Moving it in the opposite direction has the reverse effect.

Rear standard shifted to the side Moving the rear standard to the left includes more of the left hand part of the subject. Moving it in the opposite direction has the reverse effect.

Front standard swung left
Angling the lens panel to the left makes the plane of focus run from the left foreground to the right background. Shape is not altered.

Front standard swung right
This reverses the diagonal directions of the plane of focus from the previous movement.

Rear standard swung left
Angling the film plane to the left gives the same diagonal plane of focus as angling the front standard to the right, but also strongly changes the shape.

Rear standard swung right
The same effect on focus as swinging the lens panel to the left is achieved by angling the film plane to the right, but adds distortion to the shape of the image.

Front standard swung right, rear standard swung left If film and lens planes converge to the right of the camera, the plane of focus is at a sharp angle from left foreground to right background. Shape is strongly distorted.

Front standard swung left, rear standard swung right
With the film and lens planes intersecting to the left, the effect is reversed from the previous movement. Again, shape is strongly altered.

35mm and small format systems

Camera bodies The most common and generally useful small format camera is the 35mm single lens reflex (SLR), combining the two important advantages of a viewing system that shows exactly what the image will be, and accurate through-the-lens (TTL) exposure measurements.

Some advanced non-reflex cameras, which rely on rangefinder focusing, also incorporate TTL metering, but suffer the disadvantage that changing lenses is at best awkward, and with very long-focus lenses is impractical. For situations where it is important to be quiet and unobtrusive (not uncommon in indoor candid shooting), however, rangefinder cameras have the advantage of more silent action.

A recent manufacturing trend is miniaturization, resulting in both compact 35mm cameras and sophisticated improvements in the traditionally simple 110 format.

110 Instamatic

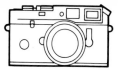

Leica M4 rangefinder camera

110 Minolta

Automatic 35mm SLR

Simple rangefinder camera

Professional 35mm SLR

Olympus XA, 35mm miniature

Minox 35GL, 35mm miniature

Lightweight 35mm SLR

Triggering accessories As many indoor photographs are taken on long exposures because of low light levels, cable releases are essential. Even with flash lighting in the studio, precise compositions can be at risk through the jarring of the camera's shutter.

Shutter cable release

Pistol grip

Soft shutter release

Viewfinders and other accessories As well as the normal pentaprism, which gives line of sight viewing, either with or without through-the-lens (TTL) metering, there are several specialized finders available. A right angled waist-level viewfinder allows composition directly on the ground glass screen, which gives a good impression of the two dimensional image. For critical focusing, magnifying viewers are useful, while an action viewfinder gives an enlarged view without the need to put the eye right up to the camera. Lens hoods and caps are essential for taking proper care of equipment and image quality.

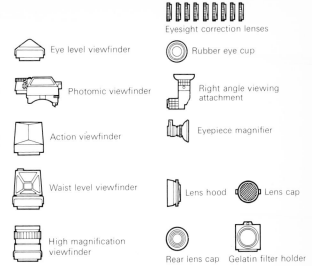

Eyesight correction lenses

Eye level viewfinder

Rubber eye cup

Photomic viewfinder

Right angle viewing attachment

Action viewfinder

Eyepiece magnifier

Waist level viewfinder

Lens hood   Lens cap

High magnification viewfinder

Rear lens cap   Gelatin filter holder

Motor drives and automatic control Although motor drives are traditionally assigned roles in covering outdoor action, they also remove the distractions of winding on by hand, so making it easier to concentrate on the image. This applies equally to indoor and outdoor work.

Intervalometers, which automatically time a sequence of exposures over a period of time, are used chiefly in technical or specialized studio photography (for example, the growth of a plant or a culture over a period of hours or days).

Among remote control systems, infrared pulsing is generally more useful than radio control, which is particularly susceptible indoors to interference and screening. A special use of remote control is to trigger a camera without vibration when a high tripod or shaky platform is being used.

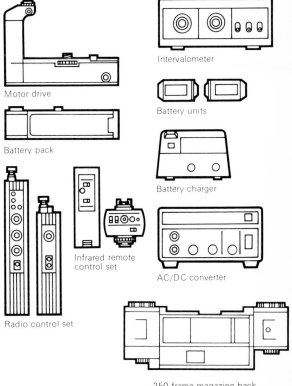

Motor drive

Intervalometer

Battery pack

Battery units

Battery charger

Infrared remote control set

AC/DC converter

Radio control set

250 frame magazine back

35mm lenses 1

Fish-eye lenses True fish-eye lenses give a circular image, but for non-scientific uses, full frame fish-eyes, such as the 16mm shown here, are more popular. The most notable characteristic is extreme barrel distortion, which gives a special, and strong, graphic character to the image. Used carelessly, this can easily overpower the content of the shot.

6mm (220°)

Fish-eye finder

8mm (180°)

16mm (137°)

Extreme wide-angle lenses Because of the restricted space in many indoor locations, and the need for wide coverage, these lenses, with angles of view ranging from about 75° to about 115°, have a valuable place in indoor photography.

15mm (100°)

18mm (90°)

20mm (84°)

24mm (74°)

Wide-angle lenses 28mm and 35mm lenses give a moderate increase in coverage over standard lenses, and so are quite useful in interiors, particularly for indoor portraits where the setting is important.

28mm (67°)

35mm (54°)

Standard lens Most manufacturers supply a 50mm lens as standard for the 35mm format. The perspective and angle of view of its image appear 'normal' to the eye.

50mm f2 (39°)

50mm f1.2 (39°)

Long-focus lens Long-focus lenses magnify the image, compress perspective and restrict the angle of view. In indoor work, where a certain amount of control is usually possible, the most important quality is the effect on perspective. Closely cropped portraits, for example, usually benefit from the flattened perspective of a long-focus lens. 105mm is the most popular for this.

85mm (23°)

105mm (20°)

135mm (15°)

180mm (11°)

200mm (10°)

300mm (7°)

Extreme long-focus Short working distances and relatively small maximum apertures limit the usefulness of very long focal lengths in indoor situations. Indoor sports stadiums are an exception. Here, the most valuable long-focus lenses are around 400mm. The relatively new internal-focusing, fast telephoto lenses, such as the 400mm f3.5 are ideal, although very expensive.

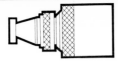

400mm (5°)

Zoom lenses One of the most valuable qualities of these lenses is that they make it possible to adjust the focusing of a shot without changing the camera position. In indoor locations, however, it is often easy to adjust the viewpoint, and this, together with the inevitably small maximum aperture, restricts the usefulness of zoom lenses in interiors.

28mm-45mm

35mm-70mm

80mm-200mm

Special lenses Perspective control, or shift, lenses make it possible to rectify converging verticals, often necessary in architectural photography (see pages 10. -10). They work on the same principle as the camera movements used in view camera work (see pages 68-71).

Night lenses are so called because they combine a very large maximum aperture (usually f1.2) with an aspherical front surface, which although expensive reduces coma. This lens fault is responsible for the flared appearance of light sources that appear in the shot, a common problem in available light indoor photography.

28mm perspective control lens

58mm f1.2 Noct-Nikkor night lens

Close-up equipment Macro lenses unlike other lenses are designed to give their best optical performance at close distances. They are ideal for most close-up work. The longer focal lengths allow a greater working distance between lens and subject, making it easier to control the quality of lighting.

Normal lenses can also be used successfully, either by adding supplementary lenses for a small increase in magnification, or by fitting extension tubes or bellows between the lens and camera. Bellows, which are often unwieldy on location, are generally more useful than extension tubes in the studio, offering greater flexibility. For high magnification work, bellows are used with short focal length lenses — a 20mm lens with a 200mm extension, for example, gives 10x magnification.

Medical lenses contain their own ring flash, making photography of small, partially enclosed areas relatively simple.

 55mm macro lens

 105mm macro lens

 200mm Medical-Nikkor

 Supplementary lenses (diopters)

 Lens reversing ring

 Extension tubes

 20mm macro lens

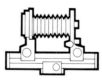 Bellows extension

6 x 6cm medium format 1

Cameras The bulk and weight of medium format cameras, which frequently makes them less convenient than 35mm equipment on location, is no disadvantage in the studio, and the larger film size helps image quality.

Twin lens reflex (TLR) models, which have either a very limited capability for interchanging lenses or none at all, are much less popular than the more flexible single lens reflexes (SLRs).

As a general rule, 6 x 6cm SLRs are best suited to studio and interior work, and many of their most useful design features — interchangeable film backs and Polaroid film backs, for example — reflect this.

The Hasselblad SWC, incorporating a special wide-angle lens design, is a non-reflex camera that is not really part of the system. Its good optics and wide coverage make it very useful in many interior situations.

4.5 x 6cm cameras differ only in scale from 6 x 6cm and 6 x 7cm formats. Most characteristics are similar.

Twin lens reflex

Single lens reflex
Hasselblad
500 C/M

Hasselblad
SWC/M

Hasselblad
500 EL/M

Film holders One of the greatest advantages of the Hasselblad is the range of interchangeable film backs. This not only makes it possible to change from, say, colour to black-and-white in the middle of shooting, it also makes it possible to use a wide variety of films, including sheet film, sprocketed, 70mm and Polaroid.

Sheet film
holder

Standard back

70mm film
magazine

Polaroid
film back

Viewfinders A simple hood, allowing a direct view of the ground glass screen (in other words, a right angled view of the subject) is standard. Other interchangeable viewfinders give a magnified view (for critical focusing), a rectified line of sight view (for faster shooting), and a TTL exposure reading.

Magnifying
viewfinder

TTL viewfinder

90" prism
viewfinder

Direct
viewfinder

Viewing screens A limited range of screens, with different etched designs, is available to suit different subjects. When a precise composition is important, a grid pattern is useful.

Standard
viewing screen

Grid-etched
viewing screen

Accessories For rapid operation — often useful in fashion photography — a crank can be fitted in place of the standard winding knob. Although most indoor situations call for a tripod, hand-held shooting is often easier with a pistol grip.

Winder knob
exposure meter

Quick focusing
handle

Pistol grip

Fish-eye lenses Similar to the 16mm full-frame fish-eye available for 35mm cameras, this 30mm lens gives the same extreme graphic treatment. The curved lines caused by the barrel distortion are usually very noticeable in interiors.

30mm wide fish-eye

Close-up The basic range of close-up equipment — supplementary lenses and extensions — is similar to that for 35mm cameras.

Extension tubes

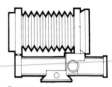

Supplementary lenses (diopters)

Wide-angle lenses These lenses fulfil the same functions as their 35mm equivalents, already described. Their coverage gives them obvious advantages in interiors.

40mm

Extension bellows

50mm

60mm

Motor drive accessories
Extension cables, automatic aperture control attachments and intervalometers are among the number of remote and automatic devices that can be used with the motor drive.

Amplifier

Automatic diaphragm control unit

Long-focus lenses Moderately long focal lengths, such as 150mm, are valuable for portrait photography, giving facial proportions that are generally pleasing. Apart from specialized uses, such as architectural details on ceilings, very long focal lengths are not commonly used indoors.

150mm

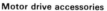

250mm

Lens fittings The best lens shade, particularly in the studio where precise control is important, is a professional lens bellows, which can be adjusted right up to the edges of the frame.

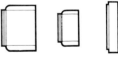

Lens shades

Standard lenses For the 6 x 6cm format, 80mm is considered 'standard', giving a normal looking perspective.

80mm

Professional lens hood

6 x 7 cm medium format 1

6 x 7cm cameras These are designed to overcome one of the real disadvantages of the 6 x 6cm frame — its square format does not lend itself to composition, so that some of the advantage of a large film size is lost through cropping. 6 x 7cm proportions are generally easier to use.

There are two types of 6 x 7cm camera: the first is an enlarged version of a typical 35mm SLR (the Pentax 6 x 7cm), the second is more convential and has many of the features of the Hasselblad (the Mamiya RB67). The choice between the two rests largely on personal handling preferences. Two particular advantages of the Mamiya RB67 are its revolving film back, which makes it possible to change from horizontal to vertical without moving the camera body, and the built-in bellows focusing system, which allows a certain degree of close-up work without complications.

Pentax 6 x 7cm SLR

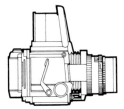

Mamiya RB67

Fish-eye lens This is similar to other full frame fish-eyes.

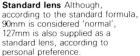

37mm

Macro lens This lens is computed to give its best optical performance at close distances.

140mm macro

Wide-angle lens Because the format is slightly larger than 6 x 6cm, the angle of coverage for lenses of the same focal length is greater.

50mm

65mm

Long-focus lenses 150mm is the most popular portrait lens for this format. The very long focal lengths have limited use indoors.

150mm

180mm

Standard lens Although, according to the standard formula, 90mm is considered 'normal', 127mm is also supplied as a standard lens, according to personal preference.

90mm

127mm

250mm

360mm

Film backs Although the Pentax 6 x 7cm functions in the same way as a 35mm SLR, the Mamiya RB67 has the facility for changing film backs, making it comparable with the Hasselblad. The rotating film back makes it easy to change from horizontal to vertical format.

Roll film back

Sheet film holder

Polaroid film back

Viewfinders A range of viewfinders is available, similar to that described for other SLRs.

TTL meter viewfinder

Magnifying viewfinder

Waist-level viewfinder

Prism viewfinder

Lens fittings The lens shades are similar to those available on other systems.

Professional lens shade

Slip-on lens shade

Screw-on lens shade

Filters

Accessories A pistol grip can aid hand-held shooting. Cable releases are essential for tripod use.

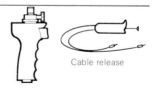

Cable release

View cameras 1

View cameras Large format photography is more closely associated with studio work than with any other. The bulk, weight and slow operation are rarely disadvantageous in the controlled environment of a studio, but the large film size and great versatility make view cameras unassailable for many subjects. For still-life work and room interiors, they are the cameras of choice. The monorail design shown below is the most advanced type of design for this format, but wooden flat bed cameras and compact technical cameras are also useful.

The system Being tailored principally for studio use, a modern monorail camera is less of a single piece of equipment than a variable assembly of parts. A rail, which is essentially an optical bench, is the base onto which different elements can be built, according to the needs of the particular shot. More control is possible over the image than with any other type of camera. It can only be used on a tripod.

Lenses Because view camera systems are so flexible, the choice of lens is not as straightforward as with other formats. Focal length, quality and coverage must all be matched to the format and type of photography. Use the table on page 63 as a guide.

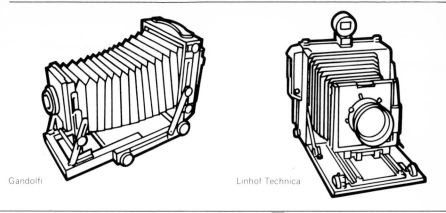

Gandolfi

Linhof Technica

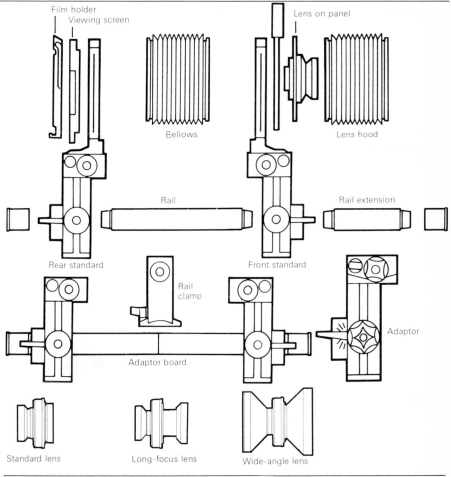

Film holder
Viewing screen

Bellows

Lens on panel

Lens hood

Rail

Rail extension

Rear standard

Front standard

Rail clamp

Adaptor

Adaptor board

Standard lens

Long-focus lens

Wide-angle lens

Film holders The three principal types of film for view cameras are sheet film (available in several sizes), 120 roll film and Polaroid instant film, and special holders are available for each. The most common formats are 4 x 5in (9 x 12cm) and 8 x 10in (18 x 24cm). As the widest range of Polaroid films is available in 4 x 5in (9 x 12cm), larger format cameras can normally be adapted to take this size.

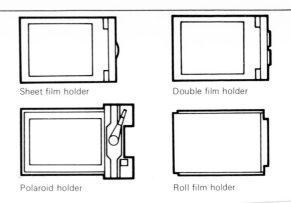

Sheet film holder

Double film holder

Polaroid holder

Roll film holder

Bag bellows When focused close to infinity, wide-angle lenses are positioned very close to the film plane. Normal bellows are inflexible when compressed so tightly, restricting the camera movements described in pages 68-71. The answer is to fit bag bellows instead. With small still life sets, however, the focus may place a wide angle lens far enough from the film plane to make bag bellows unnecessary.

Viewing aids To cut down extraneous light, which can make it difficult to view the image on a large ground glass screen, a hood may be used. One ingenious design makes use of a bag bellows with a viewer attached to one end. Other aids to clear viewing are a Fresnel screen (though this inhibits critical focusing) and a reflex viewer, which rectifies the image.

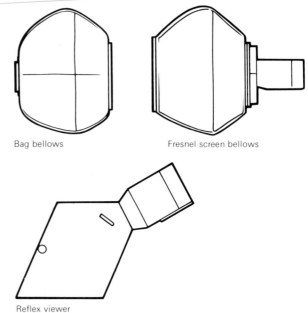

Bag bellows

Fresnel screen bellows

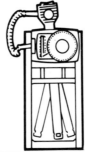

Reflex viewer

Probe exposure meter This allows TTL metering, from the screen, of very small parts of the image. The high precision possible with this exposure meter is particularly valuable with still-life subjects, because it allows very close control over the contrast range. The effects of even small adjustments to the lighting can be measured precisely.

Probe exposure meter

Special purpose cameras

Large format superwide Special adaptions from view camera systems include this 4 x 5in Sinar Handy with an extremely wide-angle lens — here 47mm — in a rigid mount. The normal movements of a view camera are sacrificed in favour of extreme coverage, particularly useful in the photography of interiors.

Rotating panoramic cameras Another approach to wide coverage is to use a lens in a motor driven rotating mount. As the mount rotates, the image is projected onto a long strip of film (either 35mm or 120 roll film, according to the model). One of the features of this type of image is strong barrel distortion, which makes it difficult to use in room interiors.

Fixed body panoramic camera Similar in principle to large format superwide cameras, the Linhof Technorama is fitted with a large format wide-angle lens — a 90mm Super Angulon — and 120 roll film. The lens covers a wide section of the film, giving an image with 3:1 proportions. Although there is no barrel distortion, there is a slight darkening of the image towards the edges. This can be corrected with a centrally graduated filter.

High speed cameras Fixed mirror SLR cameras such as the Nikon M2H, which can fire at speeds up to 10 frames per second, and the highly specialized Hulcher, which can reach 65 frames per second, have fewer applications indoors than on location, but can be useful in indoor sports. For high speed photography in the studio, a fast, repeating flash can be used in conjunction with them.

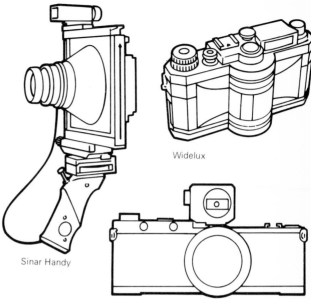

Widelux

Sinar Handy

Linhof Technorama

Hulcher 112

Nikon M2H

Equipment care and cleaning

Treat all photographic equipment as considerately as possible, protecting it from knocks and other physical damage during use, and packing it carefully between sessions. Make all mechanical adjustments gently, particularly when fitting lenses. Protect all glass surfaces with lens caps or clear ultraviolet filters. Check the equipment regularly, and clean it using the procedures shown opposite.

Some mechanisms, such as the camera shutter and fully automatic diaphragms (FADs) use springs. To avoid strain, leave them untensioned when not in use. Have the equipment serviced professionally at regular intervals – every two or three years for normal use, more frequently if you work with it constantly.

Develop a fixed sequence of maintenance checks so that you recognize malfunctions or wear before they become a problem. If you have two identical camera bodies, check them against each other. The most important check with TTL metering cameras is that the exposure measurement remains consistent. Mount the camera on a tripod in front of a constantly lit test target, note the reading and then compare it with that from different meters or bodies, all in exactly the same position. All measurements should be within one third of a stop of each other.

Cleaning Although equipment is not so likely to attract dirt indoors as outside, dust and grease are still a danger. Clean cameras and lenses regularly, being careful not to scratch surfaces by rubbing dirt into them. Start by blowing away loose particles with compressed air, then use a soft brush, and finally a cloth. Do not use oil, and if you need to apply moisture to the surface of a lens, it is better to breathe on it to form condensation than to use a lens cleaning fluid, which can spill and enter other parts of the mechanism.

Camera cleaning equipment
1. Compressed air: for removing dust, use with caution near fragile parts. 2. Lens tissues: for gently wiping lens surfaces. 3. Anti-static gun: applies a small charge to surfaces to keep them dust-free. 4. Penknife: for scraping batteries. 5. Pencil eraser: for cleaning batteries and stains from body. 6. Toothbrush: too rough for lens surfaces or delicate moving parts. Use on body or lens exterior only. 7. Anti-static brush: keep in the sealed bag. Applies small charge to keep dust away. 8. Lens cleaning fluid: use sparingly and only when absolutely necessary. 9. WD-40: an anti-corrosive, water-repellant lubricant spray. Never use inside the camera body or spray directly onto the camera. 10. Lens cloth: soft cloth can be an alternative for wiping optical surfaces. 11. Blower-brush: for removing dust. Use two – one for lenses and one for body parts, to avoid transferring grease. 12. Cotton buds: useful for cleaning in awkward angles.

Keep battery surfaces clean to ensure good electrical contact.

Cotton buds will remove dirt from difficult angles, as around lenses.

Remove dust and film fragments from the winding mechanism with compressed air.

Wipe film path clean to avoid transferring dirt to film.

Clean focusing screen, mirror or pentaprism surfaces very carefully.

Keep compressed air can upright – it may spray a deposit of propellant.

Use blower brush to keep lens surface free of dust. Cover lens with a UV filter for extra protection.

A lens cloth will remove grease or water spots. Use gently to avoid damage to the lens coating.

4. POST-PRODUCTION
Printing

Photographic printing is virtually a complete subject in its own right, and the purpose of these two pages is not to summarize all its procedures and techniques but rather to show what extra controls it allows you over the image. Even if you do not print your negatives yourself, it is important to know what results are possible and what instructions to give the processing laboratory. The very great degree of control possible in printing, particularly in black-and-white, make it a creative, part of photography.

The first control that printing gives is selective enlargement. Not only can the size and format of the image be chosen, but the negative can be cropped in any number of ways. Technically, however, printing's most important influence is on the quality of the image – density and contrast in black-and-white prints, density and colour balance in colour prints (although there is less opportunity to alter contrast in colour). Choice of paper, type of enlarger, exposure time, filters and developing techniques are the standard methods of controlling these qualities.

Just because so much can be done to improve and alter the image at the printing stage, many photographers are much less careful when using negative film than with the more inflexible reversal film, relying on darkroom techniques to save or make the shot. Although much can be done when printing, this approach completely wastes the magnificent opportunities for more subtle changes to the quality of a print. The techniques listed here can only be used to their full potential with a good negative. If, for example, you have a negative so lacking in contrast that it needs the hardest grade of paper, a condenser enlarger and vigorous development, then you are simply stretching darkroom techniques to compensate for faults in the original.

Controlling Density In the same way that some subjects can be over-exposed or under-exposed with equally acceptable although different results, some negatives can be printed as light or heavy. The normal method is quite simply to adjust the exposure time or enlarger lens aperture, although shorter or longer development also affects density (as well as contrast). Although some printers prefer to stick to a standard development time (usually 90 seconds or two minutes), you can achieve fine control by inspecting the progress of the developing print. When doing this, keep the safelight at least two feet away from the print, and remember that prints look denser under a red safelight.

Controlling Contrast In black-and-white printing, the following methods allow, in combination if necessary, very great control over contrast:

Paper grade Most black-and-white print papers are available in several grades of contrast, normally from 0 (soft) to 4 (hard), with Grade 2 designed to be normal. As a rule, soft grades allow more delicacy but hard grades give rich blacks and strong images. Variable contrast paper is used with different filters for similar results.

Paper texture and tint A glossy surface gives a visual impression of greater contrast than does a matt surface. Tinted paper – for instance, with a creamy base – gives less contrast.

Enlarger light To distribute the light from the lamp evenly over the negative, enlarger heads normally use either condenser lenses or a diffusing sheet. A diffuser head gives a more even spread of light but less contrast than a condenser.

Shading and printing-in By moving your hands or a shaped piece of card in front of the projected negative, you can give selected areas of the print more or less exposure than the rest. For example, if the contrast between sky and ground is too great, then give the sky extra exposure, shading the lower part of the print. Giving less exposure to selected areas is known as shading, or dodging, whilst giving more exposure is called printing-in or burning-in. Shading tools can be made by cutting discs or other shapes from black card and fixing them to the ends of stiff wire. For printing-in, cut holes to shape in the centre of large pieces of card. Alternatively, you can bend your hands to shape. To make these techniques blend in normally with the print, always hold the pieces of card several inches above the print and move them continuously throughout the exposure.

Altered development Using developer at a higher temperature than recommended, constant agitation and developing for longer time all give higher contrast. Conversely, less development time gives less contrast, although it can also cause unevenness of tone and streaking.

Controlling Colour In colour printing, use either colour compensating filters (see pages 36–37) or the graduated colour dials fitted to most good colour enlargers to alter the overall colour balance. A full set of gelatine colour compensating filters runs from CC05 to CC50 in six filters for each of the six primary and secondary colours – 36 in all.

High contrast The inclusion of a bright sky in this shot called for corrective printing. A test strip showed that 15 seconds exposure at f11 would give the most effective results for the mid-tones in the bottom half of the picture. This, however, would leave the sky very pale in the print and, at the same time, the man's face would be too dark (right). It was decided to give the sky an extra 30 seconds and to cut the exposure of the face by eight seconds with printing-in and shading techniques. The resulting print (below) has a much more satisfactory contrast range.

Shading face By moving a small piece of shaped card in front of the man's face, the exposure of this area was cut by eight seconds.

Printing-in sky A piece of card cut to shape and held above the foreground areas allowed 30 seconds greater exposure for the sky.

Retouching

Retouching is used increasingly as a means of achieving special effects – principally for modifying a photograph or combining two or more images. The level of skill depends partly on the medium. Prints are easier to work with than film, and black-and-white is easier than colour. Retouching also depends on the scale – it is better to work on a large original that will later be reduced than to work on a small negative or transparency that needs enlargement. The type of effect aimed for is also significant. Removing blemishes is easier than introducing large areas of superimposed illustration. Professional retouching is charged according to the time taken and is usually costly, but a wide range of techniques can be used by the photographer himself. Most retouching is concerned with tidying up images and correcting errors, although it is clearly better to avoid mistakes in the first place – by careful use of the camera, by keeping film and equipment clean, and by using the correct processing.

Choosing whether to retouch the negative, print or transparency depends on the individual circumstances and the film format. Blocking out or lightening parts of an image is easier on the negative than on the print, but the larger scale of most prints simplifies detailed work. The paper surface of a print is also more suited to straightforward retouching techniques, and allows room for mistakes which could ruin a negative. The advantage of negative retouching is that as many prints can be made from the corrected negative as wanted. Transparencies offer less choice and are generally difficult to work on. Small transparencies are better duplicated to a larger size before retouching. This gives more opportunity for detailed work and is also an insurance against mistakes (see pages 94–97).

Different techniques can affect the surface of the film or print, sometimes altering the results of earlier retouching. Carry out retouching in the following order:

1 Chemical application, such as reducing, intensifying or bleaching
2 Dye application
3 Physical retouching, such as knifing or abrasion
4 Body colour application

Plan a retouching sequence from the start, working on large areas first and fine details last. A final principle of retouching is to apply each technique in deliberately small doses, slowly building up to the desired effect. Keep retouching to the minimum necessary.

Black-and-white negatives Most of the techniques developed in the past for retouching negatives are suitable only to a large format, preferably 4×5in (9×12cm) and above. On a negative of this size, detailed work can be done using dyes, pigment, abrasion, knifing and pencil. On smaller formats, such processes are rarely satisfactory, and prints are more suited to retouching. With 35mm film in particular, the limit for retouching is normally reached with overall applications of reducer or intensifier, with occasional blocking and pencil retouching.

Reducing By treating the whole or part of a negative, the amount of silver can be reduced, effectively lightening the negative and thus darkening the resulting print or a selected part of it, as desired.
1 Swab the emulsion side of the negative with cotton soaked in water for a few minutes, until the emulsion has been softened.

2 Apply the reducer in broad, even strokes with a brush or cotton swab. If only part of the negative is to be retouched, do not allow any edges to form. Work quickly as reducers have a short life of only about 10 minutes once mixed.
3 Gently wipe off the reducer with a swab of water. Repeat the process until the emulsion is sufficiently reduced.

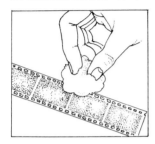
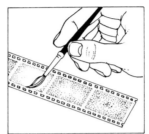

Intensifying In order to lighten a black-and-white print, the negative can be intensified – that is, the dark, silvered areas of the negative can be strengthened.
1 Soften the emulsion by swabbing with cotton soaked in water.
2 Using a two-step, chromium intensifier for the greatest control, paint or swab it on the areas to be intensified in broad, even strokes until the desired level of strengthening is achieved.
3 Redevelop the image in an ordinary (MQ/PQ) developer.

Holding back with red dye The negative image can also be slightly darkened with red dye to reduce darkness in shadows.
1 Clean both sides of the negative by swabbing with denatured (purified) alcohol.
2 If you are working on the emulsion side (this depends on the dye), soften it by swabbing with water.
3 Swab or brush a weak solution of the red dye evenly over the surface. Continue until the light parts of the negative (shadows in the print) are sufficiently darkened. Be careful not to go too far or they print as pure white. If you have applied too much, wash the negative.

Blocking with opaque In order to create strong highlights, areas of the negative can be filled in with a dense pigment known as opaque.
1 Clean the back of the negative by swabbing with denatured alcohol.

2 Using a watered-down solution of opaque, paint onto the back of the negative covering the area to be blocked or highlighted. Ragged edges on a small negative can be concealed in the printing process.

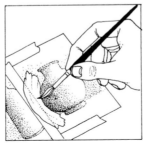

Retouching black-and-white prints

In most cases, a print is much more suitable for retouching than a black-and-white negative. Usually larger, prints allow work on a more manageable scale and mistakes are not disastrous, provided that another print can be made. Some retouching problems can even be solved while the print is being made. These include area intensification and reduction (the lightening or darkening of selected parts of the image) by printing-in and shading. These processes should be considered before undertaking the more laborious retouching.

One problem is that retouching prints tends to alter the surface of the photographic paper. If the print is intended for reproduction, this is unimportant. But if it is for display you may need to coat the surface to even out the texture after dye application or knifing. It is also important to match the colour of dyes precisely to the image, which may include a surprising amount of colour, from blue-black to brown-black. Most resin coated papers are unsuitable for retouching. The normal type used by professional retouchers is double-weight glossy unglazed.

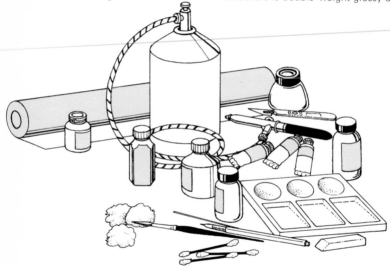

Reducing or bleaching Prints, or areas of them, can be lightened with the application of special reducers or diluted bleach.
1 Soften both emulsion and paper by soaking in water for 10 minutes.
2 On a flat, smooth surface such as a sheet of glass, swab off excess moisture.
3 If a precise area is to be reduced, mask off the surrounds with rubber cement.
4 Swab or brush on the reducer or diluted bleach with a smooth continuous action so that the effect is even.
5 As soon as the reduction is sufficient, wash the print immediately in water.
6 Peel off the rubber cement mask, if you have applied one.

Toning The use of toners can change the general hue of a print, or part of it – to sepia, for example.
1 While following the manufacturer's instructions for precise timing, soak the fixed, washed print in bleach solution for a few minutes, until the image has faded to pale yellow-brown. To apply locally, soak the print first in water, and then swab on the bleach, either using a rubber cement mask to protect the surrounding area or moving the swab constantly for a graduated border to the bleached area.
2 Transfer the print to a tray containing the toner. Toners are available in different colours, such as red, yellow and blue, and can be mixed to achieve a particular hue. Leave the print until the image has reappeared at its full intensity.
3 With some toners, a second bleach may be needed to remove the redeveloped black image that accompanies the new colour. This is largely a matter of taste, as the pure colour may appear weak on its own.

Dyeing Dye can be used to darken specific areas of a finished print.
1 Select a dye that matches the 'black' of the print exactly.
2 Soak the print in water for about 10 minutes.
3 Place the print on a tilted surface that is hard and smooth. Then swab off excess moisture.

4 Mask off any areas with rubber cement that are to be left untreated.
5 Wash the diluted dye onto the print with broad strokes, moving the brush constantly to avoid hard edges. Build up the intensity slowly in several stages. Immediate washing will remove most of the dye if you make a mistake.

Knifing Blemishes and unwanted elements in a print can be carefully removed by cutting away a thin film from the surface of the print. This procedure is frequently called for.
1 Hold a scalpel with a sharp blade well back

along its stem and at a shallow angle. Shave large areas of the surface with short strokes, moving the wrist rather than the fingers. Do not penetrate to the paper base.
2 Clear up small spots with the tip of the blade.

Spotting Small blemishes that are lighter than the surrounding areas can be filled in with dye.
1 Load the fine tipped spotting brush generously with dye, and then draw it across absorbent paper to remove most of it.
2 Test the amount of dye delivered by the tip of the brush against your thumbnail. It should not form pools.

3 On a dry print, touch the centre of the white spot, dabbing gently until it matches the surrounding tone. Touch the edges of the spot as little as possible or the dye will build up into a dark ring.
4 With grainy prints, try to match the grain size and intensity with each dab.

Air brushing This skilful process can be used to make quite extensive alterations to a print. Considerable practice will be needed to achieve effective results.
1 Mask off the parts of the image that are not to be treated. If the edges are hard, apply a sheet of adhesive masking film.
2 Knife gently around the area to be sprayed, cutting the masking film but not the emulsion.
3 Peel off the film. Start off the spray on a scrap

of paper held over the print in case there are any spurts of pigment, first pressing down on the button to regulate the air flow, and then pulling back to release the pigment.
4 Load the airbrush with pigment that has been diluted to the consistency of milk and well stirred to avoid blockages.
5 For a soft edged mask, hold a roughly shaped card about an inch over the surface of the print, moving it constantly.

Creative retouching As well as for retouching blemishes, retouching can be used to introduce new elements into a print. Here, rocket jets have been carefully airbrushed under the spaceship to give this model shot greater realism.

Colour retouching

All colour retouching is considerably more difficult than the same work in black-and-white, not simply because of the difficulty of matching and blending hues, but because the colour emulsions used in films and prints are complex and consist of many layers. Knifing and abrasion are out of the question – scraping away the top layer just removes one of the basic colours. The surface of most colour prints is not receptive to retouching with dyes, while with transparencies it is essential to use dyes that match those that make up the film. All colour retouching requires skill and is largely the domain of professionals. **Transparency retouching** The first limitation is size, and any form of colour retouching, whether spotting or more elaborate alteration, is not worth attempting on formats smaller than 4×5in (10×12cm). On smaller sizes, attempts at retouching will show when the transparency is projected or enlarged.

Retouching with coloured pencils may give an acceptable visual result, but should never be used if the transparency is going to be reproduced in a publication. The most effective method is to apply liquid dyes, matched to the make of film, with brushes. Kodak supply E–6 dyes and bleaches that are specifically designed for their films. Try never to retouch on the emulsion side unless you need more density than can be absorbed by the base side which soaks up the dye more slowly, making it easier to correct mistakes. An even safer method is to work on a transparent overlay.

As a general procedure, moisten the base side of the transparency with a solution of one drop of Kodak Photo-Flo to one ounce (30ml) of water. Then mix the concentrated dyes to the right colour, diluting them with buffer solution. Always apply a weaker colour than needed so that you can build up the effect gradually with

---

Colour transparency retouching equipment
Dye concentrates (cyan, yellow and magenta)
Dye buffer
Dilute acetic acid
Kodak Photo-Flo
Dye bleach (total)
Cyan dye bleach
Magenta dye bleach
Yellow dye bleach
14 per cent ammonia water solution

Colour print retouching equipment Prints are relatively simple to retouch. The equipment required includes cakes of dye (cyan, magenta and yellow), brushes, stabilizer and blotting paper.

several applications.

To remove dye, swab small amounts away with water-soaked cotton. Larger amounts can be removed with a 14 per cent solution of ammonia water, and for complete removal use a dye bleach.

Colour negative retouching Retouching of colour negatives is extremely difficult. As with transparencies, retouching is only likely to be successful on 4×5in (10×12cm) colour negatives and larger. Not only are tones reversed, as in black-and-white negatives, but colours also, so that red blemishes on a face appear green, for example. Also, the built-in orange mask of colour negatives makes it difficult to identify any but the strongest colours, and judging your retouching progress by eye is not easy. Coloured pencils can be used, but wet dyes, as with transparencies, are more accurate. Prepare and apply the dyes in the same way as for transparency retouching, but using colours that are complementary to the ones that are to appear in the final print.

Colour print retouching Although colour prints do not usually accept retouching dyes well as most are resin coated, they are nevertheless easier to work with than either transparencies or negatives. By making an adequate enlargement, you can work comfortably to a large scale, and you can keep a visual check on your progress. Paper manufacturers, such as Kodak and Ciba, supply retouching kits to suit their own products and it is best to use these for a proper colour match.

With Kodak papers, one set of solid dyes can be used in two quite different ways: as dry dye and wet dye. The dry dye technique is good for colouring large areas. After moistening the cake of dye by breathing on it, some of the colour is picked up on a cotton swab and applied in sweeping, circular movements to the print. This is then buffed up and made permanent by steaming the print over a boiling kettle for a few seconds. Used as a wet dye, some of the dye is diluted with water and stabilizer in a palette and applied in the same way as already described.

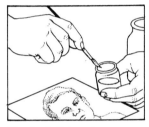

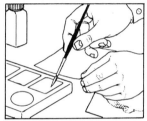

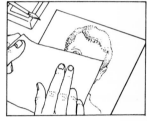

Wet dye 1. Moisten the retouching brush with water and stabilizer before starting the retouching.

2. Mix the dye to the correct intensity in a palette, testing on a spare piece of paper, and remove excess dye. Retouch from the centre of the area to be altered.

3. Use blotting paper to remove excess dye.

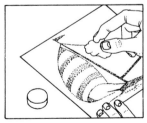

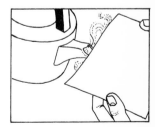

Dry dye 1. Breathe onto the surface of the dye cake to moisten.

2. Rub a cotton swab onto the dye and apply to the print in small circular motions.

3. Steaming the print over boiling water for about 10 seconds will fix the dye. Extra applications will increase the colour intensity.

Duplicating 1

Duplicating is a basic and very useful process that can be used to copy important transparencies as a form of insurance, to correct certain mistakes in the original, or to create various special effects.

Most professional duplicating is done by projection in an enlarger, with special duplicating sheet film such as Kodak Ektachrome 6121 which is balanced for tungsten lighting and placed on the enlarger's baseboard in the same way as a print. A comprehensive series of tests is needed to establish the appropriate exposures and filtration combinations for an individual enlarger system to be used in duplicating.

A simpler method of making duplicates – still of high quality – is a slide copier. This uses an electronic flash, the intensity of which can be adjusted precisely to suit the transparency. Exposure measurement is normally made with a photoelectric cell and a tungsten modelling light that varies in proportion to the intensity of the flash. An added sophistication is a contrast control attachment which fogs the film very slightly, so lightening shadows and giving an apparent reduction in contrast if desired. Slide copiers are balanced for daylight film.

A third way of making duplicates is to attach a translucent mount directly to a camera lens, with bellows or extension tubes fitted to give a 1:1 enlargement. The original is placed in the mount and the camera pointed towards a light source. Unless lighting conditions are repeated for each duplicate made, this method is unreliable.

Operationally, slide copiers are straightforward, even though different types may vary. Successful duplicating depends on appreciating the limitations of the process, and understanding some basic principles.

Fidelity Photographing a transparency is not the same as taking original pictures. The dyes in the original are themselves only an approximation of the original subject, and can reproduce in surprisingly different ways when copied. Often, the best duplicating results are made on the same make of film as the original, although there are no duplicating films balanced to match the 5,000K of flash. In all events, you should try different films and compare the results. Total colour accuracy is not possible.

Loss of quality Every stage removed from the original loses quality. This is inevitable and a close comparison will always show up the defects in the duplicate. Subjectively, there may be an improvement – in colour or contrast, for example – but resolution and graininess always suffer.

Standardization The key to consistently successful duplicates is a regular method of working. Having tested the equipment arrangement and calibrated the flash, continue to keep notes of settings, filtration and film batches for all the different types of original. Eventually, you will be able to treat duplicating as a simple and straightforward procedure.

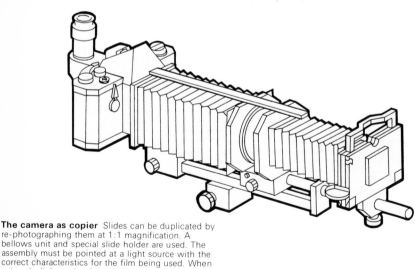

The camera as copier Slides can be duplicated by re-photographing them at 1:1 magnification. A bellows unit and special slide holder are used. The assembly must be pointed at a light source with the correct characteristics for the film being used. When using daylight, point the camera at an overcast part of the sky to achieve the correct colour temperature for daylight film. Tungsten-balanced film can also be used, with a tungsten lamp as the light source.

Slide copier For frequent duplication under more controlled conditions, this is a very useful piece of equipment. It consists of a low powered flash tube which illuminates the transparency during duplication. There is also a modelling light to aid focusing. Filters can be added for colour correction. A separate control will also reduce contrast if required by projecting a small amount of light directly into the lens.

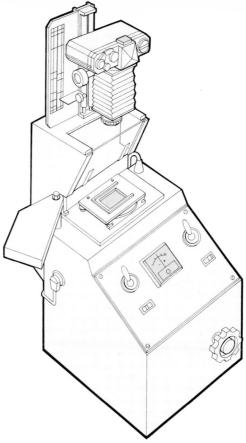

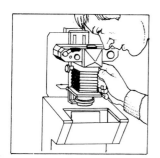

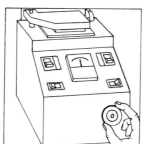

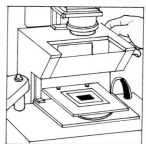

Frame the image of the transparency correctly in the camera's viewfinder and focus, using the copier's modelling light. Select the required filtration.

Stop down the lens to an aperture decided by testing or in accordance with an established working method. Position the copier's photoelectric cell over the transparency and adjust the illumination until the copier's indicator needle is centred.

Adjust the contrast control. If in doubt bracket the contrast. With practice, however, you will be able to identify the amount of contrast reduction each transparency needs. Switch over to flash and fire the camera's shutter.

When you have established a standardized equipment arrangement that allows you to make consistently accurate exposures, deliberate alteration of the results is straightforward. The following are some of the possibilities:

Increasing contrast Using a regular, non-duplicating film will automatically raise contrast.

Decreasing contrast Fog the film slightly overall, either by pre-exposing or with the contrast control attachment fitted to a slide copier (see pages 94–95).

Correcting colour Use a filter of the complementary colour to the cast on the original, and of half the strength that gives a neutral appearance when over the transparency on a light-box.

Correcting shadow colour When fogging the film to reduce contrast, add filters of the complementary colour to the cast. The highlights will be unaffected.

Selective enlargement To obtain an enlargement of part of the original, increase the bellows extension, altering the position of the original if necessary. Make the same exposure allowance for the extra extension as you would in close-up photography (see pages 200–201).

Adding effects filters Use any effects filter (see pages 36–37) as you would in normal photography.

Double exposure This is much easier and less risky when making duplicates than during original photography (see pages 186–191). Simply ensure that the light areas in one image coincide with dark areas in the other. Dark backgrounds and light subjects make the most successful marriages.

Procedure

1 Measure the exposure Consider the original as you would the scene itself. As most slide copiers have meters that average the whole picture area, you may need to make adjustments (over-exposing slightly for a light background and under-exposing if most of the original is dark). If in doubt, use the slide copier at its average settings, bracketing for extra safety.

2 Assess the contrast Unless you are using special duplicating film, contrast will be increased. If the original lacks contrast, this may be an improvement, but if the contrast is already high, you will need to fog the film slightly. A contrast control device simplifies the operation, but otherwise, before making the duplicate, expose the film with an ND2.0 neutral density filter in place of the original. This passes one per cent of the light and fogs the film very slightly.

3 Select the filtration If the original has a colour cast that you want to correct, try out complementary colour filters of different strengths on a light-box until you find one that restores the colour balance to neutral. Then use a filter of half this strength in the slide copier. For example, if a greenish original looks right with a CC10Red filter, duplicate it with a CC05Red. You can make a separate correction to just the shadow areas by fitting a complementary colour filter to the contrast control attachment or adding it to the one per cent neutral density filter in the process described above.

Unwanted contrast with dupes The adequate contrast of this Thai mother with her child was increased by the dupe (far picture). The result was less effective than the original. Steps should have been taken to reduce contrast when making the dupe.

Duping to raise contrast This shot of a Mississippi steamboat in misty conditions benefited greatly from the increased contrast provided by a dupe (lower picture). A greater range of tones resulted, and the impact of the muted colour in the scene was also raised.

Masking and stripping-in

Although multiple exposure can be an effective way of combining images (see pages 186–191). dark backgrounds are needed for it to work properly. To combine photographs with more complex or light backgrounds needs a different, extremely precise technique known as stripping-in. Because of the skill and painstaking work involved, it is almost exclusively the preserve of professional laboratories. In addition, retouching is nearly always needed to complete the effect.

Stripping-in is performed on dye transfers or on sheet transparency film (8 × 10in/20 × 25cm or even larger), and very occasionally on colour prints. A dye transfer, where the original photograph is separated into three matrices which are used to transfer dye to the final print is similar in some ways to silk-screen printing and offers the greatest control, with excellent image quality.

Dye transfer strip-ins are relatively easy for a professional retoucher, working with the same dyes as used for the print, but the production cost is high as colour prints are very difficult to retouch. Transparency strip-ins are less expensive, but even more difficult to retouch effectively.

The principle of stripping-in is the same for both dye transfers and transparencies. With two images to be combined, the unwanted parts of each image are blocked off with masks, simply made by exposing the original transparencies onto line film. These masks are then combined with the originals in such a way that the two images can be copied onto the same sheet of film without overlapping. Extreme precision is necessary, entailing the use of a system to ensure correct registration, and the work is normally done at a considerable enlargement.

Combining six photographs into one Using the techniques described on these pages, this assembly of six different subjects was possible with a high degree of realism. The foreground surface, spacecraft and rings (all models), the stars, spacecraft rocket exhaust and the disc of the setting planet (all artwork) were photographed separately on 4 x 5 in (9 x 12cm) transparency film. Following a sketched layout, each of the six transparencies was punched fit on a register bar in precise position. Line film masks, both positive and negative, were then made by contrast printing and minor retouching for the foreground surface, spacecraft and planet. Each transparency was copied onto a single sheet of film, black spaces being left for the other images with the appropriate masks. When the star background was being re-photographed, for example, masks were combined with it to give a solid black silhouette of the foreground, spacecraft and planet. The rocket exhaust and rings, being virtually white, were allowed to double expose.

Procedure

Masking First, positive and negative masks of the main image are made. For stripping-in with transparencies, negative masks are made by contact printing or enlarging the original onto line film, producing solid black images on clear film. The positive mask is made by repeating this process with the negative instead of the original. After retouching, these are ready for the next stage.

original transparency   negative mask   positive mask

Registering Using a precision-made register bar and punch, each image is aligned exactly. This is done for the original transparencies and the masks – for a two-part strip-in this means four sheets of film.

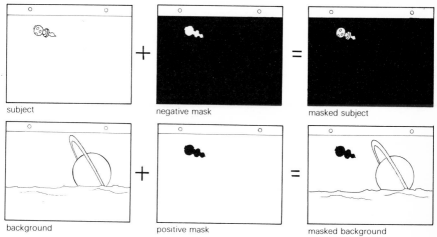

subject   negative mask   masked subject

background   positive mask   masked background

Stripping-in Using the masks to block out the unwanted parts of each image, the two transparencies are copied onto one sheet of film, by contact-printing, enlarging, or direct photography.

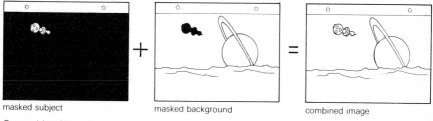

masked subject   masked background   combined image

Retouching No strip-in is perfect, and some retouching is needed to conceal the edges where the images join.

99

5. SUBJECTS
Interiors: selecting format

The first thing to be decided when photographing an interior is picture format. Usually, the choice will be straightforward but in individual circumstances it may not be immediately obvious. Deciding between a vertical and a horizontal format involves establishing the basic composition of the shot, although this will often be governed by the existing layout of the room. With some interiors, you may be able to move furniture to suit the picture, but the major features – windows, ceiling lights, doors – will inevitably be fixed.

Most modern interiors are small and have relatively low ceilings, rarely including strong vertical elements. As a result, the normal choice of format is horizontal. This view will be natural and easier on the eye. When a room does have

definite vertical components – a tall, narrow window, pillars, or a hanging chandelier, for example – then compose vertically to take advantage of them. Halls, churches and split-level domestic interiors often have striking vertical interest.

Before committing yourself to one camera position and format, experiment by walking around and trying different compositions through the viewfinder, both horizontal and vertical. Because wide coverage and a sense of space will probably be required, a camera position in the corner of the room, with a horizontal format, is standard. A wide-angle lens will often be the best choice – 20 to 28mm with a 35mm camera, 38 to 50mm with 6×6cm or 6×7cm, and 75 to 90mm with view cameras.

The standard horizontal format More often than not, a horizontal rather than vertical format suits interiors. The existing layout of this New Orleans bar, with wall racks and a long bar-top, virtually dictated a horizontal treatment. Although it is not so immediately obvious, most domestic and other small interiors have the same basic distribution of furniture and interest, while low, plain ceilings rarely encourage vertical framing. Wide-angle lenses are commonly used to cover as much of an interior as possible, and these inevitably distort lines near the corners of the frame. The danger of this is noticeable stretching of familiar shapes. Here the circular clock face is pulled out of shape, although not sufficiently to be really objectionable.

Vertical format to capture ceiling details The tubular ceiling lights in this shopping centre are a dominant part of its design, and are clearly easier to include in a vertical shot. Camera viewpoint and exposure were both chosen with them in mind. The rows of lights make a strong pattern of diagonally converging lines, emphasized by the slight under-exposure given to most of the interior which was actually the correct setting for the ceiling.

Panoramic view for grandeur and opulence Although apparently ignoring the strong vertical interest of the pillars, this super-wide frame uses the unique pictorial qualities of a special camera to give an all-encompassing sweep to a spectacular board-room. Fitted with a lens that has enough covering power for a large view camera, the wide body of the Linhof Technorama gives a picture area in the proportion three to one – a 6cm×17cm image, not much smaller than the size reproduced here. The human eye most easily scans from side to side, and a panoramic format closely matches the way we see most views. Although most commonly used for landscapes, it can be unusually effective in richly detailed interiors.

Controlling verticals

A recurring problem with all architectural photography is handling the vertical lines of a building. The normal view of an interior is from ground level, so that in large spaces and high rooms we inevitably look up. This view is so familiar that we hardly notice the perspective distortion that makes the vertical lines converge, but in a photograph the effect is inescapable and often unattractive.

There are, in fact, several ways of avoiding excessive convergence, as the examples on these pages show. The most widely used is the shift lens or rising front on a view camera, but even this cannot provide an instant and total solution to high verticals, which can only be kept parallel by trading one type of distortion for another – by introducing the unnatural stretching of parts of the image. Only convention calls for parallel verticals in formal architectural shots, and there are many situations where a deliberately chosen upward view, including the distortion caused by converging verticals, can be much more effective and even appear more natural. The least acceptable compromise is the half-hearted convergence given by a slight upward tilt of the camera, looking like a mistake, which it often is.

Using the covering power of a lens The classic answer to converging verticals is to use a wide-angle lens with such broad covering power that the height of the room can be included in the shot without having to tilt the camera upwards. Provided the camera back remains vertical, all vertical lines in the room will stay parallel in the picture. The composition is likely to be unbalanced, however, with uninteresting floor space occupying the lower part of the frame. With a view camera, the solution is to raise the lens panel or lower the film back, so shifting the whole composition upwards. A perspective-control lens on a smaller, fixed-body camera does exactly the same job. All that is necessary is to have a lens that can cover an area larger than the film format, thus recording only the desired part of the image produced by the lens.

Using the same principle, control of perspective is possible without a shift lens. Simply aim a wide-angle lens in a horizontal position, so that there is no distortion, and crop or mask the final picture at the bottom. This works particularly well with a 35mm film format, which is usually too narrow when used vertically and will benefit from trimming part of the image.

Use a very wide-angle lens – here 20mm focal length on a 35mm camera – and crop the photograph later.

If too much floor and insufficient ceiling appear in the frame with a horizontal position, shifting the lens or rear standard can raise the composition.

A high camera position for wide coverage Very few interiors offer this opportunity, but placing the camera halfway between floor and ceiling gives the best of both worlds. The camera can be aimed horizontally to avoid distortion, yet automatically includes the full vertical range of the interior. This shot of Queen Victoria and Prince Albert's tomb near Windsor was a sufficiently important project to warrant building a small scaffolding tower inside the mausoleum. From it, a Hasselblad SWC, which has a 38mm lens, was used, giving ample and undistorted coverage of the important details.

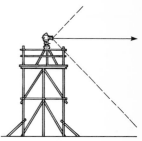

Deliberate convergence for dramatic effect No amount of technical or compositional effort will capture a high ceiling without some distortion. In this situation, it is often better to ignore the accepted rule, tilt the camera strongly upwards and make a virtue of the dramatic perspective. An argument for this treatment is that in many tall interiors this is the normal view. Here, in Thornhill's Painted Hall at the Royal Naval College, Greenwich, the deliberate convergence was doubly justified for the entrance is at the foot of a flight of steps, which allows just one dramatic upward view, exactly as in the photograph.

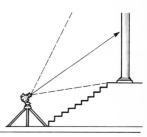

Problem interiors

Not all rooms lend themselves to straightforward horizontal viewpoints. Not even the shift lenses of view cameras can overcome every problem of restricted space or perspective effect. In addition, the design of a particular interior may place the interest in an unusual area. In very small spaces, the choice of camera position becomes very restricted indeed, and the main problem is to obtain a wide enough angle of view to cover the subject.

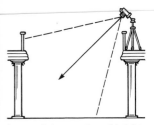

Downward-converging verticals When the main feature of interest is on the floor – here, a banquet for judges given by London's Lord Mayor – a high viewpoint may be the answer. This is usually only possible when there is an interior balcony. In this case, there was a continous balcony running completely round the hall, offering a choice of camera positions. A wide-angle lens (20mm on a 35mm camera) increased the sensation of height, and a diagonal shot balanced the pillars against the long tables. Interestingly, when verticals converge downwards, the result rarely seems awkward or unnatural.

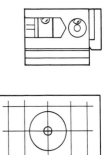

Decorated ceilings Painted or elaborately decorated ceilings usually demand a very formal and simple treatment – in a sense, vertical copying. Photograph them from directly below the centre, with the camera pointing precisely upwards. Important equipment includes a tripod, ground glass viewfinder screen etched with vertical and horizontal lines, and an accurate, two-way spirit level that can be aligned with the film plane, although the latter may not be needed with view cameras, which often have built-in spirit levels. The spirit level is especially important when there is no way of locating the point on the floor that is directly underneath the ceiling's centre. After approximate positioning, align the camera vertically, and then move it around the floor until the ceiling is centred in the viewfinder. With a wide-angle lens, even a slight error of alignment will cause convergence in one direction. If you are using a 35mm camera with a detachable prism, compose directly on the ground glass screen.

Extreme wide-angle lenses for cramped spaces The widest of all wide-angle lenses are fish-eyes, uncorrected for barrel distortion and producing strongly-curved lines, especially near the frame edges. Normally shunned by architectural photographers because of this extreme distortion, they can nevertheless be the only solution when photographing very small interiors. The floor of this beehive-shaped Navajo dwelling in Arizona, called a hogan, measured less than 20 feet in diameter. As the picture would have had little point without including the roof, the only possible lens for the shot was a 16mm fish-eye on a 35mm camera. This produces a more acceptable full-frame, rather than circular, image.

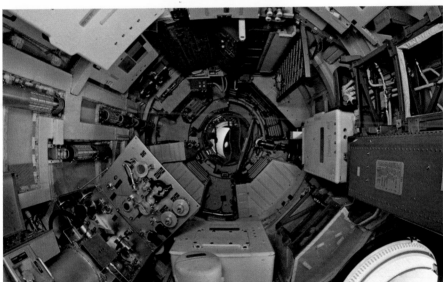

Concealing fish-eye distortion The cylindrical interior of this part of Skylab – the multiple docking adapter – was a perfect use for the same 16mm fish-eye lens. By centring the far porthole in the viewfinder, the circular barrel of the adapter matched the distortion caused by the lens, disguising it entirely. Only the slightly curved edges of the equipment panels reveal the distortion, and even then it is only apparent to someone familiar with the spacecraft.

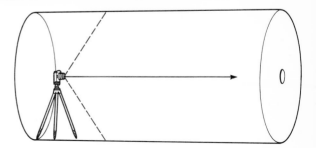

Interiors by daylight 1

The most common light source for interiors is natural daylight. Very few rooms are without windows and, although you may sometimes have the opportunity to wait until dark and rely totally on artificial lighting, more often than not the room will appear most attractive in daylight. Indeed, many old buildings – some churches are notable examples – were designed to be appreciated by daylight, before adequate artificial lighting was introduced. To preserve the authentic atmosphere of an interior, consider first whether you can photograph it using the simplest available light rather than adding any form of artificial, photographic light.

The quality of daylight indoors varies so much, being so dependent on the type, size, position and distribution of windows, that it is difficult to categorize. However, as a general rule, the proportions of window space to room area determine the contrast range in the scene. The more window space there is, the more even the illumination. Small windows or doorways, however, create a high contrast range, as the light levels fall off rapidly with distance.

When working in colour, consider the colour temperature of the daylight. Direct or diffused sunlight, and even a completely overcast sky, give illumination close to 5,500 Kelvins – mean noon daylight for which all daylight films are balanced. If, on the other hand, the windows face a clear blue sky, the colour temperature can be anything over 7,000K and will need a light-balancing filter to counteract a strongly blue cast (see pages 36–37)

The flood of light from a large window With virtually the whole of one long wall given over to window, the hall-like lobby of this old South American hotel is quite evenly lit by comparison with an average interior. With ASA 64 film, the incident light reading (see page 16) by the window was 1/4 sec at f5.6 and by the lamp in the foreground 4 secs at f5.6, a range of five stops. The exposure was set midway between the two readings, which would preserve some detail at the left.
For the greatest possible depth of field, the lens was stopped down to f45, requiring an exposure of one minute. To compensate for the reciprocity failure (see pages 38–39), the exposure was doubled to two minutes.

Light from a small window or doorway The interior of this primitive hut in one of Thailand's Blue Meo hill-tribe villages was lit by nothing more than a small open doorway and a few chinks of light from gaps in the wall. Illumination from a small source of light decreases according to the inverse square law – with every unit increase in distance, the light reduces by its square root. This interior, with no reflections from the walls or floor, came close to this extreme, with the result that there was a seven stop range of contrast from the left to right-hand edges of the shot. The exposure, using a 20mm lens on a 35mm camera, was 1/15 sec at f4, on ASA 800 film. This setting was midway between the two extremes.

Capturing atmosphere with high contrast Typical of many older churches, the interior of St. Mary Magdalene's, Oxford is quite poorly lit by the high, narrow windows, and so suffers a sharp fall-off in the light level. Allowing for reciprocity failure, the incident reading close to the windows was 1/8 sec at f16 on ASA 160 film, but only 8 secs at f16 by the bible The open pages of the bible were the key to the composition, not only to fill the foreground in this horizontally aimed shot, but to balance the windows with another light area. With the camera position carefully chosen, the photograph was deliberately under-exposed by half a stop from the reading at the bible to avoid picking up shadow detail, emphasizing the juxtaposition of book and windows.

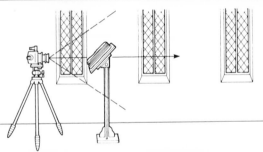

Fill-in light from reflections This enclosed alley in Iran was lit only by a row of high windows along one wall, and at most times of the day would receive very little illumination. In the late morning, however, sunlight streams through the smoke from a small metal works, and the reflections on the opposite wall act as a second light source. Although local contrast around the sunlit patches was high, this supplementary lighting lowered the overall contrast of the scene, excluding the sunlit patches themselves.

Shooting with or against the light creates special exposure conditions. With lighting from directly behind the camera, contrast is low and exposure calculations relatively simple. Backlighting, on the other hand, always needs special care, particularly when selecting the correct exposure for the view outside and inside a window in the same shot.

Silhouettes When the window or doorway is relatively large, it can serve as a bright, diffuse backdrop for a silhouetted object. Here, the distinctive shape of the Space Shuttle Orbiter is outlined against the open hangar door at N.A.S.A.'s Marshall Spaceflight Center. The exposure was calculated for the full area of the bright background to keep the spacecraft as a solid shape with minimal shadow detail.

Through a brightly lit opening When looking out from dark interiors into bright sunlight, an exposure that is correct for the outside view will show nothing of the room. The best way to treat situations like this shot in a Brazilian village is to use the doorway or window simply as a frame. Set the exposure solely for the outside lighting – here, 1/125 sec at f11 on ASA 64 film. Take care that the dark interior does not influence the meter's reading – if necessary, move to the entrance for the measurement.

Balancing exterior and interior light levels Even without resorting to artificial fill-in lights, it is often possible to accommodate the normally high contrast between the interior of a room and the view outside, even on transparency film. This photograph illustrating garden design employs four methods of keeping the scenes on either side of the window within the range of the film, all without any supplementary lighting. First, the shot was taken on a slightly overcast day, which kept the light level in the garden down. Secondly, the camera was aimed downwards to exclude the sky, which would have been over-exposed if it appeared. Next, the desk-top arrangement was made up of bright and reflective objects, angled to catch as much light as possible. Finally, the film was deliberately over-exposed by half a stop and then under-developed – a useful contrast-reducing technique described on pages 38–39. Based on an incident reading just inside the window, the exposure given was 15 secs at f27 on film rated at ASA 25. The garden is actually half a stop over-exposed, but still acceptable.

Overhead daylight

Some interiors, mainly large public and industrial ones, are lit chiefly by an open roof or skylight. This lighting direction usually appears natural, and there are few problems in working with it. Upward looking shots, however, are rarely satisfactory.

Diffuse illumination from a large skylight Washington's National Air and Space Museum was designed for the maximum use of daylight, with bright, reflecting stone walls and the whole of the ceiling and one side of the main hall given over to window area. The result, increasingly common in exhibition areas and the atriums of new office blocks, is a soft, slightly directional lighting that is very good for photographic work. The exposure on ASA 64 film followed the average reflected light reading – 1/15 sec at f5.6, using a 16mm fish-eye lens.

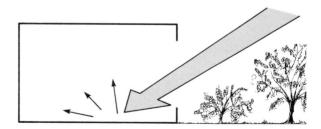

Gradual light fall-off in a tall building Although the fall-off in light level from a typical window is rapid, an overhead skylight gives much more balanced illumination, even in such a narrow interior as this test hangar for the Space Shuttle. The reason is that the light enters at a more direct angle, striking walls rather than the generally less reflective floor. The contrast range between the top and bottom of the picture – over 200 feet – is only four stops.

Flare and contrast in an upward view Shooting up towards the roof in a skylit interior brings the same problems as including a window in the composition. The contrast range in a setting like this block of flats in Calcutta is too high for any film, and the only answer, in the absence of massive artificial lighting, was to choose a compromise exposure setting. The exposure was calculated for the lower balcony by shading the camera's TTL meter from the skylight – 1/15 sec at f5.6 on ASA 200 film. Flare from the sky was accepted as inevitable.

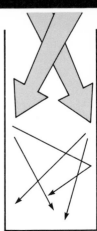

Interiors with tungsten light 1

Although gradually being superseded by the more economical fluorescent lighting, tungsten lamps are still the standard illumination in most domestic interiors and even in some larger public ones, such as restaurants. Colour temperature varies according to both the rating of the bulbs and also to voltage levels. In practice, tungsten-lit interiors hardly ever have colour temperature as high as the 3,200K and 3,400K photographic lamps for which tungsten-rated films are balanced. Even when using these films rather than daylight stock, therefore, interiors lit by domestic lamps will appear reddish unless they are compensated for with filters (see pages 36–37).

An even greater difficulty than controlling colour balance is caused by the way that most tungsten lamps are used. They are rarely concealed, as is strip-lighting, and much interior photography has to cope with light sources appearing in a shot, unavoidably leading to problems of high contrast.

Balancing the colour temperature of tungsten lamps This shot of an annual ceremony in the City of London shows the two most frequently recurring problems of available tungsten lighting. Colour temperature of non-photographic tungsten lamps is difficult to judge accurately without a colour temperature meter, but for most situations such precision is not necessary. Most domestic bulbs give a colour temperature of 2,700K, but these chandeliers were slightly higher at about 3,000K. Although warmer than the 3,200K for which the tungsten film is balanced, the result is visually acceptable. Interestingly, the same scene photographed on daylight film does not look objectionable.

The second problem is finding the best exposure when the lamps themselves are in the picture, as they often are. Using additional fill-in lighting is perhaps the ideal solution, but there are many occasions, as here, where the existing room lights are the only ones available. An average reading of this whole scene, including chandeliers, indicated 1/4 sec at f8 on film rated at ASA 320, whereas a reading of the floor area alone showed 1/4 sec at f3.5. The only acceptable compromise was a setting close to that of the floor – 1/4 sec at f4.

Choosing film to match the dominant light source With the common mixture of daylight and tungsten, daylight film is usually a better choice than tungsten. The exception is the special case of exposures of more than about 10 seconds where tungsten-balanced film is

designed to suffer less from reciprocity failure, provided an 85B filter is used to balance the film for daylight. As long as the daylight is fairly dominant in the picture, it is more acceptable, as here, to have a lamp appear reddish than the daylight deep blue. In this shot, the bedside

lamp was switched on to give 'lift' to the otherwise dark interior. It had little influence on the exposure setting, which on ASA 64 film was 1/8 sec at f5.6, carefully placed at two-thirds of a stop more than the outside reading – the greatest over-exposure acceptable.

Colour temperature meter This meter, Spectra, is one of the few that measures both green/red light as well as blue/red and can therefore be used for fluorescent lighting conditions as well as daylight/tungsten. It covers a colour temperature range from 2,800 Kelvins to 30,000 Kelvins.

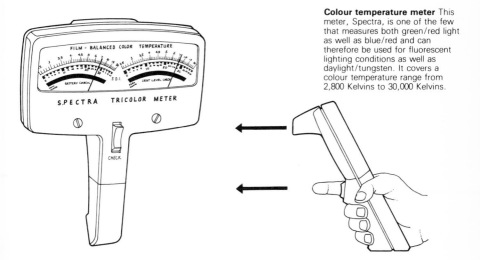

Using a mixture of light sources Four different light sources, each with its own colour temperature, illuminated the interior of this Byzantine church in Athens. With a wide-angle lens and a low tripod position, the candles, church lamps and the beams of sunlight in the cupola were all deliberately included in the frame for a sparkling, multi-coloured effect. A pale blue 82A filter enhanced the colour difference between the sunlight and tungsten, and a CC10 Magenta filter was added to correct for reciprocity failure as the exposure, on Kodachrome 64, was 1 sec at f5.6.

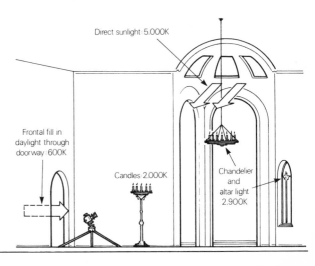

Direct sunlight: 5,000K

Frontal fill in daylight through doorway: 600K

Candles: 2,000K

Chandelier and altar light 2,900K

Exploiting the warmth of tungsten lighting In a Buddhist Temple in northern Thailand, the already low colour temperature of the candles was made even redder by the gold covering the Buddhas. While this might have seemed to suggest a corrective filter, the real attraction of the scene lay in the richness of the statues against which the kneeling monks were silhouetted. Daylight film, deliberately uncorrected, preserved this warmth, and to enhance it even further, a wide-angle lens was used to include the pillars on either side, tinged blue from the sky in contrast. The exposure (1/8 sec at f2 on ASA 200 film) was based on the brightness of the three gold figures measured with a centre reading TTL meter.

Balancing mixed lighting with filters When tungsten and daylight are fairly evenly mixed, the overall colour temperature falls somewhere between 3,000K and 5,000K, and a mild colour balancing filter is the best solution. In this library, photographed during the day, part of the illumination came from the available room lighting, and part from daylight reflected from a large white building opposite. A bluish 82A filter gives a more natural balance to the shot.

Fluorescent and mercury vapour

Although tungsten lamps and daylight generally produce an acceptable colour temperature, vapour discharge lamps do not, and are more difficult to work with (see pages 12–13). In theory, the light from fluorescent lamps, which has a greenish appearance on colour film, can be corrected to white with appropriate filters, but in practice there is often no way of calculating just how green or greenish-blue a particular lamp is. The visual appearance is always white and thus gives no guidance. The best solution is to make a colour test, whereby several shots are taken with a range of filters and the best result chosen before returning to take the final picture. Alternatively, bracket the shot with different filters, as with aperture for uncertain exposures.

Lacking even the fluorescent coating that broadens the spectrum of light from strip-lighting, mercury vapour lamps are even more difficult to balance. Depending on the type, they may be so deficient in red that no amount of filtration will help. Using stronger red filters will merely cut down the amount of light reaching the film. Again, testing various filters is the ideal answer, but if no time is available for this, try a CC20 Red or CC40 Red filter.

An ordinary colour temperature meter compares only the relative strengths of red and blue wavelengths, and is no help with fluorescent or mercury vapour lighting. A two-way meter however, measures red/blue and red/green – a specialized instrument but useful.

Taking advantage of fluorescent light's green cast Occasionally, the green colour shift in fluorescent lighting can be used to advantage. Although usually thought to be unpleasant, an unnatural green light can sometimes add to a particular effect, as in this shot of Thailand's famous Emerald Buddha. Only strip-lighting illuminated the glass case, but without corrective filtration, it actually enhanced the colour of the carved jade. A long-focus lens was used from a viewpoint beyond the doorway of the temple as cameras are forbidden inside. The reading of the TTL meter was excessively influenced by the dark surroundings, so the exposure was calculated at one stop darker than indicated. For safety, several bracketed exposures were made (see pages 16–17), the best result being obtained with 1/15 sec at f5.6 on ASA 64 film.

Balancing fluorescent lighting with filters In this silver assay office, the only illumination consisted of overhead fluorescent lamps. A rule of thumb filtration of CC20 Magenta was used, and this gave satisfactory correction with daylight film. If you know the type of lamp, refer to the filter table on pages 12–13, but remember that the age of the lamp alters colour. Otherwise, use CC20 Magenta or CC30 Magenta. If the lamps themselves are not visible in the shot, an alternative is to cover them with sheets of magenta acetate of the type supplied to the movie industry for fluorescent correction. This is useful when fluorescent lighting is unavoidably mixed with daylight. Film balanced for daylight is generally better than tungsten-balanced film, as fluorescent lamps are red deficient.

Mixed fluorescent and mercury vapour This large hangar at the N.A.S.A. facility at Houston is typical of many industrial interiors, having a complete mixture of light sources, some stronger than others. Some guesswork was involved with this shot, and several filter combinations were used for insurance. The best filtration turned out to be CC30 Magenta, as most of the lighting came from fluorescent and mercury vapour lamps. The tungsten spotlights were relatively unimportant. Such a combination of lighting is highly unpredictable, and shooting the scene several times over with a range of filters is the only safe approach.

Lighting interiors 1

When you have the time and resources, constructing your own lighting for an interior can overcome many of the problems found in the situations described so far and give you a fine degree of control over the ultimate effect.

The aim of lighting an interior is not to illuminate every corner, but to enhance the room's atmosphere. Lighting styles therefore need to be adapted to the architecture and period. Either tungsten lights or flash can be used. The choice may be influenced by the existing lighting – if natural daylight through a window is intended to play a part, then flash may be more convenient when using colour film, whereas tungsten is usually better if domestic lamps are included in the shot. Domestic lamps can be fitted with blue bulbs to balance for use with flash.

First select the camera angle and re-position the furniture for the most effective composition. A carefully sited foreground object can often give depth and balance to the shot. As a wide-angle lens is the usual choice when photographing interiors, the lighting will probably have to cover a wide area. Avoid obvious shadows cast by lights outside the picture frame as this will look artificial. Diffuse lights either by using large umbrellas or by bouncing the light off walls, ceiling or white card reflectors. Domestic lamps appearing in a shot can only be used for effect, and make little contribution to the level of illumination. Adjust the overall lighting so that they appear bright but do not cause too much flare.

Instant film as a compositional aid Photographing elaborate interiors is particularly difficult and considerable care and preparation are needed to achieve a perfectly balanced and lit shot. Polaroid film is extremely useful in this context, allowing trial shots to be taken before finally committing the scene to colour film. Here, various views were attempted, moving both camera and lights until a satisfactory arrangement was discovered.

Combining daylight, flash and room lights Daylight was chosen as the principal lighting for this extremely ornate room in Buckingham Palace, London. The four full length net-curtained windows gave an incident reading of 60 seconds at f32 at the position of the table, using film rated at ASA 16. The aperture of f32 determined all the other factors. It was the minimum lens setting that would record every detail in the shot sharply — the depth of field had been carefully worked out and the camera focused to make the best use of it. Because the exposure would have to be long, Type B film was used with an orange 85B filter, rather than daylight film, as it suffers less from reciprocity failure. At long exposures its rating is ASA 25; the 85B filter reduced this to ASA 16. Nevertheless, there was some reciprocity failure, and a test on Polaroid film (Type 55 matches Type B Ektachrome closely in speed) showed that 100 seconds gave the best result. Having set up the shot using daylight, the next step was to switch on some of the room lights, for effect only. Although distinctly warm, these

were too weak to influence the overall colour balance. Finally to even out the intensity of the lighting, two flash units were arranged close to the camera, one to brighten the far corner and the other, on an extended stand, to illuminate the ceiling area. It was important that these lights should not be obvious in order to preserve a natural atmosphere.

Lights: 750 Joule flash with large white umbrella, plus a 400 Joule flash with a medium silvered umbrella.

Film: Type B Ektachrome with 85B filter to balance for daylight and flash.

Lens: 90 mm Super Augulon on a 4 x 5in (9 x 12cm) view camera.

Exposure: 100 seconds at f32, with both flash units fired eight times.

Uneven lighting to eliminate the background In many interiors it may be impossible to rearrange objects. This old printing press was in a small, crowded museum room, and the background would have been distracting and inappropriate if it had appeared in shot. To overcome this problem, a single, diffused spotlight was aimed from overhead at the decorated headpiece and newspaper, leaving the surroundings unlit. To kill the effect of the existing room lighting, flash was used. Framing the image closely into the subject also helped to reduce the importance of the background.

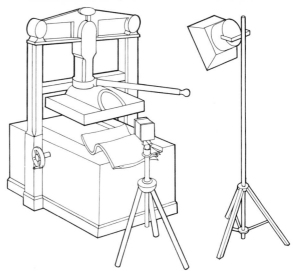

Uneven lighting to focus attention By creating pools of light in a room, rather than attempting evenly balanced illumination, specific subjects can be isolated from surrounding clutter. As this technique also tends to introduce a rather theatrical atmosphere, it does not suit every interior, and should be used with caution. In this shot, spotlighting was logical for the subject — a recently abandoned typewriter — whilst the light from a hallway provided balance and a counterpoint to the sheet of typed paper. The spotlighting came from a single flash head fitted with a snoot (see pages 22-23), suspended directly overhead on a boom arm. The light through the frosted glass was an ordinary domestic tungsten lamp, recorded with a time exposure.

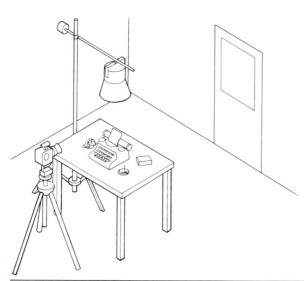

Architectural details

Shooting architectural details indoors often calls for either a long-focus lens or a special camera position for high and inaccessible subjects. A long-focus lens is less troublesome, but needs a rigid support for the long exposures inevitable with the small maximum apertures available with such lenses. In addition, it is usually necessary to shoot by available light, as the distances make supplementary lighting impractical. Constructing a camera platform can be difficult and expensive, but for an important shot such elaborate preparation makes it possible to use a variety of different cameras and lighting equipment.

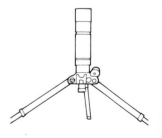

A long-focus lens for inaccessible detail With the camera in the same vertical position used when shooting an entire ceiling (see page 104), a long-focus lens needs to be held as firmly as possible to avoid camera shake. Use the tripod in its most stable position – with its legs retracted or spread wide – even if this makes viewing more awkward. This painting of Christ in the cupola of a Greek church was well lit by daylight, and there were no special problems of filtration or exposure, even with an f5.6 400mm lens on a 35mm camera. But because depth of field is very limited with a long-focus lens, alignment is especially important. If the subject is at an angle, such as on a domed ceiling, try and find a camera viewpoint that faces it square-on.

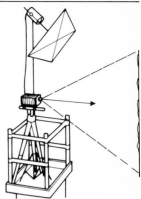

Raising camera and lights for a close view For a carefully lit direct shot of this detail, camera, tripod and flash were raised movable platform known as an air ladder. Because this restricted the choice of lighting position, the flash head was raised even higher on a stand, and fired through a large rectangular umbrella to obtain lighting that was as diffuse as possible. As this diffusion reduced the intensity of the light, 12 flashes were fired in sequence at full power to give the illumination needed for an aperture of f19 on ASA 64 film. It was necessary to pause between flashes for any slight vibration to die away.

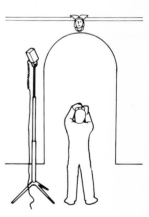

A high flash and ground level camera With little time to photograph this high detail, a portable flash unit was fixed to the top of a fully elevated stand and aimed directly at the subject. The camera was hand-held with a 180mm lens, connected to the flash by an extension synchronization lead. Far from ideal, this solution made possible a shot that could not otherwise have been taken.

Candid shots by daylight 1

With fast film, fast lenses and careful camera handling, candid photography indoors offers a wide range of opportunity. Film and lens improvements over the last few years have broken an important threshold: it is now possible to employ relatively fast shutter speeds in combination with colour film and moderately long-focus lenses in poorly lit interiors. Flash is not helpful with this kind of work, which demands unobtrusiveness. The ideal equipment is:

1. A 35mm camera for speed and compactness
2. A moderately long-focus lens, around 200mm, with a wide maximum aperture; a very fast normal lens; and a wide-angle lens for close candid work
3. ASA 400 film, push-processed when necessary (see pages 38–39)
4. The camera handling techniques described on pages 56–57. Practise them to improve your slowest workable shutter speed.

Backlighting for higher shutter speeds Even with an overall light level that is too low for the subject, it is possible to shoot against the light – from a window, for example. The shadow areas will still be dark, but the edges of face and hands define the image. In the case of this Amsterdamer drinking in a café, the backlighting was also ideal for the glass of beer. In reality, the combination of camera, lens and film were far from ideal – 6 × 6cm camera, f5.6 250mm lens and ASA 64 film – but to make the best of it, the camera was rested on a table and the shot taken at 1/60 sec at full aperture.

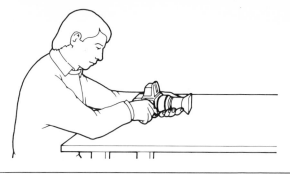

Fast film, fast lens The light level in this Indian carpet factory was low, but still sufficient for candid photography. ASA 200 film was uprated to ASA 300, to be 'push-processed' by the laboratory. With limited daylight from an open doorway, the shot was taken at 1/60 sec at f3.5, using an f2.8 180mm lens on a 35mm SLR camera. With hand-held photography in poor light, aperture and shutter speeds are nearly always close to the limits. For push-processing see pages 38–39 and 52–53.

Bracing the camera for a long-focus shot This photograph of a Thai dancer in Bangkok's Lakmuang temple was taken with a 400mm lens on a 35mm SLR camera, the long focal length being necessary for a close view. Even though 1/60 sec was just fast enough to prevent blurring during a split-second pause in the dance, it was still too slow for a handheld exposure. Using a jacket to prevent damage, the camera was jammed against a pillar, pressing hard to hold it steady. The exposure given was 1/60 sec at f5.6 on ASA 400 film up-rated by one stop to ASA 800.

Unobserved close-ups with a wide-angle lens The two virtues of wide-angle lenses in candid photography are that their great depth of field makes precise focusing unnecessary and that the wide angle of view makes it easy to line up the shot without looking through the viewfinder. This photograph taken in a Brazilian café used both techniques to avoid disturbing the subject. The camera, a Hasselblad SWC with a 38mm lens, was simply placed on the table, pointed roughly towards the subject, and the focus set approximately by the engraved scale on the lens. In this type of situation, take the exposure reading from another part of the room. In these circumstances, of course, an automatic camera can be useful.

Shooting from a car window Another useful camera support, particularly for photographing into doorways, is a car. This shot of a Hong Kong barber at work was taken with a 400mm lens on a 35mm SLR from the window of a taxi in heavy traffic. The exposure calculation in this situation is usually straightforward, as the interior is frontally lit by daylight through the doorway. Be careful, however, to avoid flare from sunlit walls on the outside. For a steady shooting position, wind the window up to a comfortable height and place the lens on a folded jacket or other soft object to cushion it from engine vibrations. Alternatively, switch the motor off temporarily.

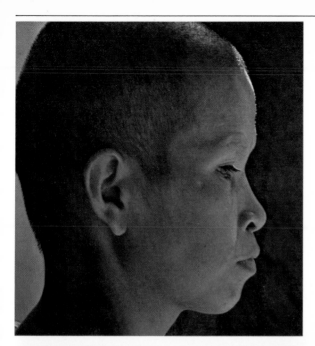

Candid photography from a tripod Although a tripod may seem an unlikely aid for quick-shooting candid work, there are situations where it is invaluable. First, it allows long-focus lenses to be used without fear of camera shake. Secondly, having set up the camera, you can take the shot while looking away, for a camera on its own is much less obtrusive than when a photographer is peering through it. This Buddhist nun, sitting motionless inside the doorway of a temple was an ideal subject for this technique. The exposure was 1/30 sec at f5.6 on ASA 64 film. Speeds between about one second and 1/60 sec need special care with a long lens used with an SLR camera even on a tripod – unless the tripod is very heavy, the mirror action can cause shake, and it is better to lock it up before shooting if the camera has this facility.

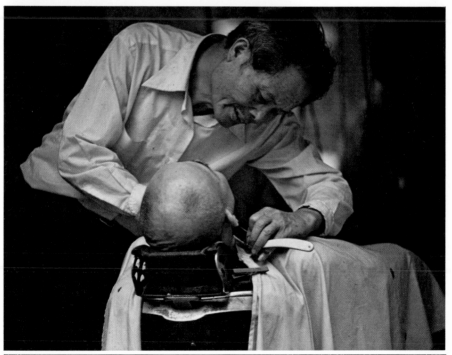

Candid shots by available light 1

Available artificial light sets greater problems for candid photography than daylight, partly because the light levels are generally lower, and also because different colour temperatures and casts need to be balanced. This is dealt with more fully elsewhere (see pages 112–117), but the difficulties in candid work are most severe. There is no possibility of using time exposures to cope with poor light, and colour imbalance is more noticeable with skin tones, to the extent that it is more objectionable than with any other type of subject matter.

Fast, up-rated tungsten film Faces and hands are less acceptable when bathed in unnatural colour than virtually any other subject. To photograph people indoors by tungsten light, daylight film is rarely acceptable without filters. Choose 3,200K tungsten-balanced film if possible, or add an 80B or 80C blue filter if you have to use daylight film. Fine-tuning the colour temperature is often not necessary in candid work, where subject interest takes precedent over technical perfection – the main priority is to capture the moment. Calculating the variance between domestic lamps and the 3,200K film is time-consuming, as is fitting filters. In this photograph of a ceremony given by the Lord Mayor of London, tungsten film was used unfiltered. The result is acceptable, although

an 82A filter would have taken the excessive warmth out of the scene. The light level was low, and to be able to use minimum speeds and maximum aperture (1/30 sec at f3.5 was the exposure), the film was up-rated from ASA 160 to ASA 320, later to be over-developed by one stop by the laboratory (see pages 38–39). Two other useful techniques were also employed. A 20mm wide-angle lens was used, not only to give good coverage of the room, but also to allow a slow shutter speed without camera shake (see pages 56–57). In addition, the shot was composed to prevent prominent light sources from appearing in the frame, keeping the contrast range in the scene down – an important consideration as the deliberate over-development of the film would raise contrast.

Tripod-mounted long lens The advantages of a steady camera platform – the possibility of using slow shutter speeds or very long-focus lens – can be employed even in tungsten-lit interiors by waiting for pauses in movement. Photographing from a gallery, a 400mm lens was used, with one second exposure at f5.6. The film was daylight ASA 400, reduced to a rating of ASA 200 with a tungsten-balancing 80C filter. At this slow speed, not only was a tripod essential, but the shots had to be timed to coincide with moments when the subjects were not moving. With this technique, provided the camera is securely locked down on the tripod, and the surroundings appear sharp, a slight movement – of a hand, for example – is acceptable.

Fast wide-angle lens Another City of London Ceremony, this time a traditional assay of the year's coinage at Goldsmiths' Hall. Here, there was less action and more time for shooting than at the event on the opposite page, and a more normal focal length lens could be used. An advantage of medium focal lengths – lenses of between about 35mm and 80mm on a 35mm camera – is that they can be manufactured with wide maximum apertures. The f1.4 35mm lens used in this shot is particularly good for low light levels. Wider maximum apertures are available on lenses with slightly longer focal lengths, but the avoidance of camera shake with the wide-angle lens allows for a slower shutter speed to produce the same result. This shot was exposed at 1/30 sec and f1.4 on ASA 160 film. An unavoidable feature of all fast lenses is very shallow depth of field. Stopping down, of course, simply cancels the advantage of great light-gathering power.

Shooting quickly with a wide-angle lens In some situations, as in this Hindu temple in Benares, the only way of taking a candid photograph is to keep the camera concealed until the very last moment and then rely on one correct exposure. As soon as this shot was taken, the boy looked up, and the moment was lost. With this kind of photograph, two valuable aids are a wide-angle lens, which has a depth of field great enough to be used without the delay of accurate focusing, and fast black-and-white film (here ASA 400) that allows a shutter speed high enough to remove the danger of camera shake.

Using the wide latitude of black-and-white film Because black-and-white negative film has so much more latitude than colour transparency film (see pages 16–17), it is much easier to use in lighting conditions that have a high contrast range. The interior of this South American village store was lit only by daylight through the doorway, and the range of contrast shooting towards the light was extremely high. A tonal range that would have been impossible to record on colour reversal film was just managed in black-and-white, with the help of a little shading and printing-in during enlargement (see pages 86–87).

Open interiors from outside
This family was sitting at the
entrance to their hut. The interior
was unlit and the only
illumination was therefore frontal
– the diffused light from an
overcast sky. Although this type
of lighting is actually quite flat,
the darkness of the room behind
gave the photograph a high
contrast range, and a considerable
amount of shading was needed
to balance the tones and make an
acceptable print.

High speed film for dim light
The light level in the Buddhist
temple where this monk was
praying was too low for most
emulsions – a speed slower than
the 1/60 sec used here would
have resulted in a blurred image.
So, a fast (ASA 400) black-and-
white film was used, uprated to
ASA 1,200 (see pages 52–53).
Development time and
temperature were increased to
compensate for the reduced
exposure.

Fluorescent light Finding the correct level of filtration is the main concern when dealing with fluorescent lighting. In the case of this shot of the London Stock Exchange, CC30 Magenta gave the correct result. This typical filtration needs an extra half stop exposure. Apart from colour balance, fluorescent light is normally quite easy to work with The overall light level is usually higher than with tungsten lighting, and the long strip lamps give a more diffused, natural lighting. For this photograph a relatively slow film, ASA 64, was used as fine grain was preferred to a high shutter spped. To convey the bustle of activity, some blurred movement was deliberately looked for. The exposure, following the centre-weighted TTL reading, was 1/15 sec at f3.5, using a 180mm lens on a tripod from a gallery.

Spotlight This peepshow was illuminated by a display spotlight in an otherwise dark hall. This kind of light gives harsh contrast and is difficult to expose effectively. It is generally ill-suited to photographing people, and shots must be composed principally out of highlights, as this is. The curved edge of the machine and its viewing hood were just enough to convey its function. When the boy was in the right position, with some of the light falling on his face, the shot was taken. Exposure was calculated for the highlights at one stop less than the shadow-influenced TTL reading but on tungsten-balanced film up-rated two stops to ASA 640. The shutter speed was 1/60 sec at f2.8, with a 180mm lens.

Stage lighting Lighting at rock concerts is composed largely of strong spotlights covered with coloured acetate. Typically, the main lighting is actually 'effects lighting', from fixed 1,000 watt lamps hung from a bar or truss above and behind the stage. These give colour and shape. A second set of lights, on towers at the sides of the stage, give fill-in, while a follow-spot is used for solo performances. All the lighting is designed for high contrast. Although light intensity varies throughout the show, the important thing to remember is that these lights are designed for effect rather than even illumination, and this allows for considerable latitude with the exposure. For the same reason, colour balance is unimportant. The on-stage photograph was taken at 1/60 sec at f4.5 with a 38mm wide-angle 6×6cm camera, the close-up at 1/60 sec and f5.6 with a 250mm lens from a tripod, also on 6×6. Tungsten-balanced film was used, up-rated to ASA 4,000. As a result, extreme over-development seriously weakened the shadow areas, but with such garish lighting the effect is acceptable.

Available light portraits 1

Portraiture can be formal or casual and, even when carefully planned and staged, does not necessarily need either a studio or special lighting. Although using available light indoors often presents problems, principally resulting from weak intensity and high contrast, these can usually be overcome by placing the subject and the camera carefully. The supreme advantage of available light is its natural appearance, but it can also help with shy subjects, who might be made nervous by having to pose in an elaborate lighting set-up.

Against the light Deliberately exploiting the flare and contrast from a window, this arranged portrait uses highlights to create strong shapes. The downward camera angle of a 38mm Hasselblad SWC, positioned diagonally to the desk, distorts the window, desk-top and books dramatically. As with the spotlight photograph on page 132, only the highlit areas are effective in the composition. In these circumstances, a useful technique is to angle bright and reflective surfaces so that they catch the light. The exposure of 1/4 sec at f11 on ASA 160 film was based on an incident reading pointing towards the window from the subject's position.

Diffuse daylight for close-up portraits The soft light from an open doorway or window that is not directly lit by the sun is ideal for head-and-shoulders portraiture. Indeed, a great deal of effort in studio work is put into reproducing this effect with flash units. Directional but diffuse, such light always gives good modelling, with moderate contrast and softened shadow edges. The easiest and most reliable direction is three-quarter frontal – to one side and slightly behind the camera, as in these two photographs. With cross-lighting, the contrast in the face may be higher. To reduce it, place a white card, sheet or other bright surface close to the shadowed side to act as a fill-in light source.

A broad light for group shots With groups of people indoors, the main problem is to light all the participants evenly. From the middle of a room, a window is a small source of light for a large subject, giving high contrast. One simple answer is to move the group right up to the largest window you can find. Not only does this spread the illumination, but it allows faster shutter speeds to be used. While single subjects can be persuaded to stay fairly still, one member of a group always seems to be moving. With a 35mm f1.4 lens, this shot was taken at 1/60 sec and f8 on ASA 200 film, as indicated by the TTL reading. The net curtains gave a welcome extra diffusion to the light coming from the window.

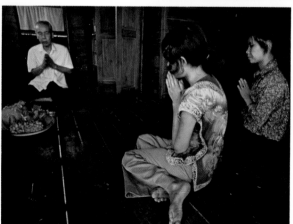

Using contrast in the subject To keep the composition clear and well-defined, look for a camera angle that sets the subject against a contrasting background. Most domestic interiors are cluttered, and can, without care, make a confusing setting that distracts attention from the sitter. This shot, of a Thai grandfather giving a family blessing on his birthday, owes its simplicity to the contrast between the three people and a plain dark background. Although the frontal lighting from an open doorway behind the camera was quite flat, the contrast in the image is high. With a 20mm wide-angle lens, the exposure was 1/15 sec at f4 on ASA 64 film, based on the incident light reading (see pages 18-19) from the position of the nearest figure.

Using room lights to lower contrast In the house of an elderly couple living just below the Acropolis in Athens, the only daylight came from a small doorway and window to the left. To balance the fall-off in light towards the middle of the room, the ceiling light — a plain tungsten bulb — was switched on. Despite the mixture of colours, including daylight, green-reflecting walls and orange tungsten, the overall effect is successful and balanced in tone.

Colour balance with mixed lighting As a general technique, switching on tungsten room lights is useful to strengthen the background of an interior, even when the lamps do not add much to the level of illumination. The entire setting was important for this portrait of London's Lord Mayor and his private secretary, and available light was easier to work with than elaborate lighting. The balance of tungsten to daylight was so even that the choice of film type was not certain. In practice, both were used, and each in its own way produced satisfactory results, despite the difference in colour.

Tungsten-balanced film

Daylight-balanced film

Portable flash for portraits

The outstanding difficulty with portable flash in portraiture is the small size of the flash head. A small light source gives harsh lighting, with a high contrast between the lit and shadow areas, and hard edges to the shadows. None of this suits the human face, and if the flash unit is used from the most convenient position on top of the camera, there is a likelihood of the effect known as 'red-eye', where the light reflects straight back from the eye's retina, tinged red.

If available light is insufficient, and if a small portable unit is the only light source to hand, the first thing to do is to diffuse it. There are two ways of achieving this: aiming it through a translucent material, or bouncing the light off a large white reflector, such as a wall or ceiling (see pages 24–25). Any form of diffusion reduces the light intensity by an amount that is difficult to calculate without a flash meter.

Automatic flash guns that have transistor circuits, and in particular integrated units, automatically compensate for the light loss, provided the flash's sensor can point independently at the subject even if the head is directed differently. There is a danger, however, that light bounced off a ceiling will be so weak that even the maximum output will be insufficient for the chosen aperture. If the flash unit offers a choice of recommended apertures, use the widest.

Despite the convenience of automatic flash, the best method is undoubtedly to use the full flash output by switching to manual. If this is not possible with your flash unit, tape over the sensor. The aperture should then be set by measuring the light with a flash meter – an essential piece of equipment if you use flash frequently. This instrument removes guesswork and gives the control you should be aiming for.

Bounced flash from a ceiling For this shot, a single flash unit was aimed at the ceiling, diffusing the light sufficiently to give a moderate spread of light over the table and diners. Diffuse lighting was particularly desirable in order to cover the field of view of the wide-angle lens. The aperture setting was calculated with a flash meter.

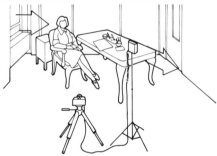

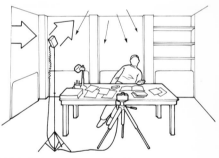

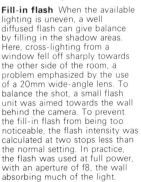

Fill-in flash When the available lighting is uneven, a well diffused flash can give balance by filling in the shadow areas. Here, cross-lighting from a window fell off sharply towards the other side of the room, a problem emphasized by the use of a 20mm wide-angle lens. To balance the shot, a small flash unit was aimed towards the wall behind the camera. To prevent the fill-in flash from being too noticeable, the flash intensity was calculated at two stops less than the normal setting. In practice, the flash was used at full power, with an aperture of f8, the wall absorbing much of the light.

Fill-in flash was also used in this shot, to give a muted lighting balance. The flash was bounced off the ceiling, and used at half-power to prevent it from being obvious. In both the photographs on this page, the existing light was nearly adequate, and the function of the flash was to give a slight correction. The use of fill-in flash is often tempting, but should be treated with care as it can destroy a natural atmosphere.

Location lighting for portraits

At the other end of the scale from casual, available light portraits are those which, although in a location, are precisely organized, with all the lighting introduced according to a predetermined plan. This may be necessary to achieve a particular desired effect, or simply to have the complete control required for near-perfect results. In effect, the location, whether office, laboratory or study, substitutes for a complete studio.

Mixed tungsten and flash For this portrait of a remarkable scholar, the detail and atmosphere of the room in which she worked was important. The lamps and yellowing wallpaper contributed to the atmosphere, but their illumination alone was insufficient and their colour temperature unreliable. Because of this, a well defined 750 Joule (watt-second) flash provided the main light, while the room lamps and a 400 Joule flash bounced off the yellow ceiling provided fill-in, particularly over the desk. To relieve the dark carpet area at the lower left, some of the scattered papers were redistributed, and a table lamp placed on the floor at the left but out of the camera's view. The main light at left was flagged from the camera, which was used with a fast wide-angle lens. The film was chosen with colour balance to match the flash, the room lights being allowed to give a distinctly warm fill-in.
Lights: 750 Joule flash through diffuser, with fill-in from 400 Joule bounced flash and domestic tungsten.
Film: Ektachrome daylight ASA 64
Lens: 90mm Super Angulon on a 4 x 5 in view camera.
Exposure: Two seconds (for room lights) at f16, with CC05 Red and CC05 Yellow filters for colour correction.

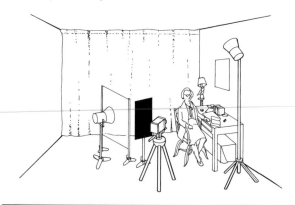

Studio flash for precision The subject here was a scientist at the University of Virginia with a highly sophisticated piece of equipment designed to test a theory of matter creation. Because the equipment had to be prominent, it determined the lighting position. The scale was small, so a single flash head was powerful enough. This allowed for complete colour accuracy, for while different exposure times on tungsten film cause slight colour shifts, a good studio flash unit is consistent. To illuminate the apparatus evenly, a diffused window-light was aimed horizontally and positioned so that there would be no reflections on the glass around the central rod. This lighting was also correct for the scientist. A black velvet backdrop removed distractions. The illuminated digital display in the foreground, actually on a recorder that could not be moved into shot, was photographed separately with a time exposure in the darkened laboratory. A second exposure added it to the first image, being correctly positioned because the composition had been lightly sketched on the 4×5in view camera's ground glass screen.
Lights: 1×750 Joule flash with window diffuser, full power
Film: Ektachrome daylight ASA 64
Lens: 90mm Super Angulon on a 4×5in view camera
Exposure: a) Main shot: f22, with CC10 Yellow and CC05 Red filers
b) Digital display: 7 secs at f8, with CC10 Blue and CC05 Red filters

Studio portraits

Lighting is only one element in portraiture: how important a part it plays depending on the aim of the photograph. In a beauty shot lighting is the critical factor, but in trying to convey character it may be subsidiary to other factors, such as the rapport between photographer and subject.

The basic configuration of the human face dictates some standard principles of lighting, but rigidly laid-down rules are not necessary. One or several lights can be used to achieve different desired effects. A standard, flexible set-up is illustrated below. A moderately diffused main light gives the principle illumination, and is responsible for the basic modelling. A fill-in light or large reflector reduces contrast and lightens shadows, whilst the lower chin, under-side of the nose and eye-sockets can be filled in even more by having the subject hold a crump-led silver foil reflector. The background can be separately lit if required, and a narrowly directed 'effects light', normally well behind the subject, can be used to pick out highlights in hair or to brighten the outline of the head and shoulders. All the suggested positions of the lights or reflectors can be changed as necessary. Over the next few pages, some of the many permutations of lights, diffuser attachments and reflectors are illustrated and described.

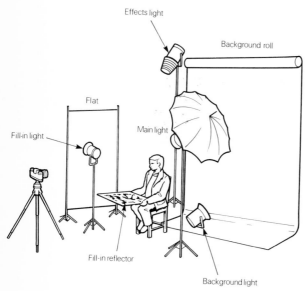

Effects light

Background roll

Flat

Main light

Fill-in light

Fill-in reflector

Background light

Portrait lighting A typical lighting set-up for head-and-shoulders portraiture uses an umbrella as the main light, and fill-in from a second light bounced off a large white board known as a 'flat'. Polystyrene or styrofoam board is often used. An effects light, high and behind the subject is fitted with a 'snoot' to concentrate the beam on a small area. Finally, a background light is placed on the floor, pointing diagonally upwards towards a wide seamless roll of background paper for a graduated effect.

Portrait lighting The shape of the human face determines to a great extent the way lighting is used in portraiture. The approach will depend on the result intended — a soft beauty shot or a vigorous portrait, for example — but some principles must always be observed. Lighting can additionally be used to strengthen the best features of a face, and play down those which are unattractive. Such decisions must be taken in relation to the circumstances — the lighting being built up and modified as you go along.

Hair The hair looks best when at least partly backlit, giving it life and sparkle.

Forehead Unless shadowed by the hair, the slope of the forehead can reflect strong lighting and appear over-exposed. Diffused lighting reduces this problem.

Eyes The sockets often need extensive fill-in to prevent them looking like deep pits.

Ears If the model has unusually large ears, only altering the pose will help. A three-quarter view will be better than straight on.

Nose There are no particular problems with lighting the nose, although it may be necessary to prevent it looking too prominent. Hard cross-lighting will cast a shadow and accentuate the nose unpleasantly. Lighting which makes it less obvious will be more effective.

Chin Because the chin can cast a hard shadow with the overhead lighting which is best for other features, a crumpled foil reflector placed beneath it is generally an effective source of fill-in.

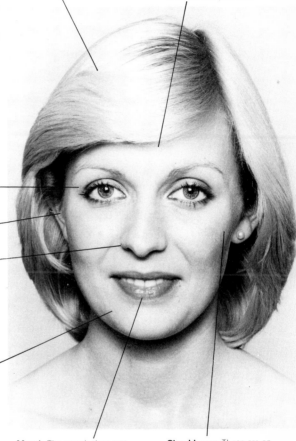

Mouth The mouth does not generally cause lighting problems. But be careful with red lipstick, which will look very dark on black-and-white film and may also be more prominent than intended in colour.

Cheekbones These are an important feature in photographic portraits. Strong, high cheekbones are particularly photogenic.

Calculating exposure
Because studio lighting can be varied infinitely in its position, quality and intensity, most exposure problems, such as contrast, can be overcome by adjusting the lighting arrangement. Incident light readings, whether you are using flash or continous lighting are much more reliable than reflected readings. They are not affected by differences in skin tone or background. Point the meter, fitted with a diffusing dome or disc, towards the camera for average readings. This is the best method for most situations.

Portrait lighting: diffused window light

Set up the studio lighting to suit the subject's face and the particular effect you want to create, not to fit preconceived rules. The permutations here and on the following pages show the basic alternatives.

One main light source is nearly always preferable to several: it is simpler and there is no danger of multiple shadows. Position this light first. Frontal lighting gives smaller shadows and less contrast. Top three-quarters is a good basic position for many situations.

The light source here is a diffused window light, directional but with slightly softened edges to the shadows. It gives less rounded modelling than an umbrella, and is therefore less frequently used, but it is less harsh than a spot. Compare the effects with pages 148–149.

Fill-in reduces contrast by lightening shadows. If a fill-in light is used, it is usually diffused to avoid secondary shadows. White or silvered reflectors give gentler fill-in.

Although the main light may serve to illuminate the background as well, an independent background light can be used. It can add depth to the picture, or fill unwanted shadows cast by the main light.

An effects light is sometimes used to highlight an area of special interest, such as the hair. To avoid an over-complicated result, use with discretion, if at all.

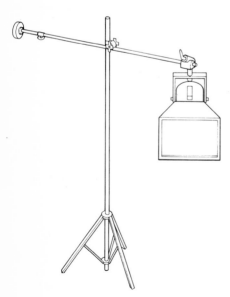

Front   Top front

No fill-in

Fill-in reflection

Fill-in light

Fill-in light and background light

Fill-in light and effect light

144

Top   Top three quarters   Side   Side/back

Portrait lighting: umbrellas

An umbrella gives a more diffuse, and generally more flattering light than a window light. It is less directional, however, and stray light is more difficult to control. A plain white cloth umbrella gives more diffused light than a silvered one, but the light will be slightly less intense. A black outer covering minimizes the risk of lens flare. Alternatively, most white umbrellas can also be used with- the light directed through them, which allows the lighting to be brought closer to the subject.

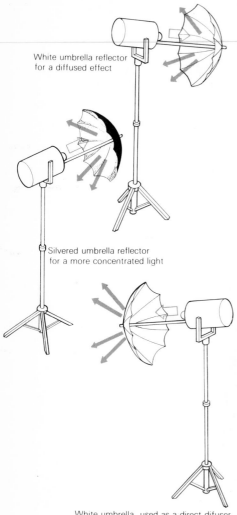

White umbrella reflector for a diffused effect

Silvered umbrella reflector for a more concentrated light

White umbrella, used as a direct diffuser.

Front   Top front

No fill-in

Fill-in reflection

Fill-in light

Fill-in light and background light

Fill-in light and effect light

Top   Top three quarters   Side   Side/back

Portrait lighting: spot light

The harshest type of studio lighting is a naked spot, normally used with a small dish reflector to concentrate the light. Although unflattering for normal portraiture, it can be used to obtain special results.

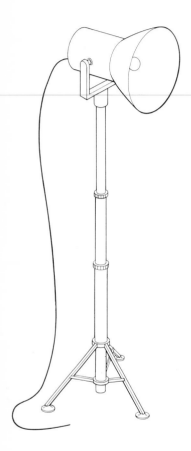

Front

Top front

No fill-in

Fill-in reflection

Fill-in light

Fill-in light and background light

Fill-in light and effect light

Top　　　　　Top three quarters　　　　Side　　　　　Side/back

Full length portrait lighting

Full length shots not only need more working space than head and shoulders portraits but also larger light sources. The main consideration is achieving even lighting from head to feet, well diffused to avoid hard shadows. The ideal light would be slightly larger than a standing person, directional to give some control over the background and well diffused iveou standard set-ups are shown here for the main lighting. Backgrounds are usually lit separately, although it is also possible to use the main light to give graduated background illumination.

Fully lit subject and background Here, a large single umbrella provided the main lighting. Fill-in came from a flat (reflector) placed close to the subject. A large white background was needed so that the photograph could be run as a magazine spread with type printed over.

Swimming pool This is a large, expensive and specialized light (see page 21). It has a high output, is diffused yet directional, and is ideal for full-length portraits.

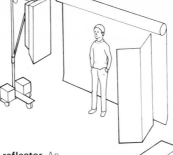

Boxed reflector An inexpensive substitute for a large area light, this can be made of wood or polystyrene (styrofoam), and resembles a walk-in cupboard. Painted white inside, it gives diffuse, directional lighting.

Large umbrellas These give a diffuse but largely uncontrolled light – a standard, uncomplicated approach, but one that gives little opportunity for subtle effects, and light inevitably spills into the background. These lights must be flagged off from the camera.

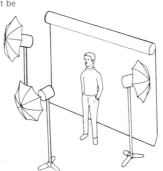

Even background lighting with strips To illuminate a background roll with no variations of tone, the ideal lights are two strips, shaped like narrow troughs, each fitted with translucent perspex (plexiglass) for even distribution. Just as in copying (see pages 206–207), aim each at the opposite edge of the background to avoid creating a hot spot. A single barn door fitted to the camera side of each strip prevents light spilling onto the subject. A similar effect is possible with four normal lamps, one close to each corner, but positioning them correctly takes longer.

Trace frame Gives a diffuse, shaped light, but the lamps themselves need to be flagged off from the camera and background.

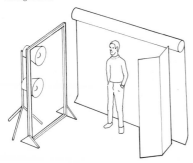

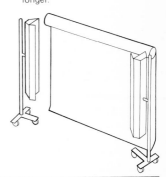

Special portrait lighting

In addition to the more straightforward permutations of lighting, there is an occasional need for special techniques to create a specific effect or to overcome particular problems. Some, such as front projection, are complex and must be used within a quite strictly determined framework. Others, such as the backlit shot of the drinker on this page, have to be constructed entirely in accordance with the immediate needs of the situation.

Silhouette To achieve a silhouette, with little or no detail visible on the camera side of the subject, the set must be strongly backlit. Here, to illustrate a magazine article on alcoholism, a silhouette was used to play on the standard interview treatment of anonymity. Translucent blinds diffused daylight from a full length window, and black card was used on either side to absorb reflected light.

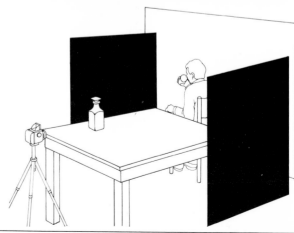

Front projection is virtually the only method of imitating a location shot in the studio with any semblance of realism. Even so, the problems of matching lenses, backgrounds and subjects, and above all the lighting restrictions, make it extremely difficult to create a believable imitation of a location. The principle is to project a transparency onto a special screen by means of a precisely angled half-silvered mirror. This mirror makes it possible to project along the axis of the camera lens. As the screen is covered with densely packed, minute glass spheres, which reflect light very efficiently back in the precise direction it came from, an even and extremely bright image of the transparency can be seen by the camera. The screen is so much more efficient at reflecting the projected transparency than the model's skin or clothes that a short exposure can be made, with the background appearing only on the screen.

The subject must be lit separately, but great care has to be taken not to let light spill onto the screen and so degrade the background image. As the purpose of the studio lighting is to imitate the lighting of the background scene, frontally lit views are generally unsuitable. Side lit scenes are best. A honeycomb grill over the area lights gives the useful combination of diffusion without spill. An unnatural edge effect around the subject is usually unavoidable.

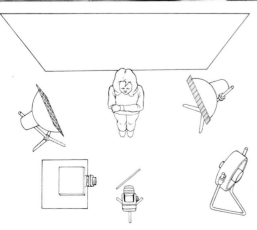

Make up and beauty 1

Make-up for photography is usually more pronounced than worn everyday, although how much more is used will depend chiefly on the lighting – a well-diffused light needs stronger make-up than a spotlight. Standard photographic make-up is used to enhance the best features of a face and suppress the less attractive ones. Definite cheekbones, for example, can be made even more striking with highlights above and darker make-up below, whilst close-set eyes can be made to seem further apart by extending eye shadow outwards.

Decide at the beginning on the purpose of a particular make-up rather than starting aimlessly. Always towards a deliberate result, in relation to the factors discussed below.

The model Each individual face benefits from certain specific make-up techniques, and most models know which effects suit them best. Professional models, by nature of their job, rarely have 'problem' faces. If you are choosing someone for a beauty shot, look for the following: fine bone structure, a balanced facial outline with small chin, unblemished complexion, unobtrusive and straight nose, eyes set fairly wide apart. Skin blemishes can be concealed by strong foundation make-up and well diffused lighting.

Lighting The more diffuse the light, the stronger the make-up should be. Conversely, a bright spotlight, giving hard-edged and deep shadows, calls for more restrained, even bland make-up. Axial lighting (that is completely frontal, from the position of the lens as with a ring-light) is flat and shadowless even without diffusion, and so needs the strongest make-up of all.

Colour or black-and-white With colour film there are no special precautions to take, although some types record certain colours more accurately than others (see pages 34-35). Black-and-white films, however, are overly sensitive to red, causing some lipsticks to seem much darker than they are. Either use an orange filter for a more natural rendering in black-and-white or use brown lipstick and shadow. An orange filter will also reduce spots and other red blemishes with black-and-white film. If they are very prominent use a red filter.

The desired effect Most beauty shots are intended to show a conventionally attractive result, but occasionally the effect may be deliberately unusual. Even with a straightforward approach, you should decide between a casual fresh appearance and formal elegance.

The Right Lens

The longer the focal length, the better the proportions of a face appear. A lens with a focal length the same as the diagonal of the film format – around 50mm on a 35mm camera or 80mm on 6×6cm format – used close enough for the model's face to fill the picture causes too much distortion, making the nose and chin seem too large. Very long focal lengths, such as 300mm on a 35mm camera, give very good proportions, but are usually inconvenient because they have to be used from a distance and need to be set at a small aperture to give sufficient depth of field. The compromise generally accepted to be the most satisfactory is 105mm on a 35mm camera and 150mm on 6×6cm. Details are, in effect, close-up shots, and invariably need supplementary lenses or better, extensions (see pages 196-203). So as not to interfere with the lighting, use a long focal length for such details – a 200mm lens for 35mm cameras or 250mm for 6×6cm are good.

50mm lens

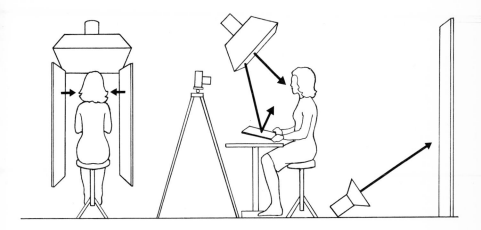

Standard Beauty Lighting

This basic lighting arrangement aims for a moderately directional effect with a great deal of fill-in. To eliminate heavy shadows. The position of the lighting is important – overhead for naturalness, frontal to reduce shadows, and in line with the camera and face for symmetry. Ample diffusion makes the edges of shadow barely discernible and gives an even distribution of light. Fill-in reflection from the sides can be adjusted by using white polystyrene (styrofoam) reflectors or sheets of white card. To light up the neck and the underside of chin and nose, the model can hold a foil-covered reflector. While the make-up is being applied, move the reflectors away and the light higher for convenience, making the final lighting adjustments after the model is made-up and dressed.

l05mm lens

200mm lens

Make-up application Make-up for photography has to take into account four factors: the model's face, lighting, film and the general style wanted for the shot. For models with a good bone structure and complexion, make-up is used to enhance the best features but it can be used to overcome problems. A broad jaw or weak cheek bones, for example, can be improved by shading the lower face, or eyes that are set close together can be widened by extending their shading outwards. A poor complexion can be smoothed with foundation and powder.

Always apply make-up under lighting the same as will be used for the photography. The highlights and shadows can then be matched to the illumination. When using black-and-white film, which is overly sensitive to red, use this colour sparingly or substitute brown make-up. Alternatively, use a red filter — it will also reduce the appearance of skin blemishes.

Finally, apply make-up with a specific effect in mind. Here, for example, the result is deliberately sophisticated rather than natural.

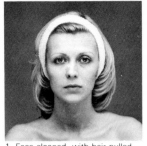

1. Face cleaned, with hair pulled back in preparation.

2. Apply foundation with a sponge to give basic colour and smooth surface.

6. Apply shading under cheek bones to give shape.

7. Powder the face to set the foundation.

11. Apply eye highlights.

12. Define edges with eyeliner.

13. Apply mascara to finish eyes.

15. Apply blusher.

16. Define shape of lips with liner.

17. Apply lipstick.

3. Foundation completed.

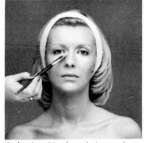

4. Apply white foundation under eyes.

5. Under-eye foundation completed.

8. Brush off excess powder.

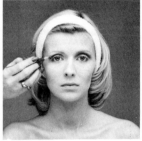

9. Pencil in eyelids.

10. Pencil under eyes.

14. Pencil in eyebrows.

18. Use lip gloss to give sparkle, if required.

19. The finished make-up with hair arranged and jewellery worn.

Still-life and props

Still-life photography is probably the most demanding of all studio work, and its standards, set largely by magazine and poster advertising, are extremely high. Because there is a great deal of time to consider, compose and prepare in most still-life sets, it is usually possible to achieve great precision.

Subjects vary enormously, from beer cans to flowers, and the original painterly definition, which embraced only living things plucked from their surroundings – *nature morte* – has long been superseded, particularly in the broader scope of the studio photographer. The limits are few: most subjects, though not all, are still but very few have seen life.

Even when a subject has been selected, the choices of setting, composition, camera angle and lighting are so open that it may be difficult to know where to start. For this reason, it is usually best to follow a set procedure, gradually refining down the possibilities until the whole set and lighting has been perfected. There is a very strong element of the constructed image in still-life photography, beginning with raw ingredients and slowly developing the final result. One example of a procedure is as follows:

1 Assemble props to go with the subject (see opposite).
2 Choose the background or setting (pages 162 to 167).
3 Make a first, casual arrangement, with the main subject prominent.
4 Try different lighting combinations until you find one that suits the set.

5 Position the camera.
6 Refine the composition.
7 Make final adjustments to the camera angle.
8 Refine the lighting.

Props Props are the basic material of still-life photography. They usually appear in a supporting role, establishing or setting off the main subject, but they can also be subjects in their own right, particularly when the purpose of the shot is to evoke a specific period or situation (see page 172). Prop hire companies exist wherever there is a television, film or photography industry, or where there are live theatres. Most carry a wide range of items, from the unusual to the everyday, although the condition of their stock, being geared mainly to film and television, is sometimes too poor for still photography, which reveals even the most minor imperfections.

Other sources of props are antique dealers and street markets. By offering a deposit to the full value of the item, you can usually find a dealer who is willing to hire to you, even if it is not normal practice. Many props are inexpensive enough to buy outright and most studio photographers have a small stock of interesting or useful props. A slab of marble and a butcher's chopping board, for instance, have obvious value to a food photographer. Props that have general uses, like those shown on the opposite page, are often useful for illustrative still-life shots. Props are so important that professional stylists are often used in advertising work, particularly when there is little time.

Glassware Items from a small collection of old bottles and glass jars can be drawn on to establish a period atmosphere, even if the piece of glass is used only as a prop and not as the main subject. The old bottle used in a food shot, for example, would suggest traditional, country cooking – particularly when combined with a suitable setting, dark wood surfaces and simple pottery.

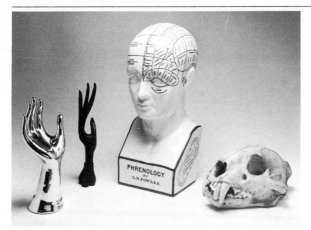

Expressive objects Some miscellaneous objects, quite different in their various origins, seem to have particularly expressive potential when incorporated in still-life shots. The phrenology head, skull and ring stands illustrated here are good examples. The photographer should try to develop the ability to spot such possibilities.

Suggesting activity Some everyday objects, whether contemporary or old as here, can immediately imply that the still-life is a casual arrangement of objects just put down in the middle of some action. An open fountain pen, for example, suggests a letter has just been written. A magnifying glass suggests something has just been examined.

Nostalgia Some historic items have the character of relics of the past. The objects shown here could all have been personal gifts and in a still-life would give the arrangement a nostalgic appeal.

Scale models

Scale models are an essential part of professional still-life work, particularly where photography is used to illustrate ideas and concepts that lack obvious visual elements. Models are used in a number of ways. Often they are made to a scale that allows the photographer to juxtapose them with another object that will appear life-size (the photograph of car and safe on page 169 is an example). The modelling technique itself can become an important part of the shot, as with the bricks and the mouse on these pages. Most difficult of all is the use of models as perfect substitutes for the real thing,

which for any of a number of reasons may not be accessible.

Although scale model construction can be a highly specialized skill, doing it solely for still photography is easier and less exacting than usual. In most cases, the model is only intended to be viewed from one position, and provided that the camera angle is worked out beforehand, only the camera-facing side need be built, rather like street frontages on movie lots. Another time-saving advantage is that models for photography hardly ever need to be permanent, so that solid construction is not necessary.

Basic Materials Simple, inexpensive materials can be every bit as effective as custom-made kits and parts. To illustrate a magazine article on the subject of hoarding, white beans were used to symbolize hoarded food. To add interest, a mouse representing the hoarder was also built up from them. The basic shape of the mouse was made in modelling clay, the beans being placed one by one to cover the surface, the whole model taking about an hour to make.

Building symbols out of model parts The complex theme for this shot was international construction finance. To reduce this non-visual idea to a simple image, model bricks were built into a wall in the shape of pound sterling, dollar and franc signs. Construction time was 10 hours.

Altering scale to suit the subjects This magazine cover called for coins and a decrepit bank to be juxtaposed. By abandoning any attempt at realism, a model bank was built to the scale of the coins, using balsa wood, cardboard, and paper printed with bricks and tiles. It took five hours to build.

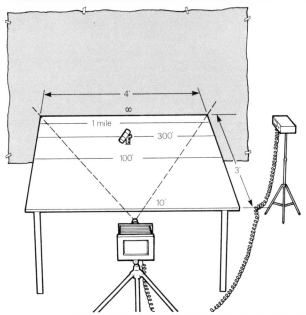

Imitating a full perspective scene There were only two possibilities for creating this fictional moonscape: expensive retouching or a model. With a board measuring four by three feet as a base, the shooting angle was chosen, and the camera locked down in position. The area covered by the lens was drawn on the base, as was the compressed distance scale, from infinity at the other side of the base to about ten feet nearest the camera. The landscape was then modelled in high alumina cement from a sculptors' supply shop. This is ideal because it can be given different textures by spraying or mixing with water. The view was constantly checked through the camera to make sure that the illusion of perspective remained accurate. Black velvet was hung for the background, and the earth and stars added later by double-exposure (see pages 186–191). The lens was stopped right down to its minimum, f64, for depth of field, and a small flash gun was used to give hard shadows.

Still-life backgrounds 1

Selecting the right background for a still-life shot can be as important as choosing other props or even the subject itself. Where the main subject is a single item or a small group of objects, the background may take up the largest area of the photograph. There are three categories of background: plain, complementary and setting. Plain backgrounds explain themselves – they are intended to be as unobtrusive as

Plain: white For the least texture, use either a slightly shiny surface, such as the white formica or flexible plastic sheeting used here, or a non-reflecting surface, such as white velvet. Coated paper and art board also have a fine texture and are acceptable for this purpose.

Plain: black For a completely black background, use a high quality cotton black velvet. Remove fluff and specks of dust with adhesive tape.

Complementary: cloth Not only can cloth be used for the texture of its basic material and weave, but folding can introduce a new textural element.

Complementary: textured paper Papers are available in a wide range of textures. This example was embossed in a lizard skin finish. To show off texture strongly, use backlight or light directed from a low angle.

possible, simply providing a colour or tone that shows off the subject clearly. Complementary backgrounds can enhance certain features of the subject and become an integral part of the shot, consisting of either matching or contrasting tones, textures, shapes or colours. Finally, settings are used to put a still-life subject in its context, and can give a more natural impression than shots very obviously taken in a studio. Many existing interiors make good settings, but their style and the objects they contain must reflect the nature of the subject itself.

Plain: graduated A carefully positioned area light, such as a window diffuser, and a smooth white surface, such as white formica, give the most easily controlled graduated tone.

Plain: backlit By separately lighting the background, a range of tones is possible. Bright lighting gives a plain white background.

Complementary: wood Wood grain can make a simple background when smooth, as here, or a more prominent one when rough.

Complementary: leather Leather surfaces are generally even, but with interesting detail in close up. This background was the cover of an old leather-bound book.

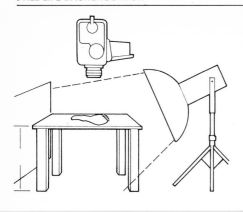

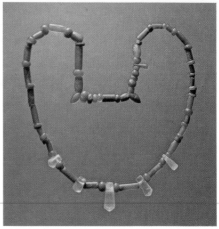

Plain: glass and coloured paper For an even, coloured background without shadows, place the subject on a flat sheet of glass, itself raised over a sheet of coloured paper. Arrange the light or lights to illuminate the subject and paper, taking care to keep the light at a low enough angle to prevent reflections from the glass. Alternatively, if the glass is raised high above the paper, subject and background can be lit separately.

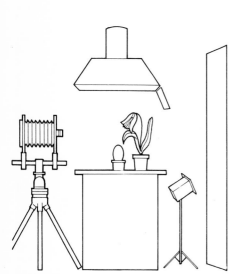

Plain: graduated colour By lighting a white background separately with coloured filters, great variety of tone and colour can be created. Here, the main white card background was shaded from the main light with a barn door (see page 22) and was lit with a small flash gun. A Wratten 58 Green filter was taped over the small flash, which was aimed from below to give a graduated effect. This method can be simpler and more economical than stocking different backgrounds.

Complementary: frontally-lit perspex Opaque coloured perspex (plexiglass) can give a variety of backgrounds, depending on how it is lit. Being reflective, it has a clean clinical appearance. When lit frontally, colour saturation is good, and reflections of light-coloured objects are picked up. Prevent specks of dust collecting with an anti-static brush.

Complementary: backlit perspex By positioning an area light further back so that it is reflected in the perspex (plexiglass), colour saturation is reduced, but reflections and contrast are increased.

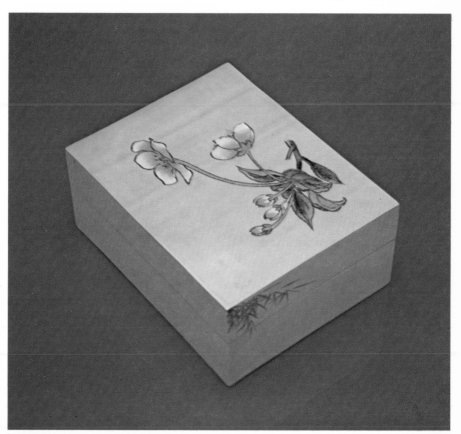

Complementary: stone The tactile quality of rough stone can often make a satisfactory contrast with smooth, well worked objects such as jewellery

Complementary: marble By usage, marble is usually associated with cool, elegant interiors, and with some aspects of cooking. A slab that is polished on one side and rough on the other side gives two types of background.

Complementary: water Water can be used as a continuous covering or, as here, in the form of droplets. The drops and their reflections can be arranged into patterns, and can make an unusual contrast for rough, solid objects.

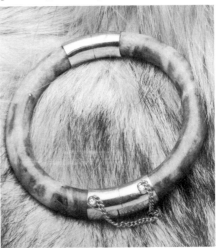

Complementary: fur For items of jewellery, fur (such as a coat) can be used fo suggest opulence and to show off hard, shiny surfaces by contrast.

Complementary: clothing Dresses and other garments can be used, particularly for jewellery and cosmetic shots.

Complementary: aggregates Large quantities of small, evenly-sized particles, such as sand, gravel, pebbles or even ball-bearings can be laid out to form a continuous background.

Settings: simple One or two uncomplicated props can convey atmosphere without being obtrusive. For these First World War greetings cards, an old plank and an army map case from the period were used.

Settings: full A more elaborate setting should attempt to remove the sense of the photographic studio, and establish the subject (in this case a book on herbal medicine) in context with a feeling for the atmosphere or period.

Diffusing light with still-life

Successful still-life photography hinges on precise control of lighting, and the most basic method of manipulating the light is to diffuse it. The raw light source, whether the head of a portable flash gun, a tungsten bulb or the coiled tube of a studio flash unit, is virtually a single point, and without modification will give high contrast and deep, hard-edged shadows. Using the diffusers and reflectors shown on pages 20–23, the quality of this light can be altered in infinitely fine stages. Adjusting the degree of diffusion to suit the subject depends partly on personal taste, and partly on the material qualities of the subject itself. It is the size of the light source in relation to the size of the subject that determines how diffused the lighting will appear. This can be controlled in two ways: by using a bigger or smaller light source, and by altering the distance at which you place it from the subject.

Basic diffused light There is no standard amount of diffusion – it depends on personal taste as much as the steadily changing fashions in still-life lighting. Even so, the degree of diffusion in this calligraphy still-life is moderate, with a two foot square window light illuminating a three foot by four foot area from a distance of about three feet. To preserve the rich colours in the set, particularly of the yellowed parchment, the light was positioned close to the camera. Any degree of backlighting would have de-saturated the colours. In addition, to give some life to the illuminated part of the parchment, a hand mirror was aimed to reflect a pool of light onto it.
Light: 750 Joule flash with window diffuser
Film: Ektachrome daylight ASA 64.
Lens: 150mm Symmar on a 4×5in (9×12cm) view camera
Exposure: f32

Pooled light With the light smaller or further away there is less diffusion. Shadows are denser and more definite, and contrast higher. Nevertheless, if the light is fitted with a diffusing head, there is still a marked difference between this and spotlighting, where the illumination is hard and focused. In this case, the lighting was used deliberately to emphasize contrast by not using fill-in lights or reflectors, and by push-processing (see pages 38–39).
Lights: 400 Joule flash with window diffuser
Film: Ektachrome daylight ASA 64
Lens: 150mm Symmar on a 4×5in (9×12cm) view camera
Exposure: f22, over-developed ½ stop

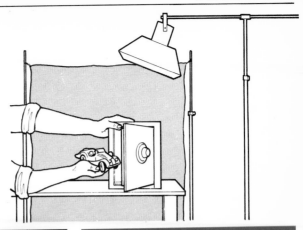

Enveloping light When the light is larger than the subject, and close, the diffusion is great. Shadows are very weak and their edges extremely soft, whilst overall contrast is fairly low.
Lights: 400 Joule flash with window diffuser
Film: Ektachrome daylight ASA 64
Lens: 150mm Symmar on a 4×5in (9×12cm) view camera
Exposure: f37

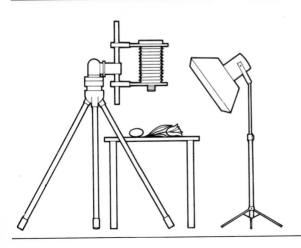

Positioning still-life lighting

The other principal control that you have over a light, after deciding the amount of diffusion, is direction. Of course, a light can be placed at any position in relation to the camera, through 360°. Some of the more unusual lighting positions are shown on the following pages. Here, however, the more subtle variations of a basic arrangement are illustrated. A single diffused window light over a curved sheet of white formica or flexible plastic – known as a scoop – is a

Slightly elevated camera With a window light directly overhead, this standard camera position gives a slight angle between the lens and light axes. The combination of directional window light and white scoop gives a tonal gradation from white foreground to very dark background. From this camera position the gradation falls near the top of the picture frame and is quite gradual. This tends to set off the subject quite well.

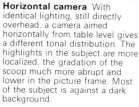

Lens axis

Light axis

Horizontal camera With identical lighting, still directly overhead, a camera aimed horizontally from table level gives a different tonal distribution. The highlights in the subject are more localized, the gradation of the scoop much more abrupt and lower in the picture frame. Most of the subject is against a dark background.

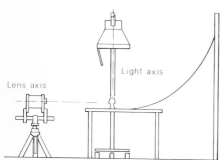

Light axis

Lens axis

standard arrangement for photographing single objects. What this lacks in originality and excitement is compensated for by simplicity and a generally pleasing distribution of tones. The shape of the scoop gives an impression of great depth, uncomplicated by edges or horizon lines. If a directional light, such as the window diffuser shown here, is used overhead, there is an even

gradation of tone from light to dark, which enhances the impression of depth and can contrast with the lighting on the subject, as the first two photographs show. Note that the white formica base acts as a natural reflector to an overhead light, relieving the shadows at the base of the subject. Paper or card can be used but wrinkles may interfere with the image.

High camera A high camera position from right next to the light results in more frontal illumination, showing detail more effectively.

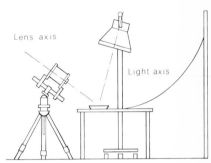

Side-lighting For vertical subjects, such as bottles or vases, a side light is usually most effective. Without the reflection from the white surface given by an overhead light, contrast is higher, and a reflector may have to be placed opposite the light. In the case of these three vases, however, no reflector was used to give an intentionally strong distribution of tones.

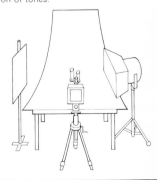

Still-life settings

In some cases, the context of a still-life is as important as the objects being shown. Carefully choosing the background or props can establish the period of the scene and increase the photograph's impact as an illustration — perhaps for a magazine article or a book jacket.

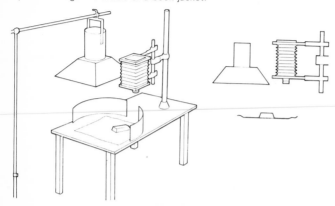

Illustrations as background Occasionally, artwork can be used to convey one of the elements in a shot, or simply to establish a particular atmosphere. Historical prints and paintings work very well in this way. The purpose of this photograph was to symbolize the beginnings of merchant banking. In common with many illustrative shots, it uses juxtaposition of two subjects. The small gold bar was naturally attractive, and to achieve a simple image, a print showing an early merchant ship in a tropical harbour was chosen. The lighting needed to reflect off the gold, and be even over the surface of the print. A single diffused window light was used, with curved white paper reflectors added to define the edges of the bar and balance the illumination.
Lights: 400 Joule flash with window diffuser
Film: Ektachrome daylight ASA 64
Lens: 150mm Symmar on 4×5in (9×12cm) view camera, at full extension, 220mm
Exposure: f19 with a CC10 Red filter

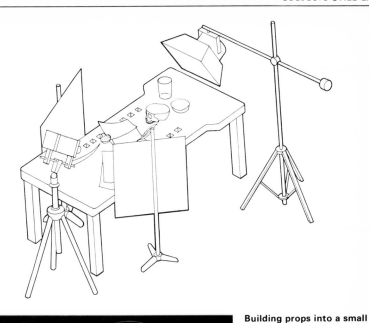

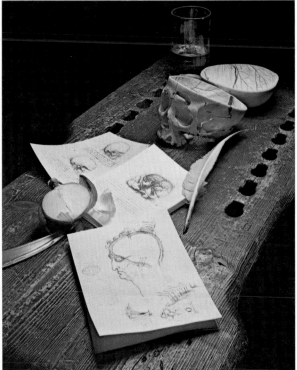

Building props into a small set Although the lighting was uncomplicated – a single window diffuser with white card reflectors – choosing and assembling the props was time-consuming. The shot was intended to illustrate Leonardo da Vinci's work on anatomy, so the content of the photography was most important. The drawings were chosen to include an element that would immediately suggest anatomy – a skull. Also, Leonardo's comparisons between the membranes covering the brain and the layers of an onion would be emphasized with more props. As it was not possible to use the originals, the drawings were photographed and printed on a textured paper. The quill came from a hire company, as did the knife, and the glass was hand made to order at a glass-maker's. Both the skull and the old operating table were lent by a local hospital museum.
Light: 400 Joule flash with window diffuser.
Film: Ektachrome daylight ASA 64.
Lens: 150mm Symmar on a 4×5in (9×12cm) view camera.
Exposure: f22 with a CCO5 Yellow filter.

Reflective objects 1

Without special precautions, reflective materials such as mirrors, polished metals and opaque glass usually reproduce poorly in photographs. The problem is that mirror-like surfaces are bound to reflect something, and at least part of the lighting will thus appear in the shot. The principle means of dealing with this is to control the shape of the light source. A broadly spread light with a simple square or rectangular shape and a completely even tone gives the least obtrusive reflection. Evenness of tone depends not only on how efficient the light's reflector is, but also on the thickness and structure of the

diffusing sheet in front. Opal perspex (plexiglass) is probably the best material.

A large area light source (see the checklist on pages 20–23) close to a small, flat surface gives the most complete reflection. The smaller the light, the further away it is, or the more curved the surface of the object, then the greater the risk of the light's edges showing. With strongly curved surfaces, such as cylinders or spheres, the light will inevitably appear as a reflection. In these cases the light should be chosen to have as uncomplicated and unnoticeable a shape as possible.

Chrome metal With many different planes of highly reflecting metal, this small sculpture was a particularly difficult subject. Ideally, some of the planes would have total reflection – but not all of them as the basic form would have disappeared. In any case, simplicity of lighting was important, as the sculpture itself was quite complex. From the possibilities considered, the final choice was an overhead window light for the horizontal planes, white card reflectors close to the camera for some of the vertical planes while the others were left to reflect the black studio surroundings. A long white formica 'scoop' (flexible plastic sheet, curved up at one end) gave a graded tone under the overhead window, and this helped define the three different tones of the sculpture. The one remaining problem was the curved surface in front, and here, with some regret, a little dulling spray (see page 176) was used to soften the edge of the reflected light.
Lights: 400 Joule flash with window diffuser, at full power
Film: Polaroid 55P/N rated ASA 25
Lens: 150mm Symmar on a 4×5in (9×12cm) view camera
Exposure: f22

Reflection and refraction combined The imperfections in the glass of this old piece of scientific apparatus give it an interesting texture which would best be revealed by backlighting. The shape of the glass, on the other hand, called for more conventional lighting, which would inevitably lead to the reflection of the light source being visible in the shot. The answer was a plain square

window light, over the retort but aimed slightly towards the close white card background. This gave equal weight to both reflection and refraction.
Lights: 400 Joule flash with window diffuser, at ⅔ power
Film: Panatomic-X ASA 32
Lens: 80mm Planar on a 6×6cm camera, with 1 dioptre close-up lens
Exposure: f19

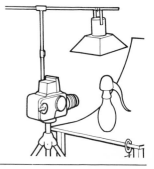

Coins: brightfield axial lighting

In one sense, a straightforward coin photograph is a copy-shot (see page 204). The film back should be parallel with the coin so that it appears truly circular. In addition, however, many coins have all the problems of reflective objects. To combine bright reflected lighting with perfect alignment use axial illumination. This is light that appears to come from the position of the camera, along the lens axis. With a special box, using a half-silvered mirror, or even very thin plain glass, any lamp can be made to produce axial lighting. The lens axis and light axis are set at right angles to each other, and the glass at 45° Part of the light is lost, passing straight through the glass, but part is also redirected down to the coin, where it is reflected straight back up to the camera. The inside of the box should be matt (flat) black to reduce unwanted reflection from the top of the glass, and the lamp should be diffused.
Light: Diffused 100 watt tungsten lamp at 12ins (30cm)
Film: Plus-X ASA 125
Lens: 55mm Micro-Nikkor at full extension (magnification $\frac{1}{2}\times$)
Exposure: 1 sec at f8

Half-silvered mirror or thin, plain glass

45°

Coin

Diffused

Coins: low angled darkfield lighting

An alternative lighting method, that works best with proof coins which have a mirror-like finish, picks out only the relief details, leaving the main surface area black. The principle is a glancing light from the side that reflects only from the raised areas. Black paper taped to the front of the camera bellows allows only the lens to show, so that nothing bright can reflect in the flat surface of the coin. A reflector – in this case gold foil – opposite the light balances the lighting.
Lights: 400 Joule flash with window diffuser, $\frac{1}{4}$ power
Film: Ektachrome daylight ASA 64
Lens: 80mm Rodagon enlarging lens on Hasselblad 6×6cm, bellows extension 260mm (magnification $3\frac{1}{4}\times$)
Exposure: f16 with a CC05 Red filter

Black paper fixed to front of bellows so that only lens shows

Coin on black velvet

Card covered with gold foil

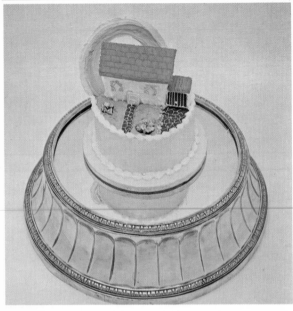

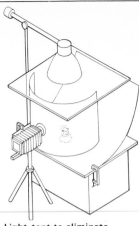

Light-tent to eliminate reflections If a simple reflective surface can be lit effectively with an evenly toned area light source, then the ultimate solution for reflective objects with complex shapes is to surround them with light on all sides. Curved mirror-like surfaces are notoriously difficult, reflecting a wide view of the surrounding studio, and are best handled in this way. The ideal method would be to construct a seamless translucent dome around the subject and shine light into it from outside – a light-tent, in fact. More practically, a makeshift version can be built from large sheets of tracing paper, thin white paper or even cotton bed sheets. Two or three evenly spaced lights will give thoroughly diffuse light, one will give directional lighting. The latter alternative was used here, to give some modelling to the cake, while completely surrounding the mirror-like surfaces of the silver stand with light. White paper was curved around the sides, with a small hole cut for the lens. The base was a white formica (flexible plastic sheet) scoop.
Lights: 400 Joule flash through a translucent sheet
Film: Ektachrome daylight ASA 64
Lens: 150mm Symmar on a 4×5in (9×12cm) view camera
Exposure: f19 with a CC05 Yellow filter

Unmodified daylight from a large window

Light-tent of tracing paper

Dulling spray

Light-tent or dulling spray With completely rounded reflective surfaces, it is impossible to remove all distracting reflections. Even with a perfect light-tent, the camera lens itself will show up as a dark patch. One alternative sometimes used is a commercially-available dulling spray, which gives the reflective surface a matt (flat) finish. This is rarely, however, a good solution – it is sticky and difficult to remove, and in close-up it introduces texture to a smooth surface. Most seriously of all, it completely alters the nature of the object. But in some instances it may seem to be the only solution. The final choice depends on personal taste.

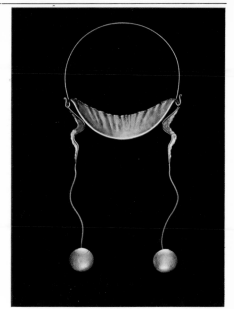

Diffuse reflected backlighting This clinical arrangement is effective for some objects, such as metal and jewellery. The single light is well diffused behind a large sheet of opal perspex (plexiglass), and its reflection is picked up in the horizontal surface of the same material, only black. The camera angle is critical, as the entire reflection must be caught. The spotlight behind the diffuser is deliberately aimed low to give a graduated effect.

Gold jewellery To emphasize shape and brilliance bright metallic objects can be placed on black velvet and illuminated by an area light source. For this shot a high window light gave a basic diffused reflection, balanced by a crumpled foil reflector. A black velvet base will absorb most of the light but use a strip of adhesive tape to pick up specks of dust.

With rounded and highly polished surfaces a light-tent may have to be used (see opposite page).

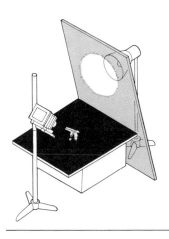

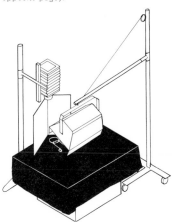

Backlighting with still-life

The main use of backlighting is to silhouette and define the outlines of objects that are difficult to photograph effectively, including those with reflective and refractive surfaces. Backlighting increases both contrast and definition. If desired, backlighting can also be used to form a part of the image itself, as in the photograph of raindrops opposite.

Backlighting for a clinical effect In photographing this experiment in magnetic levitation, there were two main problems: lighting the background to show the ball-bearing suspended in mid-air, and giving even illumination to the various reflective surfaces. The main light to the right of the camera was diffused through a translucent sheet, and positioned to give even reflections in the metal rings. The background was the front surface of a window light, its output set to give a bright tone without causing flare. For the hand and digital counter in the foreground, a small mirror was angled to fill in the shadows partly , and a separate time exposure was made of the figures, with all other lights turned off.

Lights: Main light – Diffused 750 Joule flash at full power; Backlight – 400 Joule flash with window diffuser, at full power
Film: Ektachrome daylight ASA 64

Lens: 90mm Super Angulon on a 4×5in (9×12cm) view camera
Exposure: Main shot – f32 with a CC05 Red filter; Illuminated display 5 secs at f8 with a CC05 Red filter

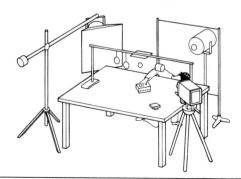

Making the backlight part of the image The theme of this shot was rain. To catch the silhouette of an umbrella in raindrops would have been impractical with a real umbrella – suspending it would have been difficult and the backlight area would have needed to be many square feet in size. Instead, a smaller window light was suspended close overhead, and a black paper cut-out taped to its front surface. Rather than water, which evaporates quickly and tends to run, glycerine was placed on the background with a dropper. A book cover was used to give a textured background, coloured blue to enhance the feeling of wetness. For maximum resolution, the normal lens was replaced with an enlarging lens, reversed, giving $1\frac{1}{4}$ times magnification. As enlarging lenses have shallow depths of field, the lens panel was tilted fully (see pages 68–69).

Lights: 400 Joule flash with window diffuser, full power

Film: Ektachrome daylight ASA 64

Lens: 80mm Rodagon on a 4×5in (9×12cm) view camera, total extension 180mm

Exposure: f32 for 9 flashes, with CC05 Red and CC05 Yellow filters

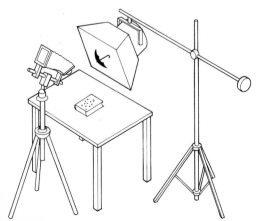

Still-life: special situations 1

Still-life shots are often expected to have strong graphic impact, perhaps for advertising or illustration purposes. A flexible and creative approach to lighting and setting up such shots is essential. Some particular solutions to special problems are illustrated on the following pages. They give a good idea of the versatility of the controlled studio environment.

Gemstones Although the brief called for these coloured, uncut diamonds to be arranged in a casual group, it was important to show their depth and colour. For refraction, a bright background was necessary. Backlighting, by placing the stones on translucent perspex (plexiglass) and aiming a light from underneath would have given the strongest effect, but at the same time the flare would have degraded the colours and contrast. Also, a soft texture would make a good contrasting background for the hard diamonds. White velvet was used – the dense texture of the fibres softening and absorbing much of the shadows.
For the reflections, a diffused window light was positioned almost overhead, illuminating the stones from the top left corner. Each large stone was angled to catch the reflection in one interesting face, and a silver foil

and white card reflector were arranged opposite the light, the first to add secondary highlights, the second to balance the illumination.
Light: 750 Joule flash with window diffuser
Film: Ektachrome daylight ASA 64

Lens: 150mm Symmar on a 4×5in (9×12cm) view camera, with a total bellows extension of 250cm
Exposure: f22

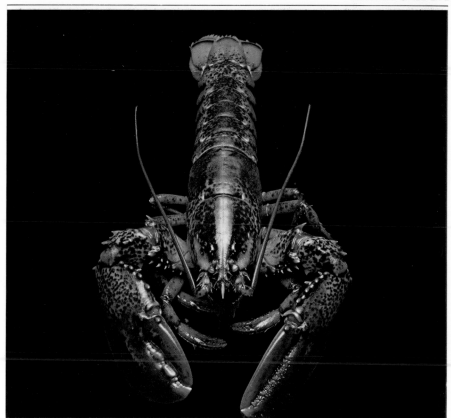

Isolating the subject The most obvious ways of photographing a lobster would be either in a setting that suggested its habitat, such as rocks or the sea, or one that suggested food, perhaps a marble slab. In this case, however, the intention was to treat the lobster as a still-life object, without any associations. For a simple, strongly lit photograph, a single overhead flash was used with a background of black velvet to absorb all light. For additional simplicity, the arrangement was symmetrical, and no reflectors were used.
Light: 400 Joule flash, with window diffuser
Film: Ektachrome daylight ASA 64
Lens: 150mm Symmar on a 4×5in (9×12cm) view camera
Exposure: f14 with CC10 Red and CC05 Yellow filters

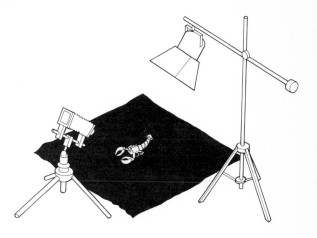

Catching laser beams on film

A particularly difficult shot to control was this photograph of an experimental laser beam apparatus. The arrangement of mirrors and beam-splitters created a complex geometrical pattern. Like all light rays, a laser beam is only visible when it strikes particles in the air. A hazy atmosphere is ideal, and the most effective solution in this case was to blow cigarette smoke over the entire set. As this would be unsuitable for the standard lighting, two separate exposures on the same film were necessary.

The apparatus was laid out on black velvet to show up the laser beams by contrast, with a main side-light and a small effects light opposite, covered with a blue gelatin filter to add some variety of colour. For maximum depth of field, the smallest aperture was used. Because the portable flash units available were not powerful enough, several repeat flashes were fired with the room in darkness.

For the second exposure, cigarette smoke was blown over the set to reveal the laser beams and the shutter left open for 90 seconds. Exceptionally, reciprocity failure at this long exposure produced no colour shift, as the laser emits at only one wavelength.

Lights: 1st exposure – 750 Joule flash with window diffuser, full power, with 2,013 BCPS pocket flash gun and CC100 Cyan filter, full power; 2nd exposure – Helium neon 1 milli-watt laser
Film: Ektachrome daylight ASA 64
Lens: 150mm Symmar on a 4×5in (9×12cm) view camera
Exposure: 1st exposure – f45 (main light flashed 9 times, effects light once); 2nd exposure – 90 seconds at f45

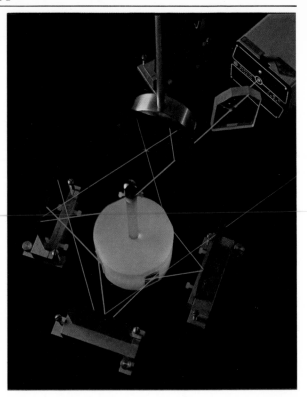

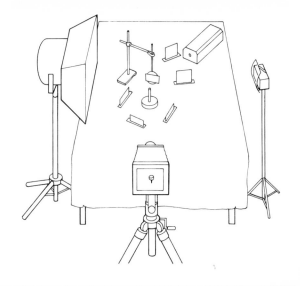

Flame and Smoke Here, the problem was to photograph a candle twice in sequence, while burning and having just been extinguished, to illustrate a magazine article on moonlighting. The flame needed a time exposure, but to catch the wisp of smoke, only flash would be fast enough. In both cases, a dark background to the top of the candle was needed for contrast. With the modelling light and all studio lights switched off, a 15 second exposure was made, with the flash fired once only. No filters were used for the flame, as it added very little to the overall illumination.

Lights: 400 Joule flash with window diffuser, at full power
Film: Ektachrome daylight ASA 64
Lens: 150mm Symmar on a 4×5in (9×12cm) view camera
Exposure: f37, plus 15 seconds for the flame, with a CC05 Red filter

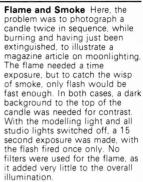

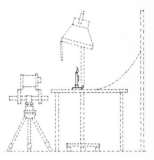

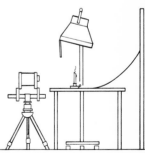

Lighting glass by reflection

For this magazine cover to illustrate the dual creative and analytical aspects of personality, a glass head was partially painted. Photographically, there were two problems: lighting the painted areas without flare and capturing the qualities of the glass below. The fairly high camera angle was determined by the design on the head, which was lit by a single diffused light. The top of the forehead was treated with dulling spray to reduce the highlight.

For the glass, a second light and crumpled silver foil were used as a completely localized light source behind the head. The thin foil, matt side up, was cut to a shape that would be concealed from the camera position, and the beam of light from a snoot aimed at it. The reflection illuminated the transparent glass. The snoot itself was flagged off from the camera to prevent flare.

Lights: Main light – 400 Joule flash, with diffused window light; Second light – 750 Joule flash, with snoot

Film: Ektachrome daylight ASA 64

Lens: 150mm Symmar on a 4×5in (9×12cm) view camera

Exposure: f27

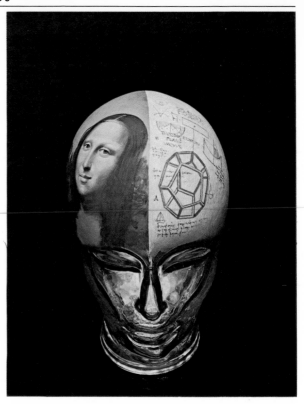

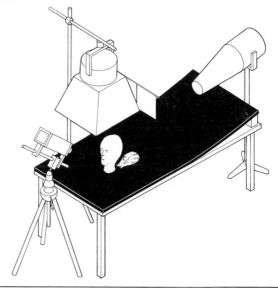

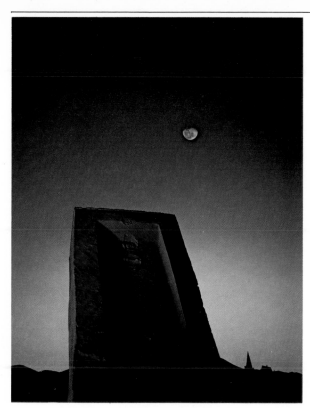

Forcing perspective with a false horizon To make an ordinary brick seem the size of a large building, a wide-angle lens had to be used from a very short distance and angled to give a deliberate convergence of verticals (see pages 102–103). However, if it had been set up against a real landscape, the depth of field would have been insufficient to keep the whole scene sharp. Instead, a twilight setting was used, and a false horizon cut out of black card with the recognizable outlines of a church and house to make it obvious. This was laid on a thick sheet of translucent perspex (plexiglass) and backlit.

A small portable flash unit was used to light the brick, at a grazing angle to emphasize texture. This helped the illusion of a large scale, because the small flash tube cast very detailed, hard shadows. In addition, being aimed from such an acute angle, the lighting did not include the horizon or 'sky'. For a realistic evening sky, two sheets of transparent coloured acetate were taped under the perspex (plexiglass) – blue for the upper sky and plum-coloured for the area close to the horizon. By shaping them so that they fell away in the middle of the picture area, the transition was smooth and natural. To help 'key' the illusion even further, one last refinement was to add a moon by making a second exposure on the film from an existing transparency with a slide copying machine.

Lights: Brick – 2,000 BCPS portable flash; Sky – 750 Joule flash, with bowl reflector.
Film: Ektachrome daylight ASA 64
Lens: 90mm Super Angulon on a 4×5in (9×12cm) view camera
Exposure: f38 (14 flashes of portable flash gun, four flashes of backlight flash).

Blue acetate

Plum acetate

Multiple exposure 1

To achieve certain desired effects, images can be built up or combined on the same film by means of multiple exposure. The technique requires careful planning and precise execution, but can produce startling and imaginative res- ults. It is most suited to work with large-format view cameras, but it can be extended to roll-film and even 35mm cameras using the procedures described on these pages.

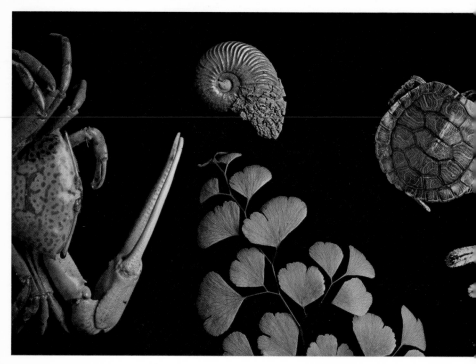

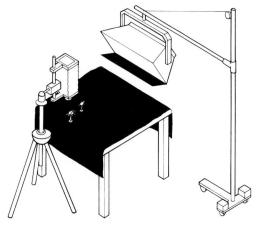

When loading film holders, use adhesive tape to fix the film firmly in place to avoid slight movement between exposures.

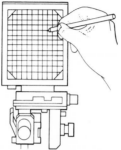

Trace the image of each exposure directly on the view camera's ground glass screen with a felt-tip pen.

Remove the pentaprism from a 35mm camera and trace the image on the focusing screen.

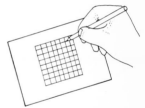

Alternatively, sketch the position of each exposure in a notebook.

Basic technique: objects on a black background For clear multiple exposures to be produced, two things are necessary – some way of ensuring that the different images do not overlap, and areas of unexposed, totally black, background for the second or subsequent images.

Methods of registering depend on how much accuracy is needed. With this collection of natural subjects, it was quite sufficient to draw the outlines of each on the camera's ground glass screen as it was exposed, using a felt-tip or draughtsman's pen. Provided that some space can be left between the different objects, this method can even be used with 35mm SLR cameras, provided that the prism head can be removed. An alternative is to trace the shape of the ground-glass screen onto paper, and sketch the images there. For this method, a grid-etched screen is invaluable.

By using a black background, most of the film remains unexposed. This is essential for multiple exposure, as even a slight tone will affect the clarity of the subsequent images. The more exposures made on the same piece of film, the more important it is to have a dense black background, and good quality black velvet is much more effective than ordinary black paper or card. To make sure that no light at all was reflected from the velvet, each of these objects was supported on a short rod and raised above the cloth. A barn door then prevented light from spilling onto the velvet. The lighting was calculated for each object individually, as if it were a fresh shot.

The film must remain securely in position in the camera. Methods of cocking the shutter without winding on the film vary, but most 35mm cameras have either a rewind button or special double-exposure lever. With cameras that have interchangeable backs, simply remove the back before cocking. With view cameras, the only precaution is to tape the film sheet down to prevent slight movement inside the holder.

Using these techniques, objects of any size can be juxtaposed at different scales, and the lighting can be adjusted to suit each one individually. Here, the terrapin and crab were slightly reduced in scale.

Repeating the subject To strengthen and add drama to this shot of a mailed fist, it was superimposed against its own silhouette. The photograph was taken in two stages, both exposures being made on the same sheet of film. To make sure that the two images were in register with each other the outline of the fist was sketched on the camera's ground glass screen.

The fist was first photographed normally, on black perspex (plexiglass) with an overhead window light. Black velvet was hung behind for a completely black background. Then, without moving the fist or camera, the velvet was replaced with a large white card and the light angled towards it, a barn door cutting off direct light to the fist so that it would appear in silhouette. The lens was changed to a longer focal length and the exposure was made with a strong red filter. The flash of light was added later.
Lights: 400 Joule window diffuser, full power
Film: Ektachrome daylight ASA 64
Lens: 1st – 90mm Super Angulon on a 4×5in (9×12cm) view camera; 2nd – 150mm Symmar
Exposure: 1st – f27, with a CC05 Red filter; 2nd – f9, with a Wratten 25 Red filter

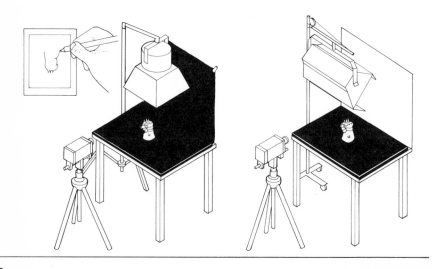

Overlapping multiple exposure Multiple exposure can be used not only to juxtapose images but to superimpose them. To illustrate a magazine article on cross-infection in laboratories – a fairly specialized theme – it was decided to show an overlapping series of culture dishes receding from a microscope.

By planning the shots in advance, this could be done entirely in the camera. A black background was used to simplify the multiple exposures (see previous pages) – a gently-curved sheet of black perspex (plexiglass). The overhead light was positioned carefully so that its reflection would not show in the background.

The first exposure was made of the microscope and culture dish, the outline being sketched on the ground glass screen for reference. Then the microscope was removed, the camera lowered slightly but at the same angle, and the dish separately photographed. Three exposures were made of the dish alone, and the position of each one was checked against the sketch on the viewing screen. The lighting and exposure were exactly the same for all four exposures.
Light: 400 Joule flash, with window diffuser
Film: Ektachrome daylight ASA 64
Lens: 150mm Symmar on a 4×5in (9×12cm) view camera
Exposures: f27 for each

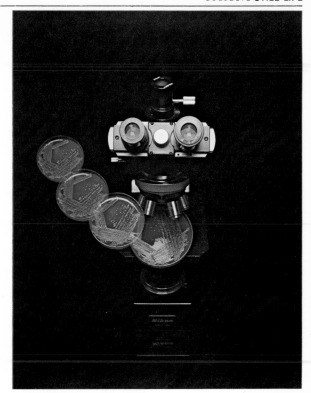

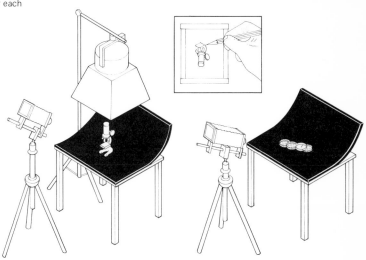

Defying gravity with double-exposure This finely machined quartz assembly was for a space-shuttle trial and needed extremely careful handling, with no possibility of suspending or clamping part of it. In order photograph it opened up, two exposures were made, with the camera and lighting unmoved. In the second exposure, the smaller part of the assembly replaced the larger, and the film was reversed in the holder. With a smaller format, such as 35mm, the whole camera could be turned over to achieve the same result.

As usual, the main limitation of the multiple exposure was the need for a black background, but in this case, the strong refraction in the quartz actually showed up best against a dark setting.

Lights: 750 Joule flash, with window diffuser
Film: Ektachrome daylight ASA 64
Lens: 90mm Super-Angulon on a 4×5in (9×12cm) view camera
Exposure: First – f32 (eight flashes); second – f32 (four flashes)

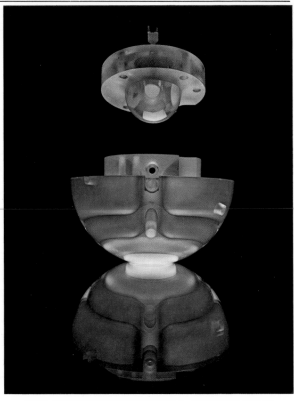

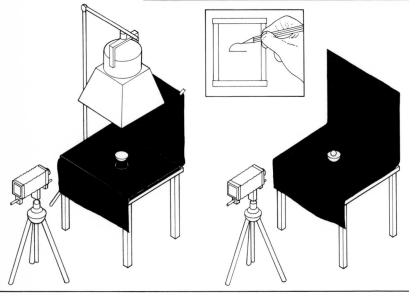

Separate lighting for different surfaces To light this camera dramatically without showing detail two lights were used: one to pick up the top edges of the body, and the other to create as much refraction as possible in the wide angle lens. However, as both were from opposing-directions, they would have acted as fill-in lights for each other if used in one exposure, destroying the intended effect. Instead, the shot was made in two exposures.

For the diffused strip of light across the top of the body, a large area light was suspended behind, illuminating the camera only through a narrow gap between the top of a sheet of black velvet background and a barn door. As well as controlling the light, this barn door also shaded the view camera lens from flare.

The second exposure was made with the smaller window light alone. During the first exposure it had been covered with a black cloth to prevent reflections in the lens. A piece of black card, cut to shape, was positioned in front of the view camera to mask off the body. As it was positioned close to the view camera, its outline was out of focus and too indistinct to show in the photograph.

Lights: 2 × 5,000 Joule flash, one with a large area diffuser, the other with a window diffuser.
Film: Ektachrome daylight ASA 64.
Lens: 150mm Symmar on a 4 × 5in (9 × 12cm) view camera.
Exposures: First (body) – f45 (two flashes); Second (lens) – f45 (with flash at three quarter power). Both exposures used CCO5 Red, CCO5 Yellow and 81A filters.

Food 1

By convention, food photography is concerned mainly with making its subjects look appetizing. This limits the techniques that can be used and the photography of food tends to be conservative in style in order to present dishes in a familiar and largely idealized way.

Authenticity There are a limited number of ways of presenting dishes and in many cases there is only one accepted appearance. For this reason, expert knowledge is important, and home economists or food stylists are normally used in commercial food photography. Without this service, research the dish you are planning

to photograph, using several authoritative sources, and buy the best ingredients available.

In order to make food look right in a photograph, it is often necessary to use a number of tricks that go beyond normal cooking. This may be because a dish suffers from the photographic process – frozen foods can melt and fresh vegetables tend to wilt under studio lighting. Some food is not particularly photogenic to start with. There are no set ways of approaching this kind of problem. As with still-life work, ingenuity is usually required.

With advertising work, it is important not to

Standard food set The basic light for a simple shot of a single dish uses an overhead window light, moderately well diffused to avoid hard edges to the shadows. Here, it was positioned to the rear of the set and pointed very slightly towards the camera to achieve good contrast, with a white card

reflector in front of the camera to give broad highlights.
Lights: 750 Joule window light, diffused, with card reflector
Film: Ektachrome daylight, ASA 64
Lens: 150mm Symmar on 4 x 5in (9 x 12cm) view camera
Exposure: f22

present the food in such a way that you may be liable to charges of misrepresentation. Artfully sculpting the flow of cream over a pudding to look well proportioned is acceptable in an advertising shot, improving the contents of a canned stew with fresh meat is not.

Studio administration Timing is important as most foods look their best when freshly prepared. An average dish will not normally survive the length of time needed to compose and light a shot, so position the camera and lighting in advance, as far as is possible. With all the other props arranged, except for last minute adjustments, it is a good idea to have two identical dishes, one prepared a few minutes ahead of the other. Use the first dish to check

composition and lighting, and then replace it with the second, fresher serving for the photography.

Arrange for a short and clear line of delivery from the stove to the set, but do not have the camera so close to cooking food that it is in danger of being splashed with fat or other ingredients. Ideally, the kitchen and studio should be separate but adjacent (see the floor plan on page 30).

For shots of food actually cooking, a portable gas burner can be useful. This can be positioned anywhere in the studio, and when the dish is almost ready it can be transferred to the smaller cooker or stove to keep it in good condition for the shot.

Portable stove To photograph these langoustines while they were actually cooking, a portable gas stove was used in the set itself. The lighting and composition were established in advance and the fat then brought to a high temperature in the heavy cast-iron pan. The heat was turned off

before the langoustines were added, but the pan's heat was sufficient to keep the food sizzling
Lights: 2,000 Joule area light
Film: Ektachrome daylight, ASA 64
Lens: 150mm Sonar on a 6 x 6cm camera
Exposure: f32

Lighting To make food look as appealing as possible, use a moderately diffused area light (described on pages 168–169). Exactly how you position it depends largely on the relative importance of texture, detail and colour – an overhead position to the front gives the best detail and colour saturation, while a position slightly behind the food gives more pronounced highlights to liquids and shiny surfaces and often reveals texture strongly. Avoid large and deep shadows by using fill-in reflectors.

With reflective surfaces, such as glasses, bottles or the surface of liquids, use a well diffused light with an unobtrusive shape (rectangular, for

example). The still-life problems described on pages 174–177 apply.

Transparent liquids such as spirits, wine or vinegar are a special problem. If you are photographing the liquid on its own, then backlighting may be the answer (see pages 178–179). If it is part of a set, however, this may not be possible. In this case, position a reflector, such as a small mirror, a sheet of silver foil, or a white card, behind the glass or bottle, and angle it to catch the light and reflect it through the liquid to the camera. If the reflector is approximately the same shape as the glass or bottle, its outline will not be noticeable when refracted by the liquid.

Equipment

In addition to normal cooking utensils, these extras can be useful in preparing foods for the camera:

Scalpel For cutting thin slices and precise trimming without disturbing an arrangement.

Tweezers For repositioning small pieces and tidying up.

Dropper For placing small drops of liquid and removing pools.

Water spray To simulate condensation and give an appearance of freshness to vegetables.

Freezer spray Creates condensation and keeps frozen dishes cool.

Glycerine Looks like water, but its greater surface tension makes more substantial drops. In addition, it does not evaporate quickly.

Thick copper wire For propping things up out of sight

Paint brushes and make-up brushes For applying liquids and tidying up.

Acrylic ice cubes Custom-made to avoid the problems caused by melting. In a drink shot it is usual to pack them into the glass, as unlike real ice cubes they do not float.

Glass bubbles Another custom-made item. Real bubbles burst and are difficult to position precisely. Spherical bubbles are used for side-on shots of the surface of a liquid. Half-bubbles are used for shots looking down

Mood in food shots To establish an atmosphere of rustic simplicity, this Roquefort cheese was placed in an carefully constructed setting on an old pewter plate, with a natural looking slate shelf above. The glass of wine, corkscrew and apple were added to lend the shot informality. The dark shadows under the shelf contrast well with the cheese. Overall, the shot makes the food appetizing by association rather than by directly stressing its edibility.
Lights: Well diffused 2,000 Joule window light
Film: Ektachrome daylight, ASA 64
Lens: 150mm Sonar on a 6 x 6cm camera
Exposure: f32

Imitation ice To avoid the problems caused by melting ice, custom made pieces of acrylic can be used. These have to be carefully placed in the glass as they only appear natural from one or two sides. The shot was backlit, with the glass placed on black perspex (plexiglass).
Lights: 1,000 Joule area light
Film: Ektachrome daylight, ASA 64
Lens: 150mm Symmar on a 4 x 5in (9 x 12cm) view camera
Exposure: f32

The close-up image

The small scale of the close-up subject makes it possible to control the lighting very precisely. Although the close working distances sometimes make it difficult to position lights near to the subject, and there is occasionally a danger of the lens casting a shadow over the picture area, a very wide range of diffusion is possible, from the spotlight effect of a small portable flash unit to the broad wash of light from a regular window light. The important factor is the ratio of the subject's size to the area of the light (see pages 168 to 169). If you need more working

Patterns in close-up Because the scale of close-up subjects is smaller than the human eye is accustomed to, many of its images appear new and unusual. Patterns in particular can be interesting. Cropping in close so that they fill the frame disassociates them from the objects of which they are a part. Photographing a flat surface, such as this snakeskin, poses no depth of field problems, provided that both the camera and subject are aligned correctly. Here, by aiming the camera vertically, a spirit level could be used on the camera back and the subject. As the magnification was greater than life-size, the lens was reversed for the best resolution, and a wide-angle lens was used so that its short focal length would give a high magnification for the available bellows extension. The short focal length reduced the working distance between the lens and snakeskin, however, so that the light had to be aimed from the side to exclude the camera's shadow. This cross lighting, deliberately emphasized by the use of a naked flash tube, suited this subject well, revealing the texture of the overlapping scales. A white card was placed opposite the flash as a fill-in reflector. The magnification was adjusted by extending and shortening the camera bellows until just the right part of the pattern was framed. With a 35mm or medium format camera fitted with a bellows extension, the procedure would be substantially the same.
Light: 400 Joule flash, naked tube
Film: Ektachrome daylight ASA 64
Lens: 90mm Super Angulon, reversed, on 4×5in (9×12cm) view camera
Exposure: f27, eight flashes

room fit a longer focal length lens, although this will need greater extensions to reach the same magnification as a shorter lens.

More often than not, maximum sharpness is desirable. For the greatest depth of field, stop the lens right down to the minimum, even though you may then sacrifice some resolution because of diffraction (most lenses are optimized to work best at two stops less than their minimum aperture). Depth of field is always very shallow at large magnifications and it is most important to position the subject and camera carefully. By tilting one or the other you can often improve the overall sharpness. With a view camera or some types of extension bellows, tilt or swing the front or rear standards to make the plane of sharp focus coincide with the plane of the subject (see pages 68 to 71).

Using camera movements to control sharpness These tightly rolled banknotes had to be photographed at an angle in order to introduce a sense of perspective. At this magnification (3.75×), the depth of field alone would not have been great enough to render all the banknotes in focus, even at the smallest aperture. To overcome this, both the front and rear standards of the view camera were tilted as shown, so that the plane of sharp focus was made to lie along the row of banknotes (see pages 68–71). For good resolution at this high magnification, an 80mm enlarging lens was used, reversed. The camera angle made it possible to introduce a diffuse light without problems. A white card close to the camera filled in the shadows. The exposure was calculated in exactly the same way as the shot opposite, measuring first the light with a flash meter, and then the compensation for the bellows extension – a total of 380mm from the film plane to the lens. The precise exposure was checked with a test on Polaroid film (see page 45). The lens was stopped down fully, for maximum depth of field.
Light: 400 Joule flash with window diffuser
Film: Ektachrome daylight ASA 64
Lens: 80mm Rodagon enlarging lens, reversed on a 4×5in (9×12cm) view camera
Exposure: f32, for six flashes

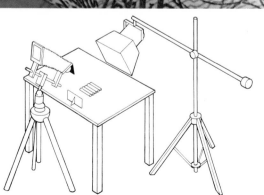

Close-up and macro

The reproduction ratio in most photography is less than 1:7. In other words, the majority of subjects are reproduced on film at less than one seventh of their size. All the considerations of lighting, exposure and depth of field discussed so far have been geared to this scale. When the reproduction ratio is greater than 1:7, however, new factors come into play, and special techniques have to be used. The most significant problem is calculating the correct exposure, because the normal method is to increase the distance between the lens and the film plane, inevitably reducing the light reaching the film.

Close-up photography includes the range of reproduction ratios from 1:7 to 1:1, which is life-size. Photomacrography (macro), which involves fresh problems, takes over at 1:1 and extends to about 20:1. Beyond this, ordinary camera optics are not really satisfactory, and a microscope must be used.

Supplementary close-up lenses The strength of a close-up lens is measured in diopters – the higher the number, the greater the magnification. The extra focal length that the close-up lens adds to the camera's lens brings the point of focus closer. For instance, a +1 diopter lens, with a focal length of one metre, will make the camera lens focus on one metre when its nominal setting is infinity. Add different diopters together for greater magnification, with the stronger diopter next to the camera lens. Image quality deteriorates with strong diopters.

Extension rings Fitted between the lens and camera body, these give a fixed increase in magnification. This makes exposure calculation easy, because the exposure compensation for a particular focal length lens never varies. The better makes connect the lens aperture mechanism to the body, and so allow a fully automatic diaphragm (FAD) to continue working.

Extension tubes These are longer versions of exposure rings, for greater magnifications, but work in exactly the same way. If the length of the tube is the same as the focal length of the lens you are using the magnification will be life-size.

Extension bellows Bellows perform the same function as rings and tubes, but their flexibility allows intermediate levels of magnification. For studio work they are ideal, and their fragility and slowness of operation are less of a disadvantage than when working out-of-doors. For macro work they are essential. Some makes can be used with a double cable release to allow FAD operation. The best models permit swings and tilts of the lens panel, so that the plane of focus can be altered to suit the subject as with view cameras (see pages 68–71). Because of the magnification, the lens covers a much greater area than the film format.

Reversing the lens Because most camera lenses are designed to work at scales where the distance to the subject is greater than the distance to the film, image quality suffers at reproduction ratios greater than 1:1. So, in macro work, for greater than life size images, turn the lens around. Reversing rings are available for this.

Macro lenses Using a special lens designed for macro work is even better than reversing the lens. Because these are designed to be used with extension bellows, most lack focusing mounts. An enlarging lens is another good alternative, although the depth of field is limited.

View cameras View cameras have no limits to their focusing range. Extra sets of bellows can be added for what ever magnification is needed.

Medical lenses These are highly specialized, and incorporate a ringflash for shadowless lighting. Focusing is achieved by moving the camera and lens bodily towards the subject – the easiest method for all macro work. Magnification can be changed by adding matched supplementary lenses.

Bellows extension

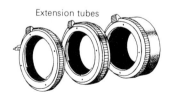

Extension tubes

Reproduction ratio is the relationship between the size of the image and the size of the subject. For instance, if an object 12cm high appears 3cm high on the film, the reproduction ratio is 1:4 (ie 3cm:12cm). **Magnification** is another way of expressing the same thing. It is the size of the subject divided by the size of the image. For the same example, the magnification would be 0.25×or, expressed as a fraction, $\frac{1}{4}$.

The basic method of magnifying the image is to extend the lens forward, away from the film. This, in fact, is the way that most lenses are focused for normal enlargements, but the distance that a lens has to move away from the film when focusing between several feet and infinity is quite small. For cameras with rigid bodies, which include all 35mm models and most medium format ones, the answer is to fit an extension between the lens and the body. View cameras, which have flexible bodies to start with, need only be extended further, inserting extra bellows if necessary.

In addition to lens extension, there is a simple method for achieving limited magnification – supplementary close-up lenses. These simple meniscus lenses are fitted in front of the camera lens in the same way as a filter and can be used to give reproduction ratios up to about 1:5. Beyond this, image quality suffers. Their advantage is simplicity, and they need no extra exposure compensation.

Lens extension: reproduction ratios and magnification

Extension (mm)	50mm Lens		100mm Lens		200mm Lens	
	Reproduction ratio	Magnification	Reproduction ratio	Magnification	Reproduction ratio	Magnification
5	1:10	0.1×	1:20	0.05×	1:40	0.025×
10	1:5	0.2×	1:10	0.1×	1:20	0.05×
15	1:3.3	0.3×	1:7	0.15×	1:13	0.075×
20	1:2.5	0.4×	1:5	0.2×	1:10	0.1×
25	1:2	0.5×	1:4	0.25×	1:8	0.125×
30	1:1.7	0.6×	1:3.3	0.3×	1:7	0.15×
35	1:1.4	0.7×	1:2.8	0.35×	1:6	0.175×
40	1:1.2	0.8×	1:2.5	0.4×	1:5	0.2×
45	1:1.1	0.9×	1:2.2	0.45×	1:4.4	0.225×
50	1:1	1×	1:2	0.5×	1:4	0.25×
55	1.1:1	1.1×	1:1.8	0.55×	1:3.6	0.275×
60	1.2:1	1.2×	1:1.7	0.6×	1:3.3	0.3×
70	1.4:1	1.4×	1:1.4	0.7×	1:2.8	0.35×
80	1.6:1	1.6×	1:1.2	0.8×	1:2.5	0.4×
90	1.8:1	1.8×	1:1.1	0.9×	1:2.2	0.45×
100	2:1	2×	1:1	1×	1:2	0.5×
110	2.2:1	2.2×	1.1:1	1.1×	1:1.8	0.55×
120	2.4:1	2.4×	1.2:1	1.2×	1:1.7	0.6×
130	2.6:1	2.6×	1.3:1	1.3×	1:1.5	0.65×
140	2.8:1	2.8×	1.4:1	1.4×	1:1.4	0.7×
150	3:1	3×	1.5:1	1.5×	1:1.3	0.75×

Supplementary close-up lenses (diopters)

Reproduction ratio (magnification), 50 mm lens on 35 mm format

Diopter	$+\frac{1}{2}$	+**1**	+**2**	+**3**	+**4**
lens focused on infinity	1:40 (0.025×)	1:20 (0.05×)	1:10 (0.1×)	1:6 (0.17×)	1:5 (0.2×)
lens focused on 1 metre	1:20 (0.05×)	1:10 (0.1×)	1:6 (0.17×)	1:5 (0.2×)	1:4 (0.25×)

Close-up: lighting quality

As with full-scale still-lifes, the quality of lighting is probably the single most important factor in close-up photography. It is not enough simply to deliver the right quantity of light to the subject – consider the essential qualities of the subjects you are dealing with and develop the lighting to enhance them.

Backlighting Many close-up and macro subjects are thin enough to be translucent, and sometimes transparent. This is often the case with living things, such as leaves, or these sand shrimps in oil polluted water (the subject of an ecological experiment). Backlighting can offer an interesting way of showing internal structure, producing a different type of close-up image. The procedure is straightforward. Here, a window light was upturned and a glass dish containing the shrimps and oil placed on its perspex (plexiglass) surface. A sheet of black paper, with a hole cut to the exact size of the picture area, was then slid under the dish, to mask down the light and minimize flare. A range of exposures was made, based on an incident reading with the flash meter aimed down towards the light, with the appropriate compensation made for the magnification (0.5×, using the closest focus of a macro lens).
Light: 400 Joule flash with window diffuser
Film: Ektachrome daylight ASA 64
Lens: 55mm macro on a 35mm camera
Exposure: f22

Reflective objects The basic approach described for reflective objects (pages 174–177) holds true for close-ups, and angling the shot so that the light from a broadly diffused lamp is reflected in the surface generally works best. The extra difficulty in close-up, however, is the short working distance between lens and subject, which often allows little room to introduce an area light. In this shot, the subject was a detail of a small coin, at a magnification of 3.5×. The camera and light were angled as shown in the illustration. There was no tilt facility on the bellows, so that a slight loss of focus towards the top of the frame was accepted as inevitable, even with the reversed lens at minimum aperture. An additional refinement was needed to add green to the coin as the shot was illustrating a magazine feature on the two Irelands – hence the shamrocks and colour. An overall green cast from a filter would have been uninteresting, so it was decided that the colouring should be selective. At this small scale, painting would have appeared clumsy, so the coin was submerged in a shallow dish of water, and a few drops of green ink added. The ink, being heavier than the water, sank to form a layer at the bottom. The exposure was worked out as described on pages 196–197:

Exposure

$$= \left(\frac{\text{lens focal length} + \text{extension}}{\text{lens focal length}} \right)^2$$

$$= \left(\frac{21 + 94}{21} \right)^2 = \left(\frac{115}{21} \right)^2 = 5.5^2 = 30$$

or an increase of $4\frac{1}{2}$ stops.

Light: 400 Joule flash with window diffuser
Film: Ektachrome daylight ASA 64
Lens: 21mm, reversed, on a 35mm camera
Exposure: f32, over 4 flashes

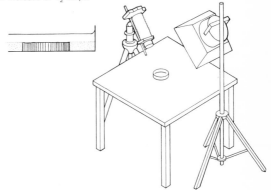

Close-up exposure

The main technical problem with close-up photography and photomacrography is calculating the correct exposure. Compensation needs to be made for the lens extension and the lighting is normally placed so close to the subject that even very small adjustments can have a significant effect. If you are using continuous lighting (daylight or tungsten lamps), the simplest method is to use a camera with TTL metering – the system measures only the light reaching the film, and so removes the need for complicated calculations. Even so, at great magnifications the lighting may be too weak to allow really small apertures at an acceptable shutter speed. Slow shutter speeds can cause a lack of sharpness due to vibrations even if the subject is static. At great magnifications, even traffic outside the building may affect the shot. For long exposures, refer to the reciprocity failure tables on page 39.

For these reasons, and because the heat from tungsten lamps in close proximity can damage subjects and camera, flash is infinitely preferable for most close-up and macro work. A modelling light close to the flash tube makes it easier to judge the final effect. However, as virtually no cameras have the facility of measuring flash exposures through the lens, separate calculations need to be made.

With any close-up or macro arrangement, first calculate the light falling on the subject and then work out the compensation for the lens extension to be employed. Use either a continuous light meter or a flash meter, taking incident readings rather than reflected light readings (see pages 18 to 19). If you do not have a flash meter, use the flash unit's guide number. To make the extension adjustment, you can use one of the three methods given here: *formulae, table* or *scales.*

Formulae

1 Exposure increase =
$$\left(\frac{\text{Lens focal length}+\text{extension}}{\text{Lens focal length}}\right)^2$$

So, if a 25mm extension is added to an 80mm lens, increase the exposure by

$$\left(\frac{80+25}{80}\right)^2 = \left(\frac{105}{80}\right)^2 = 1.3^2 = 1.7.$$

Reading off this exposure factor from the table opposite, add two thirds of a stop.

2 Exposure increase = $(1+\text{magnification})^2$
If the magnification is 1.2×, increase the exposure by $(1+1.2)^2 = 4.8$.
In other words, add $2\frac{1}{3}$ stops in accordance with the table.

Positioning the flash

1 If you have decided on the aperture you want to use, calculate the magnification, and use this formula:
$$\text{Flash to subject distance}=$$
$$\frac{\text{guide number}}{\text{aperture} \times (\text{magnification}+1)}$$
So, if the guide number (in feet in this example) is 80, the aperture is f32 and the magnification is 2×, position the flash 10 inches away from the subject

$$\frac{80}{32 \times (2+1)} = \frac{80}{96} = 0.83 \text{ feet, or 10 inches.}$$

2 If the flash is already in position, use this formula to find the aperture:
$$\text{Aperture}=$$
$$\frac{\text{guide number}}{\text{flash to subject distance} \times (\text{magnification}+1)}$$

6×6 format (for 6×7, use shorter side)

f-stop increase	4	3	2	1⅔	1⅓
Exposure increase	16.0	8.0	4.0	3.2	2.5

35mm format

f-stop increase	4	3	2	1⅔	1⅓	1	⅔
Exposure increase	16.0	8.0	4.0	3.2	2.5	2.0	1.6

Close-up exposure increase

If you have worked out the reproduction ratio or magnification, increase exposure in accordance with this table. **R** = reproduction. **M** = magnification. **E** = exposure increase. **F** = exposure increase in f-stops and **X** = decrease in flash to subject distance . The latter is an alternative to **F**

R	M	E	F	X	R	M	E	F	X
1:10	0.1×	1.2	$\frac{1}{3}$	1.1	1.2:1	1.2×	4.8	$2\frac{1}{3}$	2.2
1.5	0.2×	1.4	$\frac{1}{2}$	1.2	1.4:1	1.4×	5.8	$2\frac{1}{2}$	2.5
1:3.3	0.3×	1.7	$\frac{2}{3}$	1.3	1.6:1	1.6×	6.8	$2\frac{2}{3}$	2.7
1:2.5	0.4×	2	1	1.4	1.8:1	1.8×	7.8	3	2.8
1:2	0.5×	2.3	$1\frac{1}{3}$	1.5	2:1	2×	9	$3\frac{1}{3}$	3
1:1.7	0.6×	2.6	$1\frac{1}{3}$	1.6	2.2:1	2.2×	10.2	$3\frac{1}{3}$	3.2
1:1.4	0.7×	2.9	$1\frac{1}{2}$	1.7	2.4:1	2.4×	11.6	$3\frac{1}{2}$	3.5
1:1.2	0.8×	3.2	$1\frac{1}{2}$	1.8	2.6:1	2.6×	13	$3\frac{1}{2}$	3.7
1:1.1	0.9×	3.6	$1\frac{2}{3}$	1.9	2.8:1	2.8×	14.4	$3\frac{2}{3}$	3.8
1:1	1×	4	2	2	3:1	3×	16	4	4

Quick Exposure Guide

To correct the exposure in close-up or macro work, read off the lens to film distance against the lens focal length. Then open the lens by the number of f-stops indicated. For example, with a lens to film distance of 80mm and a focal length of 50mm, increase exposure by $1\frac{1}{3}$ f-stops.

Lens focal length (mm)	50	60	70	80	90	100	110	120	130	140	150	160	170	180	190	200	210	220
35	$1\frac{1}{3}$	$1\frac{1}{2}$	2	$2\frac{1}{3}$	$2\frac{2}{3}$	3	$3\frac{1}{3}$	$3\frac{1}{2}$	$3\frac{2}{3}$	4	$4\frac{1}{3}$	$4\frac{1}{3}$	$4\frac{2}{3}$	$4\frac{2}{3}$	5	5	$5\frac{1}{3}$	$5\frac{1}{3}$
50	—	$\frac{1}{2}$	1	$1\frac{1}{3}$	$1\frac{2}{3}$	2	2	$2\frac{1}{2}$	$2\frac{2}{3}$	3	$3\frac{1}{3}$	$3\frac{1}{3}$	$3\frac{1}{2}$	$3\frac{2}{3}$	4	4	4	$4\frac{1}{3}$
55	—	$\frac{1}{3}$	$\frac{2}{3}$	1	$1\frac{1}{3}$	$1\frac{2}{3}$	2	$2\frac{1}{3}$	$2\frac{1}{2}$	$2\frac{2}{3}$	3	3	$3\frac{1}{3}$	$3\frac{1}{2}$	$3\frac{2}{3}$	$3\frac{2}{3}$	4	4
60	—	—	$\frac{1}{2}$	$\frac{2}{3}$	$1\frac{1}{3}$	$1\frac{1}{2}$	$1\frac{2}{3}$	2	$2\frac{1}{3}$	$2\frac{1}{2}$	$2\frac{2}{3}$	3	3	$3\frac{1}{3}$	$3\frac{1}{3}$	$3\frac{1}{2}$	$3\frac{2}{3}$	4
80	—	—	—	—	$\frac{1}{3}$	$\frac{1}{2}$	$\frac{2}{3}$	$1\frac{1}{3}$	$1\frac{1}{2}$	$1\frac{2}{3}$	$1\frac{2}{3}$	2	$2\frac{1}{3}$	$2\frac{1}{3}$	$2\frac{1}{2}$	$2\frac{2}{3}$	3	3
90	—	—	—	—	—	$\frac{1}{3}$	$\frac{1}{3}$	$\frac{2}{3}$	$1\frac{1}{3}$	$1\frac{1}{3}$	$1\frac{1}{2}$	$1\frac{2}{3}$	$1\frac{2}{3}$	2	2	$2\frac{1}{3}$	$2\frac{1}{2}$	$2\frac{1}{2}$
105	—	—	—	—	—	—	—	$\frac{1}{3}$	$\frac{1}{2}$	$\frac{2}{3}$	1	$1\frac{1}{3}$	$1\frac{1}{3}$	$1\frac{1}{2}$	$1\frac{2}{3}$	2	2	2
120	—	—	—	—	—	—	—	—	$\frac{1}{3}$	$\frac{1}{3}$	$\frac{1}{2}$	$\frac{2}{3}$	1	$1\frac{1}{3}$	$1\frac{1}{3}$	$1\frac{1}{2}$	$1\frac{1}{2}$	$1\frac{2}{3}$
135	—	—	—	—	—	—	—	—	—	$\frac{1}{3}$	$\frac{1}{3}$	$\frac{1}{2}$	$\frac{2}{3}$	1	1	$1\frac{1}{3}$	$1\frac{1}{3}$	
150	—	—	—	—	—	—	—	—	—	—	—	—	$\frac{1}{3}$	$\frac{1}{2}$	$\frac{1}{2}$	$\frac{2}{3}$	$\frac{2}{3}$	1
180	—	—	—	—	—	—	—	—	—	—	—	—	—	—	—	$\frac{1}{3}$	$\frac{1}{3}$	$\frac{1}{2}$
200	—	—	—	—	—	—	—	—	—	—	—	—	—	—	—	—	—	$\frac{1}{3}$

Exposure increase scale

Having composed the shot and corrected the focus, point the camera at the scales below, without re-focusing, so that the arrow touches the left hand edge of the frame. The right hand frame edge will then indicate the required exposure increase in f-stops.

1

2.0

2/3

1.6

1/3

1.3

Copy shots 1

Copying can be used to record documents or illustrations, or as part of other photographic techniques such as photomontage. The three most important considerations are alignment, lighting and fidelity. The latter includes colour, tone and contrast.

Alignment The two most convenient positions for copying are horizontally on the floor or a table, and vertically against a wall. With small originals, the horizontal position is easier, but with large originals it may be necessary to photograph them hanging in place. A custom copying stand is useful if you do this type of work frequently, or you can adapt an enlarger. Otherwise, use a regular tripod for vertical

copying against a wall or a tripod with an extended horizontal arm (see pages 60–61) for copying horizontal originals.

Alignment is a critical procedure, and even a slight error can cause the effect known as 'keystoning' which will turn the rectangular borders of a painting into a trapezoid and throw part of the image out of focus. There are four methods of aligning the original to the film plane, shown below.

1 Use a spirit level to check that both the camera back and the original are precisely horizontal or vertical.

2 Where the original has to remain at an angle (a hanging painting, for example), measure this

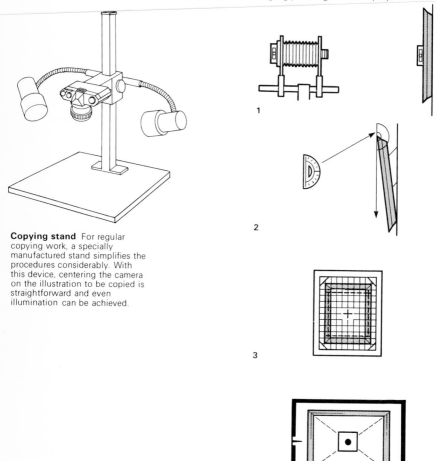

Copying stand For regular copying work, a specially manufactured stand simplifies the procedures considerably. With this device, centering the camera on the illustration to be copied is straightforward and even illumination can be achieved.

1

2

3

4

angle with a clinometer or a plumb-line and protractor, and then adjust the camera back to the same angle.

3 Use a grid focusing screen and compare the edges of the artwork with the etched lines. Occasionally, however, the original itself may not be exactly rectangular. When using a view camera, try not to use rear standard movements as a means of alignment – it nearly always introduces new problems of focus and lighting angle.

4 Place a small mirror flat against the surface in the centre of the original, focus the reflection of the camera sharply in the viewfinder, and align either the original or the camera until the reflection of the lens is centred in the viewfinder. Adjust the focus again before shooting. This is a very accurate method.

Fidelity As in duplicating, completely accurate reproduction is not possible and some colours may be distorted by certain types of film. As an independent check, place a Kodak Color Separation Guide alongside the original. This is an accepted standard, and if the shot is intended for reproduction the printer can then correct colours and tones without viewing the original illustration.

Contrast is often a problem, and you may have to alter the processing (see pages 38–39) to achieve the right balance. With many colour films there is insufficient contrast. For the best results, eliminate flare by placing the original against a dark background, such as black velvet, and use naked lamps unless the painting or its frame may show reflected highlights, in which case you will need to diffuse the lights.

Correct colour and tone reproduction When copying paintings or illustrations where accurate reproduction of colours and tones is important, use the guides produced by some film manufacturers – Kodak, for example. These should be photographed beside the original illustration. By comparing the reproduced colours or tones with the guide, printing can be adjusted to achieve precise fidelity. When making a colour print, for example, they can be used to assess the correct filtration.

Lighting – reflections To avoid the reflections which are most obvious in varnished oil paintings but can still be troublesome on matt surfaces causing the colours to appear less saturated, position whatever lights you are using at about 45° to the original. A position closer to the camera will cause reflections and a shallower angle will show texture. There is even less risk of reflections if the camera is positioned farther back, with a moderately long-focus lens.

For absolute control of reflections, cover the lights with polarizing sheets and the lens with a polarizing filter. Rotate the filter until the reflections are reduced, but beware of small violet highlights from very bright reflections. Because the light has to pass through two polarizing screens, an extra three stops exposure is needed.

When the original is behind glass which cannot be removed, use the same techniques but in addition hang a sheet of black velvet or black paper in front of the camera with a small hole cut for the lens.

Lighting – even coverage The most even lighting is equally from all sides. The ideal lighting arrangement uses four identical lamps positioned at the corners and equidistant. To avoid a hot-spot in the centre, aim each light towards the opposite corner. A simpler arrangement, but also effective, uses just two lights. Again, aim each at the opposite edge of the original, but position them at a greater distance than with four lamps. Even a single lamp, or daylight from a window, can be used provided it is diffused and a reflector is placed at the opposite side.

To measure the evenness of the lighting from more than one lamp, place a plain card against the original and hold a pencil perpendicular to it. The shadows cast by each lamp should be equal in length and density. Alternatively, hold an incident light meter at the centre of the original and aim it at each lamp in turn, shading it from the others. Each measurement should be identical. If the original is large, take incident readings towards the camera from the centre and at each corner. Again, they should all be equal.

Always flag off the lights from the camera with pieces of card attached to stands, or use a professional lens shade.

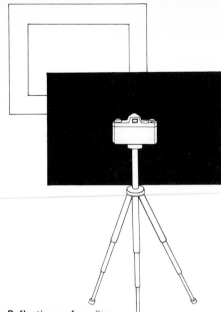

Reflective surface Pictures covered with glass or with a varnished surface can be a particular problem. To cut down unwanted reflection, place black card or velvet in front of the camera, with a hole for the lens.

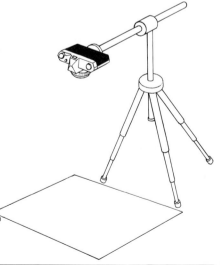

Vertical copying One straightforward way of keeping the illustration flat and level is to place it on the floor and photograph it from above. An extended horizontal arm will keep the camera clear of the tripod. A plumb line or spirit level can be used to centre the camera vertically above the picture.

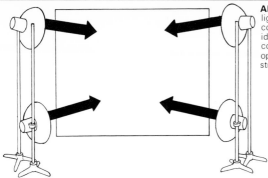

All-round lighting The best lighting arrangement for a completely even spread uses four identical lights, one at each corner. Direct each lamp at the opposite corner to avoid a strongly lit centre.

Two lamps A good result can also be achieved with two light sources placed at either side. They should be aimed at opposite sides of the illustration.

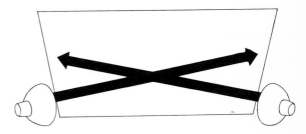

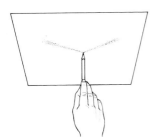

Checking the lighting If more than one light source is being used, hold a pencil vertically at the centre of the illustration. The shadows cast by each lamp should be of equal length.

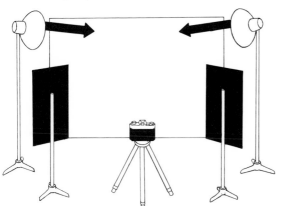

Shading the lens Because it is particularly important to avoid flare to reproduce the full contrast in the subject, the lights should be flagged from the camera with pieces of dark card.

Museums and galleries 1

The regulations that affect photography in museums, art galleries and other buildings open to the public vary greatly. In most public buildings in the United States there are fortunately very few restrictions, but in other countries there may be different levels of prohibition, from tripods being disallowed to a complete ban on photography. Check first.

If you have special permission to photograph as you wish, then you can use some of the still-life and interior lighting techniques already described. Otherwise, whether you are photo-graphing exhibits, people or complete interiors, you will have to make the best of the situation.

Use a tripod wherever possible, and if this is prohibited rest the camera on a bag or folded jacket or hold it firmly against a convenient pillar or railing. Not only do the generally low light levels demand long exposures, but a time exposure of about half a minute or longer will reduce people moving around in the shot to an undetectable blur. Depending on the film you are using, such long exposures may cause reciprocity failure (see pages 38–39).

Time-exposure to eliminate crowds Although this view of the Air and Space Museum in Washington DC seems deserted, there were people walking around the exhibits the whole time. Using tungsten-balanced film and an 85B filter to suit the long exposure (see pages 38–39), the shutter was left open for forty seconds. Moving people did not register on the film, and when anyone stood still in the picture area, a black card was quickly placed in front of the lens to interrupt the exposure.

**Remove a cluttered
background** Backgrounds to
exhibits, particularly large ones,
are not often suitable for
photography. One answer,
shown here on a shot of an
Apollo command module, is to
retouch the background so that it
appears black or white. On a
large transparency or negative
this can be done directly, using
opaque or bleach (the latter
needs great care). A print can be
retouched using either body
colour or bleach. If the
photograph is being published,
the separation makers or printers
are best equipped to do this.

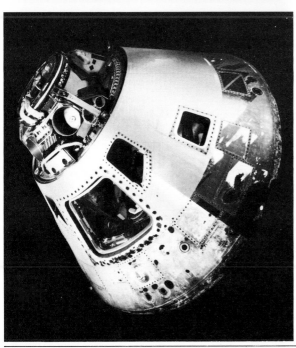

Portable flash through glass The best way of lighting exhibits behind glass is to hang a sheet of black velvet in front of the camera, allowing only the lens to show through, and aim the lights from above or the sides. Without special permission, however, this is rarely possible. The simple answer, used with this tree snake in a public zoo, is to leave the flash mounted on the camera, stand slightly to one side, and take the shot at an angle to the glass. There is no danger of reflections from the flash and the short shutter speed reduces the risk of reflections from ambient lights. Bracket exposures, as the glass absorbs some of the light and may also cause the sensor on an automatic flash unit to produce an incorrect exposure.

People in museums Often, visitors to museums and galleries make interesting subjects in their own right. Juxtapositions between exhibits and people are usually worth waiting for. Use the techniques for candid photographs described on pages 124–133.

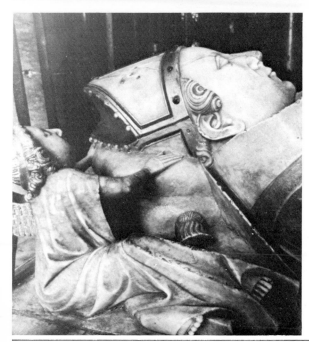

Close-ups without a tripod To photograph this effigy in Canterbury Cathedral a one second exposure was required. A tripod could not be used as they were not permitted, so the camera was jammed between two uprights of the enclosing railing. A wide-angle lens (20mm on a 35mm camera) was fitted to compensate for the very close working distance of two feet.

6. PREPARATIONS
Shooting check

Before starting a photographic session, go through the checklist below to avoid basic mistakes. Although obvious, each of these steps is surprisingly easy to miss, and the results can be disastrous.

35mm cameras 1. Check whether the camera contains film by gently turning the rewind knob clockwise. If there is tension, it is loaded.

4. Set the film speed dial correctly, and if the camera back has a slot for the film carton end, slip it in as an extra reminder.

5. Check that the right filters, if any, are fitted, and that the lens cap is removed.

8. When using flash, check that the shutter speed is correctly set if the camera has a focal plane shutter.

9. Set the aperture and shutter speed.

View cameras 1. Having set up the camera and composed the shot, shade the lens as close as possible to the picture area.

2. With the lens stopped down, check that there are no obstructions in front of the lens.

2. If the camera is empty, open the back and clean away particles of dust or film chips.

3. Load the film, checking that it is properly located on the take-up spool and sprockets, shut the back and wind on to the first frame.

6. Check that the TTL meter coupling to the lens is working, and is accurate (see pages 16–17).

7. Operate the battery check, if there is one.

3. Check that the aperture is set and closed before loading film.

4. Load the film holder and withdraw the dark slide.

Release form

If you take an identifiable photograph of a person without his or her written consent and it is published, you run the risk, however slight, of a lawsuit based on invasion of privacy or libel. The law in this respect differs between countries and states, but if you feel that the photograph may well be used later in a publication, the best insurance against such problems is to have the person sign a model release form. There are no standard forms, but the one reproduced here covers most possibilities. Photocopy it and ask the 'model' to sign it. You should ask the parent or guardian if the model is a minor – the age differs between countries.

Model Release

Name of photographer
_____

Number or description of photograph(s)
_____

Date of photograph
_____

For consideration received, I give ....* and all licensees and assignees the absolute right to copyright and use the photograph(s) described above and any other reproduction or adaptations thereof, in whole or in part, alone or in composite or altered form, or in conjunction with any wording or other photographs or drawings, for advertising, publicity, editorial or any other purpose.

I understand that I do not own the copyright in the photograph(s), and I waive any right to inspect or approve the finished use of the photograph(s).

I hereby release and discharge ....* and all licensees and assignees from any liability whatsoever, by reason of any distortion or alteration or use in composite or other form, whether intentional or not, which may occur in the making or use of the photograph(s).

I have read this release and am fully familiar with and understand its contents.

**I am over the age of majority and have the right to enter into this contract.
**I am not over the age of majority, but my parent/guardian agrees to these conditions.

Name
_____

Signature _____ Date _____

Address
_____

_____

Name of parent/guardian
_____

Signature
_____

Witness
_____

Address
_____

*insert photographer's name   **delete as applicable

Lens angles of view

90 °

60°   45°   30°   20° 15° 10° 5°

5°   10°   15°   20°   30°   45°   60°

90°

Estimating angles When choosing the lens for the angle of view you require, hold these pages up to your eye and point them at the subject. The angles of view can then be read off the top edge of the page. Check the angle chosen against the table on page 125 for the correct focal length.

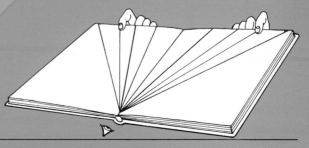

Metric measurements

Most measurements in connection with photography are given in metric units — focal length, for example. Some readers will find metric measurements convenient for all dimensions and calculations, but for those who prefer feet and inches metric measurements can be converted with the tables on these pages.

Ounces to grams	
oz	gms
1	28.3
2	56.7
3	85.0
4	113.4
5	141.7
6	170.1
7	198.4
8	226.8
9	255.1
10	283.5

Grams to ounces	
gms	oz
1	0.04
2	0.07
3	0.11
4	0.14
5	0.18
6	0.21
7	0.25
8	0.28
9	0.32
10	0.35

Pounds to kilograms	
lbs	kg
1	0.45
2	0.91
3	1.36
4	1.81
5	2.27
6	2.72
7	3.18
8	3.63
9	4.08
10	4.54

Kilograms to pounds	
kg	lbs
1	2.20
2	4.41
3	6.61
4	8.82
5	11.02
6	13.23
7	15.43
8	17.64
9	19.84
10	22.05

Pints to litres	
pts	l
1	0.47
2	0.94
3	1.41
4	1.88
5	2.35
6	2.82
7	3.29
8	3.76
9	4.23
10	4.70

Litres to pints	
l	pts
1	2.08
2	4.16
3	6.24
4	8.32
5	10.40
6	12.48
7	14.56
8	16.64
9	18.72
10	20.80

Fluid ounces to millilitres	
fl oz	ml
1	30
2	59
3	89
4	118
5	148
6	177
7	207
8	237
9	266
10	296

Millilitres to fluid oz	
ml	fl oz
10	0.3
20	0.7
30	1.0
40	1.3
50	1.7
60	2.0
70	2.4
80	2.7
90	3.0
100	3.4

Inches to millimetres		Millimetres to inches		Yards to metres	
ins	mm	mm	ins	yds	m
$\frac{1}{2}$	13	10	0.4	10	10
1	25	20	0.8	20	18
2	51	30	1.2	30	27
3	76	40	1.5	40	37
4	102	50	2.0	50	46
5	127	100	3.9	60	55
6	152	150	5.9	70	64
7	177	200	7.9	80	73
8	203	250	9.8	90	82
9	229	300	11.8	100	91
10	254	350	13.8	200	183
11	279	400	15.8	300	274
12	305	450	17.8	400	366
		500	19.7	500	475
		600	23.6	600	549
		700	27.6	700	640
		800	31.5	800	732
		900	35.5	900	823
		1,000	39.4	1,000	951

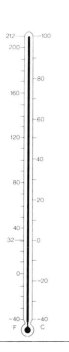

Feet to metres		Metres to feet	
ft	m	m	ft
1	0.30	1	3.28
2	0.61	2	6.56
3	0.91	3	9.84
4	1.22	4	13.12
5	1.52	5	16.40
6	1.83	6	19.68
7	2.13	7	22.97
8	2.44	8	26.25
9	2.74	9	29.53
10	3.05	10	32.81
20	6.10	15	49.20
30	9.15	20	65.61
40	12.20		
50	15.25		
100	30.50		
200	61.00		
300	91.50		
400	122.00		
500	152.50		

Index

Acknowledgements

Permission to reproduce photographs has kindly been granted by the following:

Harry N. Abrams Inc: 110. Bankers Magazine: 160 (below), 172, 176 (top), 185, 188, 197, 201. De Beers Ltd: 180. Michael Busselle; 143, 144-145, 146-147, 148-149, 154-155. Drive Magazine: 183. Richard Lobel: 163 (above), 182 (below), 164, 166-167. Nursing Times: 167, 173, 189. Pan Books Ltd (courtesy of Gary Day Ellison): 186-187. Roger Phillips: 193-194. Reader's Digest Association Ltd: 107 (top). Smithsonian Magazine: 140-141. Courtesy of Spink & Son: 175. Tony Weller: 36-37. By gracious permission of Her Majesty The Queen: 103 (top), 118-119, 123 (top).